D1180119

REINCARNATION
THE RING OF RETURN

"O, how could I not be ardent for Eternity,
and for the marriage-ring of rings, the ring
of return?"

NIETZSCHE

"Thou hast made me endless, such is thy pleasure.
This frail vessel thou emptiest again and again,
and fillest it ever with fresh life."

RABINDRANATH TAGORE

REINCARNATION

THE RING OF RETURN

compiled and
with an introduction by

EVA MARTIN

UNIVERSITY BOOKS *New Hyde Park, New York*

First American Edition, Fall, 1963
Library of Congress Catalog Number: 63-18492
Thanks are due the Buffalo and Erie County Library, Grosvenor Reference Division, for providing a copy of this book for reproduction purposes.
Manufactured in the United States of America

RETURN OF THANKS

To the following authors and publishers thanks are due for permission to quote copyright poems and prose passages :

To Dr. Robert Bridges, Poet Laureate, and Mr. Humphrey Milford for a passage from the former's translation of Virgil ; to Lord Chalmers, the Pali Text Society, and Mr. Humphrey Milford for quotations from the former's translation of *Dialogues of the Buddha* ; to Mr. A. T. A. Dobson and Mr. Humphrey Milford for a poem by Austin Dobson ; to the Clarendon Press for a translation from Kabir by M. A. Macauliffe, from *The Sikh Religion* ; to Sir John Murray for a passage from *The Thread of Gold*, by A. C. Benson, and for extracts from the following volumes in *The Wisdom of the East* Series : *The Lute of Jade, A Feast of Lanterns, Musings of a Chinese Mystic* (*Chuang Tzu*), and *Buddhist Psalms* ; to Messrs. John Lane for quotations from the poems of Stephen Phillips and Margaret L. Woods, for poems by K. Balmont and V. Brusov from *Modern Russian Poetry, an Anthology*, and for a poem by Natalia Crane from *The Janitor's Boy* ; to the Theosophical Publishing House for passages from the writings of H. P. Blavatsky, A. P. Sinnett, Annie Besant, C. Jinarajadasa, Olive Stevenson Howell, G. S. Arundale, C. W. Leadbeater, E. D. Walker, J. J. van der Leeuw, and F. L. Woodward ; to Dr. James Cousins for two poems from *The Garland of Life* ; to Messrs. Martin Secker for a sonnet by Lord Alfred Douglas ; to Mr. G. R. S. Mead and Mr. John Watkins for extracts from the former's versions of the *Pistis Sophia* and the Hermetic Books ; to Mr. John Watkins for passages from *Clothed with the Sun* and

Return of Thanks

The Perfect Way, by Anna Kingsford and Edward Maitland; to Mr. John Masefield for his poem, *A Creed* (from *Ballads and Poems*); to Messrs. W. Heinemann for passages from *The Prophet,* by Kahlil Gibran, and from *The Man Who was Born Again,* by Paul Busson; to Mr. Clifford Bax for quotations from *Poems Dramatic and Lyrical, The Traveller's Tale,* and *Inland Far,* and to Mr. Basil Blackwell and Messrs. Heinemann for confirming the two latter permissions; to Mr. Basil Blackwell for two verses from Edward Storer's *Narkissos*; to Mrs. William Sharp for extracts from the prose and poetry of William Sharp (' Fiona Macleod '); to Messrs. Mills & Boon for a passage from *The Jacket,* by Jack London; to Dr. Moses Gaster for a passage from his *Exempla of the Rabbis*; to Messrs. Kegan Paul, Trench, Trübner & Co. for passages from *The Light of Asia, The Epic of Hades, The Spirits' Book,* and *A Talmudic Miscellany,* and from the poems of Longfellow and Whittier; to Mr. Arnold Bennett and Messrs. Chapman and Hall for a passage from *The Glimpse*; to Mr. Walter De La Mare and Messrs. W. Collins for a passage from *The Return*; to Messrs. W. Collins and M. Charrier for extracts from *From the Unconscious to the Conscious,* by Gustave Geley; to Messrs. Rider & Co. for passages from the writings of G. Baseden Butt, Prentice Mulford, W. Gorn Old, Elsa Barker, W. L. Wilmshurst, and Violet Tweedale; to Lady Haggard and Messrs. Longmans Green for quotations from *The Mahatma and the Hare,* and *She,* by Sir Rider Haggard; to Miss E. G. Roper for passages from the prose and poetry of Eva Gore-Booth; to Mr. Bernard Shaw and Messrs. Constable for passages from *Back to Methuselah* and *Saint Joan*; to Messrs. Constable for passages from *Sweet Rocket,* by Mary Johnston; to Mrs. Leo for a passage from *Esoteric Astrology,* by Alan Leo; to Mr. Oliver Douglas and the editor of the *Observer* for the former's poem, *Recognition*; to Mrs. C. A. Dawson Scott and Messrs. Arrowsmith for a passage from *From Four Who Are Dead*; to Professor G. Lowes Dickinson and Messrs. J. M. Dent for passages from *Religion and Immortality*; to Sir A. Conan Doyle and Messrs. Cassell for a passage from *A History of Spiritualism*; to Mr. Algernon Blackwood and Messrs. Cassell for passages from *Julius Levallon* and *Episodes before Thirty*; to Sir Oliver Lodge and Messrs. Hodder & Stoughton for a passage from *The Making of Man*; to Sir Oliver Lodge and Messrs. Methuen for passages from *Man and the Universe* and *Reason and Belief*; to Professor W. Flinders Petrie and Messrs. Methuen for extracts from the former's version of *The Two Brothers* (in *Egyptian Tales*); to Messrs. Methuen for a Sonnet by Oscar Wilde, and a passage from *Ardath*, by Marie Corelli; to Mr. Frank Archer for a passage from William Archer's translation of Ibsen's *Emperor and Galilean*; to Mr. Edward Carpenter for passages from *Towards Democracy* and *The Art of Creation*, and to Messrs. G. Allen & Unwin for confirming the latter permission; to Mr. Henry Nevinson and Messrs. Allen & Unwin for a poem from *Lines of Life*; to Dr. Oscar Levy and Messrs. Allen & Unwin for extracts from Thomas Morrow's translation of *Thus Spake Zarathustra* (Nietzsche); to Messrs. Allen & Unwin for a quotation from *The Treasure of the Humble*, by Maurice Maeterlinck; to Mr. Talbot Mundy and Messrs. Hutchinson for passages from the former's novel *Om*; to Mr. A. E. Waite for quotations from his *Collected Poems*; to Mr. H. G. Wells and Mr. Jonathan Cape for a passage from *The Dream*; to Mr. Jonathan Cape for passages from *Later Days*, by W. H. Davies, *The Travel Diary of a Philosopher*, by Count Hermann Keyserling, and *The Notebooks of Samuel Butler*; to Mr. Wilfred Meynell for quotations from the poems of Alice Meynell and Francis Thompson; to Mr. H. A. Vachell and Messrs. T. Nelson for a passage from *The Other Side*; to Mr. Herbert Thomas for a quotation from his *Ballads of Evolution*; to Mrs. Frances Cornford and The Poetry Bookshop for the former's poem, *Pre-existence*; to Mr. Greville MacDonald for quotations from the prose and poetry of George MacDonald; to

Return of Thanks

Miss Rose Macaulay and Messrs. Sidgwick and Jackson for a poem from *The Two Blind Countries*; to Mr. John Drinkwater and Messrs. Sidgwick & Jackson for a verse from *The Fires of God*; to Professor A. A. Bevan, Dr. C. D. Broad, and Messrs. Edward Arnold for extracts from *Some Dogmas of Religion*, by J. E. McTaggart; to Mr. Rudyard Kipling and Messrs. Macmillan for quotations from *The Sack of the Gods* and *The Finest Story in the World* (from *The Naulahka* and *Many Inventions*); to Mr. James Stephens and Messrs. Macmillan for an extract from *A Prelude and a Song*; to Mr. George Russell ('A. E.') and Messrs. Macmillan for the poem *Babylon*, and for a prose passage from *The Candle of Vision*; to Messrs. Macmillan for poems by F. W. H. Myers, W. E. Henley and Rabindranath Tagore, also for passages from *Amiel's Journal*, translated by Mrs. Humphrey Ward, and from *The Soul of a People*, by H. Fielding Hall; to Messrs. Philip Allan for a poem from *The White Road*, and for a passage from *The Vein in the Marble*, by Stephen Tennant and Pamela Grey; to Mr. H. E. Palmer and The Hogarth Press for the poem, *Various Reincarnations* (from *Songs of Salvation, Sin and Satire*); to Mr. W. L. Wilmshurst for part of his poem, *Nox Nivosa*; to Mr. Robert Hillyer for two poems from *The Halt in the Garden*; to Mr. J. Caldwell-Johnston for a poem from *The Book of the Beloved*; to Messrs. Harper Bros. for a passage from *Peter Ibbetson*, by George Du Maurier; to Messrs. Funk and Wagnalls for passages from *Victor Hugo's Intellectual Autobiography*; to Mrs. Glaspell and Messrs. Ernest Benn for a passage from *The Road to the Temple*; to Mr. Henry Alsberg and Messrs. Ernest Benn for extracts from *The Dybbuk*; to the Open Court Publishing Co. for a passage from Empedocles, translated by W. Ellery Leonard.

To Mrs. C. A. F. Rhys Davids, D. Litt., M.A., President of the Pali Text Society, for translations of some ancient Buddhist Scriptures; for permission to use translations by Professor T. W. Rhys Davids; and for very helpful advice in connection with the quotations from Buddhist sources.

To Mr. Fred Rothwell, B.A., for permission to quote from his translations of Edouard Schuré's *Pythagoras* and T. Pascal's *Reincarnation* ; for several translations of passages from other French authors ; and for most patient and valuable assistance in the compilation of the Anthology. Also to Mr. Bernard Fielding for similar assistance, and for some valuable notes for the middle portion of the Introduction.

Finally, a special word of thanks is due to the many authors who have expressed so warm an interest in this Anthology that they have most generously waived the customary fees ; and to the publishers who have equally generously confirmed these authors' permissions, or who have themselves given free permissions.

A few apt quotations have perforce been omitted for copyright reasons, but it is hoped that these, and others that have been overlooked—for, like most Anthologies, this one makes no claim to having attained 'completeness'—may be included in any future editions.

EVA MARTIN

Cornwall, 1927

CONTENTS

I
INTRODUCTION

THERE have existed, from earliest ages, certain universal images which symbolise the deepest truths the human mind is capable of conceiving, and one of the chief of these pictures the soul of man as a traveller, a sojourner in a strange land, the wandering heir to a lost inheritance. In the lamentations of Isis for Osiris, of Demeter for Persephone; in the parable of the Prodigal Son who had gone 'on a far journey'; in the stories of Cinderella mournful among the ashes, and of the Sleeping Beauty awaiting love's magic kiss; in the fantasy of the lost Princess in *The Immortal Hour*, loved by an earthly king, but drawn back by her immortal lover to the 'Country of the Young'; in many another folk-tale, legend, and poem is the same idea repeated, age after age, in varying forms.

There is a very remarkable poem about eighteen hundred years old, called *The Hymn of the Robe of Glory*, which speaks of the soul as a little child dwelling in its father's house, and tells of its being sent down into the Land of Egypt to seek the Pearl 'that lies in the Sea, hard by the loud-breathing Serpent.' But when it reached the Land of Egypt—that is, the body—the soul forgot its royal birth, forgot the Pearl, and sank into a deep sleep. From this it was aroused by the receipt of a letter, urging it to awaken and to remember the object of its journey; whereupon, after overcoming the Serpent with magical charms:

> I snatched up the Pearl,
> And turned to the House of my Father. . . .
> My Glorious Robe that I'd stripped off,
> And my Mantle with which it was covered,

The Ring of Return

Down from the Heights of Hyrcania
Thither my Parents did send me. . . .
And I stretched myself forth to receive it,
With its beauty of colour I decked me,
And my Mantle of sparkling colours
I wrappèd entirely around me.[1]

Thus garmented, in what might be described as the 'aura' or 'body of light,' in what St. Paul called the 'spiritual body,' the soul returned to the Presence of the King, its Father.

We are reminded of this old Gnostic poem when we find William Blake describing how the soul of Milton discards 'the Robe of the Promise' before descending to 'Eternal Death,' or in other words to rebirth in the 'Sea of Time and Space'; and again when among the quaint and lovely thoughts of Henry Vaughan, that wise physician, we come upon such a verse as this:

If a star
Should leave the Sphere,
She must first mar
Her flaming wear,
And after fall, for in her dress
Of glory she cannot transgress;

while many another seer, ancient or modern, has looked upon the body as a 'Land of Egypt,' a place of darkness and captivity. In the Orphic Mysteries, we are told, the cry of the believer, like that of St. Paul, was, '*Who shall deliver me from this body of death?*'; St. Clement of Alexandria speaks of the soul being 'yoked with and buried in the body as in a tomb'; and Thomas Vaughan, twin-brother to the poet just quoted, says that 'the soul of man, whiles she is in the body, is like a candle shut up in a dark lanthorn.'

It is not surprising that the poets and mystics of all ages should have been more fully conscious than other men of this state of separation and imprisonment, and also more successful in expressing the soul's ardent

[1] Translated by G. R. S. Mead

desire for reunion, and its joy at even temporary accomplishment of this desire. Thus Crashaw tells how·

The self-remembering soul sweetly recovers
Her kindred with the stars ; not basely hovers
Below ; but meditates her immortal way
Home to the original source of Light and intellectual Day.

Francis Thompson cries :

My soul remembers its lost Paradise,
And antenatal gales blow from Heaven's shores of spice ;

and F. W. H. Myers writes of man's ' incommunicable, homeless pain,'

Until his soul so yearns to reunite
With her Prime Source, her Master and Delight,
As if some loadstone drew her, and brain and limb
Ached with her struggle to get through to Him.

Avicenna describes how the soul :

was hurled
Midst the sign-posts and ruined abodes of this desolate world.
It weeps, when it thinks of its home and the peace it possessed,
With tears welling forth from its eyes without pausing or rest ;

and Jalālu'd-dín Rúmí, the Sufi poet, puts the same thought in original fashion :

Every moment the voice of Love is coming from left and right.
We are bound for heaven : who has a mind to sight-seeing ?
We have been in heaven, we have been friends of the angels
Thither, Sire, let us return, for that is our country.

Jacob Boehme says that we are

with our soul (in this world) in a strange lodging, and yet we certainly know that we must travel, either into heaven to God or into hell to the devil. . . . Yea, but in what misery we lie captivated, in what lodging we are, for we are captivated by the spirit of this world.

The Ring of Return

And in Arthur O'Shaughnessy's poem *En Soph,* the unborn soul prays:

> Oh, let me not be parted from the light,
> Oh, send me not to where the outer stars
> Tread their uncertain orbit. . . .
> I fear to live the life that shall be mine
> Down in the half lights of that wandering world.

Among contemporary poets, perhaps none has more beautifully expressed the soul's secret knowledge of the 'Robe of Glory' which once it wore than Laurence Binyon, in *Unsated Memory*:

> Where is that world that I am fallen from? . . .
> Ah, surely I was rather native there
> Where all desires were lovely. . . .
> O, we go shrouded from ourselves, and hide
> The soul from its own splendour, and encrust
> The virgin sense with thinking. Then some chance
> Moment reveals us: we are deified,
> Feeling and seeing; gold gleams from the rust;
> And, marvelling at our lost inheritance,
> We breathe the air of beauty.

Again, Evelyn Underhill has the same thought:

> Let me whilst yet I can
> In this life's span,
> Stretch to the Only Fair
> And teach my homing heart to breathe its native air;

and A. E. Waite describes how:

> in that time when I was lifted up,
> Refreshment from an everlasting cup
> To take with spiritual lips, Thou didst
> My soul sustain, its angel-peers amidst.
> Then at Thy board I sat, all sane and whole,
> Clothed in the proper garment of my soul;

and how, since then,

> Far as my paths might from Thy throne divide,
> Deep as the gulfs might be which I plunged in—
> Conduits and cesspools of the House of Sin—
> In the strange tavern and the stranger's bed
> I do remember still Thy wine and bread.

So again Dante, in *The Banquet*, writes:

> The strongest desire of everything and the one first implanted by Nature, is to return to its source. And since God is the Source of our soul and has made it like unto Himself . . . therefore this soul desires above all things to return to Him. And like a pilgrim who is going by a road he has never travelled, who believes each house that he sees from afar to be his inn, and, disappointed in this one, puts faith in the next, and so on from house to house until he comes to the inn, so our soul, as soon as she enters upon the new and never-travelled path of this life, directs her eyes towards her supreme good.

This symbolism of the traveller or pilgrim appears and reappears, in various guises, times innumerable throughout human literature. 'Death ought to be looked upon only as one stage in our journey,' writes Claude Saint Martin. 'We reach this stage with tired, worn-out horses, and we start again with horses that are fresh and able to take us farther on our road'; 'the Earth,' says William Blake, 'is a Vortex not yet pass'd by the traveller through Eternity'; and Walt Whitman urges us 'to know the Universe as a road, as many roads, as roads for travelling souls.'

It has been necessary to lay stress on the prevalence of this particular world-symbol, as it may be called, before passing to a consideration of the idea with which this Anthology is specially concerned—the idea of Reincarnation as an integral part of the scheme of Evolution, involving *repeated* sojourns in this place of exile, pleasure-ground, prison, or school of experience, as our earth may variously be described by those of differing temperament and outlook. For the idea of the pilgrim soul's pre-existence in some diviner sphere is so closely bound up with that of its recurrent visits to earth that it is far from easy to disentangle the two. They cannot, indeed, be entirely separated, and if any quotations are found in the body of this book which seem, to some readers, to suggest merely such pre-existence, we can only say that we have done our best in the very difficult task of selection and elimination.

The Ring of Return

The well-known lines from Wordsworth's *Ode on the Intimations of Immortality*,

> Our birth is but a sleep and a forgetting.
> The soul that rises with us, our life's star,
> Hath had elsewhere its setting,
> And cometh from afar,

were rejected for the reason that they offer no suggestion of the poet's having believed that this spiritual rising and setting might take place more than once ; and for similar reasons other well-known names will be found missing. Keats, for example, having a vision of great spirits 'standing apart upon the forehead of the age to come,' believed that 'these will give the world another heart and other pulses '—thus definitely indicating the conscious existence of souls before their incarnation upon earth, but not necessarily a repetition of the experience. Indeed, the conception of the soul existing, not in embryo, but, as it were, full-fledged and in possession of all its faculties, in some heavenly region before birth, is one which has strongly appealed to poets of all ages, and a large Anthology could be compiled along this line alone. It is interesting to remark in passing that there is one poet, at least, who, while obviously believing in the soul's divine origin, regrets, instead of welcoming, childhood's evidences of it. Thus Edmund Gosse, in his lines *To My Daughter Teresa,* shows no delight in such 'bright shootes of everlastingnesse' as rejoiced the heart of Henry Vaughan, but looks upon them merely as 'cold immortal lights' ; and instead of deploring, like Wordsworth, the inevitable gathering of the 'shades of the prison-house,' can write with all sincerity :

> I joy in every childish sign
> That proves the stranger less divine—

a novel point of view which may appeal to the more human side of parents in general.

On the other hand, Thomas Hardy, so-called pessimist,

and opposed (perhaps?) to the theory of personal immortality, speaks sympathetically of the ghosts who surround him when 'Copying Architecture in an Old Minster,' and suggests that,

> Perhaps they speak to the yet unborn,
> And caution them not to come
> To a world so ancient and trouble-torn,
> Of foiled intents, vain lovingkindness,
> And ardours chilled and numb—

a very definite suggestion of the existence of individual souls before birth, whether or no their survival after death be admitted.

Not one of these poets, however, attempts to explain how each human soul has attained those varying qualities and faculties which they obviously believe it to possess at birth; not one of them offers any solution of the eternal problem as to the why and wherefore of its temporary sojourn upon earth under circumstances differing so widely, and apparently so unjustly, for each individual; though some of them do seem to be aware of the fact that this sojourn is, in many cases, too tragically short to allow of any benefit being reaped from what must, at the least, be an experience of universal importance and great educative value.

Well may Thomas Hardy ask—as he does in his *Chorus of Pities* in *The Dynasts*—

> To what tune danceth this Immense? . . .
> Why the All-Mover,
> Why the All-Prover
> Ever urges on and measures out the chordless chime of Things?

And though he supplies as answer to his own question—

> That the rages
> Of the ages
> Shall be cancelled, and deliverance offered from the darts that were,
> Consciousness the Will informing, till It fashion all things fair—

there are those for whom that answer, satisfactory as far as it goes, is too abstract to carry either comfort or conviction.

It is, in part, the knowledge that there are still many people vainly seeking an answer to this pregnant question that has led to the compilation of an Anthology remarkable, we venture to think, both for the extent of time that it covers and for the variety of names that it includes. This company of writers, from such widely separated lands and periods, united here in common thought, will provide many seekers, we confidently believe, with an answer to 'the everlasting Why' that is both satisfying and unique. In any case, a book which includes between its covers such various names as Empedocles, Plato and Virgil; Shelley, Ibsen and Victor Hugo; Browning, Nietzsche, Tennyson and Martin Tupper; Walt Whitman, Marie Corelli, Bernard Shaw, 'A. E.' and H. G. Wells—such a book is not likely, whatever its shortcomings, to be found dull reading.

For it seems as if there could scarcely be a time in human history when some such doctrine as this—be it called Reincarnation, Metempsychosis, Palingenesis, or the Transmigration of Souls—had not been formulated in thoughtful and speculative minds as a possible explanation of the Riddle of the Universe, a possible indication of the tune to which 'danceth this Immense,' a possible solution of the way in which 'deliverance' shall be offered, and all things fashioned fair at last.

We find its traces in such unexpected regions: not only in the organised philosophy of Hinduism and Buddhism, but in the customs of untaught savage tribes; in the speculations of lonely heterodox thinkers; in the scornful parodies of some old Roman satirist; in the didactic allegories of some early Christian Father.

The idea that the soul with its inexplicable memories, its inborn characteristics, tendencies and gifts, must inevitably be the product of former experience in a similar material environment, as well as of intervening periods in some 'heavenly' realm; the idea that it is compelled by the mysterious laws of its being to seek out ever new habitations, new bodies, new circumstances, until in the course of ages it has learnt all that such experiences can teach it, and is ready to enter into a state of blessedness beyond the grasp of mortal speech or thought—this is an idea that appeals powerfully to man's innate sense of justice, to his innate yearning for eternal progress and hope.

And though in various schools of metaphysical speculation it has assumed a confusing and perhaps rather forbidding complexity, though much that has been said and written about it by well-meaning but not very well-instructed enthusiasts may have tended to arouse prejudice against it, yet the fact remains that, stripped of accretions, it appears before us as a teaching of extraordinary dignity, simplicity and spirituality.

In the ancient faith of Brahmanism, the vision of the continuity of the Self, or individual consciousness, treading again and again a path of purgation and illumination was, for millions of men and women, a force that made for righteousness, a curb on animal passions, an impetus to virtue. It is noteworthy that the Founder of Buddhism did not reject it from his reformed religion. His mind, so merciless to superstition, accepted this doctrine of Reincarnation and Karma—the harvest of results reaped in succeeding lives from the good or evil done in previous ones—as at once rational and sincerely religious. During his lifetime, it appeared also in Greek philosophy, derived from either Egyptian or Indian sources, or possibly from both. The legends told of Pythagoras, of his circumstantial recollection of events in previous incarnations of his own, may, or may not, be accepted as literally true; but they supply, in any case, strong evidence of the trend of his teachings, and of the influence of the doctrine upon his thoughts and actions. Plato, inheriting the tradition, touched it with his own eloquent genius, and to such a degree did he associate it with his philosophy that later believers, in various periods and places, were, as we know, to rediscover it by the light that he had kindled, and to speak of the doctrine as *Platonic*; while many people to-day owe all their knowledge of it to the immortal *Dialogues*, and to the wealth of critical and explanatory literature that has grown up around them.

It is true that orthodox Christianity for many centuries looked coldly upon it, but it has been mistakenly supposed that the opinions of Origen on the point were condemned by the fifth General Council of Constantinople. What now seems established is that the condemnation was, as a matter of fact, merely that of a local synod held at Constantinople in A.D. 543. The doctrine had, in any case, Christian adherents of some number and note, for it appears again and again in writings of the first centuries after Christ; and the fact that it was commonly accepted in Palestine during His lifetime is borne witness to by the various references to it in the Gospels (p. 71). In this connection the reader will find it interesting to compare the views of three such different writers as Joseph Glanvill (p. 123), Anna Kingsford (p. 190), and Eva Gore-Booth (p. 265); while, in *The Great Law*, Williamson definitely expresses the opinion that the words 'resurrection of the body,' in the Nicene Creed, should be rendered 'in a body,' and that but for this mistranslation the phrase 'might be recognised for what it is, neither more nor less than an affirmation of the doctrine of rebirth.' At the same time, one of the chief aims of Christian teaching having been to stress the importance of the present life, and the need for attaining grace and salvation here and now, it is not surprising to find that this doctrine was allowed to drop into the background, and, by most exponents of the Christian faith, definitely rejected. In the present day, however, the view that its acceptance is not consistent with a profession of Christianity seems to be rapidly dying out, as a glance through the sections of this Anthology devoted to the nineteenth and twentieth centuries will make apparent; and, in surveying the subject dispassionately, it is well to bear in mind that a teaching which forms a main bulwark of the religious faith of two-thirds of the population of the world is one that cannot be lightly dismissed. Its prevalence is not, of course, a proof of its truth; neither is its antiquity, nor its persistent reappearances throughout long periods of history; for 'nothing worthy proving,' as Tennyson has remarked, 'can be proven nor yet disproven.' Its prevalence, however, its persistence, and its vast antiquity must all be taken into account before passing judgment.

Among many primitive tribes the belief, in a variety of crude forms, is found to flourish quite independently; for instance, among the Fijians, many African tribes, and the North American Indians. Examples can be found in any text-book of Anthropology, and it seems unnecessary to repeat them here. Of greater interest to the general reader is the fact that it also flourished among the early inhabitants of our own islands, and that here again, according to the view held by most students of the subject, it was original and spontaneous, not derivative. 'The ancients,' says Max Müller, 'were convinced that this belief came from the East; they imagined that Pythagoras and others could have got their belief in Metempsychosis from India only' . . . but 'it can easily be shown that a belief in the transmigration of souls sprang up in other countries also, which could not possibly have been touched by the rays of Indian or Greek philosophy.' With regard to Ancient Britain it is impossible to speak positively on this point, the evidences being too scanty. During the Druidic Ages teachings of this kind were only allowed to be transmitted orally, and any that were written down later are fragmentary, though extremely interesting. We may quote a Druidic proverb—'*The true home verily is heaven*'; and one of the Triads, obscure but suggestive, will be found on p. 110. As to the idea of a human being's reincarnation in animal forms, so commonly accepted among savage and primitive peoples—this, it must be remembered, finds no place in the more logical and more spiritual interpretation of the doctrine which prevails among civilised men to-day. It is well to make a definite distinction between Reincarnation (rebirth in human bodies) and Transmigration or Metempsychosis (the flitting of the soul through sub-human shapes). Whether even Pythagoras ever held the belief, so generally attributed to him, of the possible return of a human soul to the animal kingdom, seems extremely doubtful. Modern students of his teachings declare emphatically that he stood but for the fact that souls must always find expression of their strongest tendencies, and that it would be 'as impossible for a gallon to be contained in a pint measure as for a human spirit to inhabit an animal body'; while Dacier, in his *Life of Pythagoras*, says equally emphatically:

> A sure token that Pythagoras never held the opinion attributed to him lies in the fact that there is not the faintest trace of it in the symbols we have left of him, or in the precepts his disciple, Lysis, collected together and handed down as a summary of the Master's teaching.

This may be compared with the statements of Hierocles on p. 56, of A. P. Sinnett on p. 194, and of Max Heindel on p. 242.

In Buddhism the idea of rebirth in animal bodies was derived from ancient folk-tales, but this rather childish teaching appears to have been held only by the monks and by their often totally uneducated hearers. It is considered more than doubtful, by informed opinion, whether Gotama and his co-teachers ever subscribed to it. At the same time, we must remark that Gotama, like many other seers, did, on looking back, behold himself in various sub-human shapes. The point is that he saw it all as an orderly progress:

> Life's upward steps long-linked, from levels low
> Where breath is base, to higher slopes and higher.

Introduction

As Tennyson's 'Evolutionist' has it, the sceptre of the Human Soul must rule the province of the Brute, until

> I hear no yelp of the beast, and the Man is quiet at last
> As he stands on the heights of his life with a glimpse of a
> life that is higher.

It is surprising that this eminently rational idea of the age-long evolution of the soul through repeated sub-human and human lives should have been largely ignored by those who have given so much attention to the age-long evolution of the body. Life and form, soul and body, spirit and matter—call them by what names we will, the two seem inextricably intermingled. The slow æonian growth of the one parallels the slow æonian growth of the other. Who can maintain that the souls inhabiting the bodies of pre-historic men were at the same stage of development as those inhabiting the bodies of average mankind to-day? Or that the soul of a Hottentot is as fully evolved as that of a civilised human being of fine character and high intellectual powers? Mere increase of physical brain-capacity fails to explain the differences—the immense differences—in outlook, in achievement, in aspiration, between the early stages and the later ones. 'Men rise on stepping-stones of their dead selves.' . . .

It has been left to a Frenchman, Gustave Geley, to remark that against this theory of palingenesis 'no objections of a scientific kind can be raised'; and to a German philosopher, Carl Du Prel, to point out that it is 'completely compatible with Darwinism' (pp. 273 and 137). We have been able to quote only a few short passages, but the whole of the second part of Geley's remarkable book, together with Du Prel's chapter on 'The Monistic Doctrine of the Soul,' will repay close study. So will, from the religious and philosophical, rather than the scientific, point of view, the very valuable contributions to modern thought of the late Dr. McTaggart, quoted on pp. 222–5. Hume also, it is true, admitted that metempsychosis is the only system of immortality 'that philosophy can hearken to' (p. 171); Huxley, though no believer, paid definite tribute to it as one of the most logical theories put forward in explanation of the meaning of the universe (p. 198); and Sir Oliver Lodge has pertinent and suggestive passages in several of his books, some of which we are privileged to quote (pp. 226–8), and all leading up to the conviction that 'humanity has a future, a potential future, beyond our wildest dreams!'[1]

Bergson, in his *Creative Evolution*, does not touch on the Reincarnation theory, but he does remark that our character is 'the condensation of our history since birth, or even before birth, since we bring pre-natal dispositions with us'; and an older philosopher, Henry Drummond, more than once comes very near to the doctrine—so near as to make us wonder why he held back from that one step farther which would so satisfactorily have completed his 'scheme of things.' 'Natural Law,' he says, 'could it be traced in the Spiritual World, would have an important scientific value—it would offer Religion a new credential. . . . It is not plain that the one thing thinking men are waiting for is the introduction of Law among the Phenomena of the Spiritual World?' And again he remarks that the continued existence of the discarnate souls of either men or animals—as 'ghosts,' that is to say—in a material environment, limited by space and time, does not constitute *eternal life,* 'because their environment is not eternal. . . . An eternal life demands an eternal environment.' And more suggestively still: 'The materialistic Evolution, so to speak, is a straight line. . . . But as Evolution unfolds everything else, it is now seen to be itself slowly unfolding. The straight line is coming out gradually in curves. . . . What we are reaching, in short, is nothing less than the evolution of Evolution.' Is it too much to say that the theory of soul-growth by means of innumerable successive lives in the lower and higher worlds does indicate a 'Natural

[1] *Ether and Reality*

Law' among spiritual phenomena, does provide discarnate souls with 'an eternal environment,' and does constitute what may very well be called 'the evolution of Evolution'—with the capital letters reversed?

Another writer—not scientist, but novelist—who comes near to the theory without actually adopting it, is George Du Maurier. In that remarkable book, *Peter Ibbetsen,* he certainly suggests the evolution of the spirit in this and other worlds when writing of 'that ever-growing Conscious Power. . . . That which is slowly, surely, painfully weaving Itself out of us and the likes of us all through the limitless Universe, and Whose coming we can but faintly foretell by the casting of Its shadow on our own slowly, surely, painfully awakening souls.' But at the same time he limits human reincarnation on this earth to those who marry and have children, thus excluding all the unmarried, and all who, though married, are childless, in a wholesale fashion that seems scarcely reasonable (p. 197).

Samuel Butler, rather similarly, involves himself in contradictions through his theory that the only form of human immortality (or reincarnation) is that of those who, either for their achievements or for themselves, live on in the memories of succeeding generations. Even this is a strictly limited 'immortality,' for, as he admits, 'Shakespeare and Homer may live long, but they will die some day, that is to say, they will become unknown as direct and efficient causes.' He seems here to mean that the 'persons' known as Shakespeare and Homer will die, together with their work, even in the memory of man; but as he says quite definitely elsewhere that 'the immortal constituents do not cease and never will,' we are left with a suspicion that he had not fully faced the problem. At any rate, whether he consciously believed in the possibility of any other kind of reincarnation or not, he appears to imply such a belief in the verse quoted on p. 209; just as George MacDonald, while frequently veering towards the doctrine in his prose writings, expresses it openly only in his verse

(p. 189). Another such case may be cited in Oscar Wilde who, when speaking of the soul's innate, ancestral memories, declares that 'it is not our own life that we live, but the lives of the dead, and the soul that dwells within us is no single spiritual entity. . . . It is something that has dwelt in fearful places, and in ancient sepulchres has made its abode'—explaining all this, and much more, as merely 'the result of heredity . . . concentrated race-experience.' Yet in his sonnet to Sarah Bernhardt (p. 200) the same writer unreservedly adopts the idea of individual reincarnation. It may perhaps be argued that he looked on it merely as an attractive fancy, to be used for the sake of poetic effect, yet the frequency of such instances does suggest the presence of some intuitive knowledge which had not fully penetrated to the writer's conscious, everyday mind, and could therefore only find expression when subconscious inspiration was at work through the medium of poetry.

A similar solution presents itself when we consider De Quincey's famous *Confessions of an English Opium-Eater*. Here it seems as though the subconscious mind, stimulated to unnatural activity by the drug, called up vivid, though chaotic, memories of former lives—just as we know has happened even more definitely in experiments on subjects under hypnosis. Hear the opium-eater describe how he sometimes saw 'a crowd of ladies, and perhaps a festival and dances. And I heard it said, or I said to myself, "These are English ladies from the unhappy times of Charles I." . . . This pageant would suddenly dissolve; and at a clapping of hands would be heard the heart-quaking sound of *Consul Romanus*; and immediately came sweeping by, in gorgeous paludaments, Paulus or Marius, girt round by a company of centurions.' The intense horror with which his visions of the Orient always filled him suggest some particularly unhappy life (or several such) in an Eastern environment. 'The causes of my horror lie deep,' he says—and perhaps they lay deeper than he knew, in some long-buried substratum of memory. 'I ran into pagodas, and was fixed for centuries at the summit, or in secret rooms; I was the idol; I was the priest; I was worshipped; I was sacrificed. . . . I was buried for a thousand years in stone coffins, with mummies and sphinxes in narrow chambers at the heart of eternal pyramids. . . . Over every form, and threat, and punishment, and dim sightless incarceration, brooded a sense of eternity and infinity that drove me into an oppression as of madness.' The fantastic, nightmare quality of these visions was no doubt due to De Quincey's abnormal state of body and mind; but it does not seem unreasonable to suppose that there was something more than diseased imagination at work. It is interesting to compare the experiences of a modern poet (p. 222).

We do not know whether Shelley's beautiful but rather obscure poem, *The Triumph of Life,* has ever been interpreted in the light of reincarnation. Because it *is* obscure we have refrained from placing it with the other much more definite extracts from this poet's work (pp. 174–6), but that some such idea was in his mind seems not improbable. The poem begins, indeed, with an intimation that the whole vision partook of the nature of a recollection:

> I knew
> That I had felt the freshness of that dawn,
> Bathed in the same cold dew my brow and hair,
> And sate as thus upon that slope of lawn
> Under the selfsame bough.

And what were those 'shadows of shadows' sent forth from themselves by the great crowd of beings, if not the passing selves of various earthly incarnations?

> Each one
> Of that great crowd sent forth incessantly
> These shadows numerous as the dead leaves blown
> In autumn evening from a poplar tree . . .
> Mask after mask fell from the countenance
> And form of all. . . .

It is illuminating to compare this with a sentence from that little book of mystical wisdom, *The Voice of the Silence*: 'Have perseverance as one who doth for evermore endure. Thy shadows live and vanish.'

But, apart from any such 'dark horses,' perhaps it is as well to state here that not all the authors quoted in this Anthology are claimed as *believers* in reincarnation, even in a broad sense. Our aim has been to collect 'references' to the doctrine, and we have, in consequence, quoted some who openly scoffed at it, and a few whose views, while not actually including it, seem of peculiar interest when read in conjunction with those of convinced adherents.

Of the definite unbelievers, John Donne, while deliberately making fun of the idea, yet can very happily describe the body of a sparrow as 'this soul's moving inn'; and it is interesting to find that he has remarked elsewhere upon the unreasonable shortness of the life of man, as usually envisaged. 'Who lives to age,' he asks, in his *Anatomy of the World*,

> Fit to be made Methusalem his page?
> Alas! we scarce live long enough to try
> Whether a true-made clock run right or lie. . . .
>   Nor are we grown
> In stature to be men till we are none—

a disturbing thought which must have occurred to many.

A few of the authors quoted have possibly made use of the idea of reincarnation in their work merely because it appealed to their imagination—as suggested in the case of Oscar Wilde—and because they found it useful for the purpose of that work. If such cases exist, all we need say is that the use these authors have made of it is extremely effective. Several, however, will be found to have treated it quite seriously in prose (apart from fiction) as well as in verse. It appears definitely in Mr. Bernard Shaw's *Back to Methuselah*; and the late Sir Rider Haggard has not only used the idea most successfully in fiction, but, in his recently published autobiography, *The Days of My Life*, has declared his belief that 'the Personality which animates each one of us is immeasurably ancient, having been forged in many fires, and that, as its past is immeasurable, so will its future be.' He adds that he himself feels no wish to live again upon earth and does not hold the reincarnation theory to be susceptible of proof; yet—'unless we have lived before, or the grotesque incongruities of life are to be explained in some way unknown to us, our present existence, to my mind, resembles nothing so much as a handful of what is known as "printer's pie" cast together at hazard.'

It should be noted that when Sir Rider Haggard speaks of the 'immeasurably ancient' Personality, he obviously means what most writers on the subject would call the 'inner man,' or 'ego' or 'individuality.' The 'personality' is usually understood to be the transient garb or mask (*persona* =a mask) assumed by the soul for one incarnation only. Schopenhauer, equally obviously, when he speaks of throwing off 'our individuality, like a worn-out garment' (p. 133) is referring to the non-reincarnating personality, while he describes the individuality as a 'Being,' meaning a permanent Being of which the other is only a temporary manifestation. Du Prel, again (p. 136), calls this Being 'the transcendental Subject.' If these differences of terminology are kept in mind, any confusion of thought can be avoided.

Certain differences, however, not of terminology but of opinion, will be found to exist on three points. One we have already dealt with—the possibility of a human soul entering an animal body. The others are (1) the desirability, or otherwise, of remembering our past lives, and (2) the rigidity of the Law of Karma. Most writers hold that the loss of memory with each new incarnation—for indeed 'body is the true river of Lethe' as Plotinus has said—is a wise dispensation of Providence, by means of which we are enabled to take up our responsibilities and renew our adventures with fresh strength and courage every time. Others express a contrary opinion, and look upon the recovery of the spirit's memory as a thing greatly to be desired. Probably both are right; and, in the earlier stages, loss of memory with each rebirth is helpful, as well as inevitable, although in later stages of soul-development its recovery becomes at the same time possible and desirable. With regard to the Law of Karma, while certain schools have held that every event and experience must be looked on as the direct result of the individual's own acts and thoughts in the past, the more recent—and more reasoned—view appears to be that there are other forces to be reckoned with as well, forces for which individual human beings are not responsible (though in some cases mankind as a whole may be, in the form of what is known as 'racial Karma'). The reader is especially referred to the quotation from A. P. Sinnett on pp. 195–6.

The extreme frequency with which this idea of repeated earth-lives appears in modern philosophy, fiction and verse, gives peculiar point to the following passage written by Lafcadio Hearn more than thirty years ago:

> Proof that a reconstruction of the problem of the Ego is everywhere forcing itself upon Occidental minds, may be found not only in the thoughtful prose of the time, but also in its poetry and romance. . . . Creative art, working under larger inspiration, is telling what absolutely novel and exquisite sensations, what hitherto unimaginable pathos, what marvellous deepening of emotional power, may be gained in literature with the recognition of the idea of pre-existence.[1] Even in fiction we learn that we have been living in a hemisphere only, that we have been thinking but half-thoughts, that we need a new faith to join past with future over the great parallel of the present, and so to round out our emotional world into a perfect sphere.

All this is as true now as it was towards the end of the nineteenth century—perhaps even more strikingly true. And when Hearn goes on to say that the knowledge of the Ego as infinite can never be reached until that

[1] i.e., pre-existence upon the earth

'blind pride which imagines Self unique shall have been broken down,' and the *feeling* of self and of selfishness 'utterly decomposed,' we may begin to question whether this also is not still an applicable truth, and whether the sense of the vast importance of the personal 'I' is not still as deeply rooted in the Western mind as it was when those words were written. Perhaps insufficient time has elapsed since Lafcadio Hearn's day for us to be able to judge how far the West has ceased to 'think half-thoughts,' or how far it has moved towards finding 'a new faith to join past with future'; but it is certain that those who cling to a conviction of the supreme importance of the *personal* self, its joys and sorrows, losses and gains, will not willingly or easily accept this doctrine of Reincarnation, with its belief in a Higher Self whose enrichment is the sole aim and purpose of our transitory earth-experiences. The increase of individuality, of power, life and love; the enlargement of consciousness; the hastening of the steps of the Eternal Pilgrim towards his rightful Home—these, according to this philosophy, form the object of human incarnation and reincarnation, and whether we, *as persons,* suffer or rejoice in the process is of little moment compared to the attainment of our transcendent End.

On the other hand, the Western mind, though it may fail to grasp the Eastern point of view in some respects, yet has surely gained something in breaking away from the pessimistic attitude which this doctrine has induced in many of its adherents. Severe criticism has been levelled at certain modern believers in Reincarnation by a recent writer[1]—criticism which appears somewhat unreasonable when we consider that a fusion of the ideas of West and East on any such subject is bound to result in the appearance of something new, and not merely in a repetition of the old. Where the East sees all earthly experience merely as illusion, *maya,* a thing to be escaped from with all possible speed, the

[1] Count Hermann Keyserling, in *The Travel-Diary of a Philosopher*

West, more hopefully, holds that our earthly lives, while admittedly far removed from the sphere of Supreme Reality, are yet of incalculable value, in that they offer us a field for the development of our faculties, for mental, moral and spiritual growth. Here, it seems to an unbiased observer, the West undoubtedly gives something of value to the East, while receiving much of value from it. The value of what it receives has been put very clearly in an article in the *Hibbert Journal,*[1] where the Eastern and Western attitudes of mind are compared, and the conception of God and man as found in Eastern philosophy and religion is upheld as a most desirable antidote to Western materialism.

> The Gospel of Spiritual Evolution, as preached by Buddha, and preached again five centuries later by Christ, is the practical embodiment of that sublime conception. And it is for the Gospel of Spiritual Evolution that the world is waiting now. Until the higher thought of the West is able to enter, with some measure of understanding and sympathy, into the ideas that dominate the Upanishads, it will continue to waver, as it has long done, between supernaturalism and materialism, seeking rest and finding none—finding none, because it does not see that the only rest which can refresh and revivify the soul is the inward peace which comes from the progressive realisation of our potential oneness with God, the peace which passeth all understanding, the rest of infinite unrest.

In the doctrine of Reincarnation this 'Gospel of Spiritual Evolution,' in its most reasonable form, finds expression.

We are not, however, concerned here with adducing arguments for or against acceptance of the belief. That can be done much more forcibly by the writers gathered together between these covers. We would merely point out, in conclusion, that the appeal made by it to so many of the greatest minds throughout human history can be effectively illustrated by tracing a few analogies.

It will be found a fascinating and most suggestive

[1] 'The Ancient Wisdom of India,' by Edmund Holmes (*Hibbert Journal*, January 1925)

occupation to compare the startling similarities, both in thought and expression, between such writers as Plutarch (p. 72) and W. H. Davies (p. 290); between the Chinese philosopher, Chuang Tzu (p. 98) and the French poet, Victor Hugo (p. 149); between the Hindu *Upanishat* of unknown antiquity quoted on p. 39 and the saying of Bernard Shaw's Serpent (p. 276)—'Why not be born again and again as I am, new and beautiful every time?'; between the old Chinese poet (p. 100) imagining his friend's spirit passing into 'some far-towering pine' and the two American poets quoted on pp. 162 and 167; between the French philosopher, Dr. Pascal (p. 157) and the English poet, Francis Thompson (p. 197); between the ancient Buddhist and the modern French descriptions of the sensations of one about to be reborn on earth (pp. 43–4 and 236–7); the vision experienced by A. C. Benson (p. 239); and the statement of the 'Living-Dead Man' (p. 261)—'Do you know what they call death? It is rebirth into the world. Yes, even so.' A contrasting point of view, however, is expressed by Eva Gore-Booth in her poem (pp. 261–2), where the soul, weary of wings, is glad to find itself once more 'safe among shadowy, unreal human things.'

With regard to divine, not human, reincarnation the *Bhagavad-Gîtâ* (p. 41), dating from long before the Christian era, is in perfect accord with a German poet, Friedrich Rückert (p. 131)—the latter directly influenced, no doubt, by a study of Eastern philosophy; while a woman-poet of the twentieth century, the late Alice Meynell, has extended the same thought to its farthest compass, and has clothed in words of rare and dignified beauty the conception of the Divine Being assuming new and different forms, not on our own small globe, but in other worlds throughout the immensities of the stellar Universe (p. 258).

Finally, attention may be called to the verses which close the modern section of the Anthology, from the pen of an American child-poetess, aged ten. So, from old

The Ring of Return

Egypt to new America, the extremes of antiquity and modernity meet full-circle ; and so may we fitly conclude this brief survey of what, whether accepted as truth or rejected as fantasy, must still be admitted to merit honourable inclusion among those

> Large heroic hopes, whereby should thrive
> Man's spirit as he moves
> From dawn of life to the great dawn of death.[1]

[1] John Drinkwater

II
PRE-CHRISTIAN ERA

ANCIENT EGYPT

HAIL! I have become helpless! But I go forward. . . . I have come forth from the uttermost parts of the earth and received my apparel. . . .

Make thou smooth for me the ways and let me go round about [to visit] my thrones; I have renewed myself and raised myself up. . . .

Grant thou that my soul may come unto me from wherever it may be. . . . Let me have possession of my soul and let me triumph therewith in every place wheresoever it may be. . . .

O keep not captive my soul! O keep not ward over my shade; but let a way be opened for my soul and for my shade and let them see the great God. . . . Let not injury be inflicted upon me [but let me be], clothed on the day of those who go forward to every good thing.

Nebseni, the lord of reverence, saith: ' I am Yesterday, To-day and To-morrow, [and I have] the power to be born a second time. I am the divine hidden Soul who created the gods, and who giveth sepulchral meals unto the denizens of Tuat [the underworld], Amentot, and heaven."

Homage to thee, O Governor of those who are in Amenti, who makest mortals to be born again, who renewest thy youth.

I am the Swallow: I am the Swallow. I am the Scorpion-bird [or white bird] the daughter of Ra. . . . And that which I went in order to ascertain, I am come to tell. Come, let me enter and report my mission. And I, entering and ascertaining who cometh forth through that gate of the Inviolate one, I purify myself at that great stream, where my ills are made to cease and that which is wrong in me is pardoned, and the spots which were on my body upon earth are effaced. Here am I, and I come that I may overthrow mine adversaries upon earth, though my dead body be buried. For I am the Crocodile-god in all his terrors. I am the Crocodile-god in the form of man. I am he who carrieth off with violence. I am the almighty Fish in Kamurit, I am the Lord to whom one bendeth down in Sechem. . . . Oh, thou who bringest ; oh, thou runner who dwellest in thy keep, thou great god ; grant that my soul may come to me from whatsoever place wherein it abideth. . . . Let my soul [*ba*] be caught, and the spirit [*khu*] which is with it wheresoever it abideth. Track out among the things in heaven and upon earth that soul of mine, wherever it abideth. . . .

From *The Book of the Dead*

AND they came to the acacia, and they cut the flower upon which was the soul of Bata, and he fell dead suddenly. . . . And Anpu, the elder brother of Bata . . . wept when he saw his younger brother verily lying dead. And he went out to seek the soul of his younger brother. . . . He found a seed. He returned with it. Behold this was the soul of his younger brother. He brought a cup of cold water, and he cast the seed into it. . . . Bata shuddered in all his limbs, and he looked on his elder brother ; his soul was in the cup. Then Anpu took the cup of cold water, in which the soul of his younger brother was ; Bata drank it, his soul stood again in its place, and he became as he had been. They embraced each other, and they conversed together.

And Bata said to his elder brother : " Behold I am to become as a great bull, which bears every good mark ; no one knoweth its history, and thou must sit upon my back." . . .

And when the land was lightened, and the next day appeared, Bata became in the form which he had told to his elder brother. And Anpu sat upon his back until the dawn. . . .

And . . . the bull entered the purified place ; he stood in the place where the princess was ; he began to speak with her, saying, " Behold I am alive indeed." And she said to him, " And pray, who art thou ? " He said to her, " I am Bata. I perceived when thou causedst that they should destroy the acacia of Pharaoh, which was my abode, that I might not be suffered to live. Behold I am alive indeed, I am as an ox." . . .

And the King sent one of the chief butchers of his Majesty, to cause the ox to be sacrificed. And when he was sacrificed, as he was upon the shoulders of the people, he shook his neck, and he threw two drops of blood over against the two doors of his Majesty. . . . They grew as two Great Persea trees, and each of them was excellent. . . .

And his Majesty sat beneath one of the Persea trees, and it spake thus with his wife : " Oh, thou deceitful one, I am Bata, I am alive, though I have been evilly entreated. I knew who caused the acacia to be cut down by Pharaoh at my dwelling. I then became an ox, and thou causedst that I should be killed."

And many days after these things the princess stood at the table of Pharaoh, and the King was pleased with her. . . . And he hearkened unto all she said. And after this his Majesty sent skilful craftsmen, and they cut down the Persea trees of Pharaoh ; and the princess, the royal wife, was standing looking on, and they did all that was in her heart unto the trees. But a chip flew up, and it entered into the mouth of the Princess ; she swallowed it, and after many days she bore a son. . . .

His Majesty made him heir of all the land. . . . He was thirty years King of Egypt, and he died, and his elder brother stood in his place on the day of burial.

The Two Brothers
An anonymous story dating
from about 1400 B.C.
(Translated by W. FLINDERS PETRIE)

The Ring of Return

(THE sorcerer Horus, son of Panishi . . . knowing that Egypt was menaced by the incursions of an Ethiopian invader, insinuated himself into the body of the Princess Mahîtuaskhît, and was reborn into the world under the name of Senosiris, and as the son of Satmi-Khâmoîs. He traversed afresh all the stages of human existence, but he retained the acquirements and consciousness of his former life, and only returned to Hades after having victoriously accomplished the patriotic task he had imposed on himself.)

" The Ethiopian plague knew that he was incapable of combating the sorcerer of Egypt ; he performed a deed of magic by written spells, so that no one saw him any more in the court of audience, and that with the intention of going to the land of the Negroes, his country. But Horus, the son of Panishi, recited a writing over him, he unveiled the enchantments of the Ethiopian, he caused Pharaoh to see him, as well as the people of Egypt who were in the court of audience, so that he appeared as a wretched gosling ready to start. Horus, the son of Panishi, recited a writing over him, he turned him over on his back with a fowler standing over him, a pointed knife in his hand, on the point of doing him an evil turn. While all this was being done, the signs which Horus, the son of Tnahsît, had arranged between him and his mother occurred all of them before her. . . . She did not delay to go up to Egypt in the form of a goose, and she stopped before the palace of Pharaoh ; she called with all her voice to her son who had the form of a wretched bird menaced by the fowler. Horus, son of Panishi, looked up to the sky ; he saw Tnahsît under the form in which she was, and he recognised that she was Tnahsît, the Ethiopian ; he recited a writing against her, he turned her over on her back with a fowler standing over her with a knife ready to deal death. She cast off the form in which she was, she assumed the form of an Ethiopian woman, and she prayed him, saying, 'Do not come against us, Horus, son of Panishi, but forgive us this criminal deed! If thou wilt but give us a boat, we will never come back to Egypt again.' Horus, the son of Panishi, swore by Pharaoh, as well as by the gods of Egypt, to wit, 'I will not stay my work of magic by written spells if you will not swear to me never to return to Egypt under any pretext.' Tnahsît raised her hand as witness that she would not come to Egypt for ever and ever. Horus, the son of Tnahsît, swore, saying, 'I will not come back to Egypt for fifteen hundred years.' Horus, the son of Panishi, reversed the deed of magic, he gave a boat to Horus, son of Tnahsît, as well as to Tnahsît, his mother, and they departed to the land of the Negroes, their country."

This discourse Senosiris uttered before Pharaoh while the people listened to his voice, and Satmi, his father, beheld all, the Ethiopian plague being prostrated with his forehead to the ground; then he said; "By the life of thy countenance, my great lord, the man here before thee is Horus, the son of Tnahsît, the same whose doings I recount, who has not repented of that he did before, but who has come back to Egypt after fifteen hundred years to cast his enchantments over it. By the life of Osiris, the great god, lord of the Amentît, before whom I go to rest, I am Horus, son of Panishi, I who stand here before Pharaoh. When I learnt in Amentît that this Ethiopian enemy was going to hurl sacrilege against Egypt, as there was no longer a good scribe or a sage in Egypt who could contend with him, I implored Osiris in Amentît to allow me to appear again on earth to prevent his reporting the inferiority of Egypt to the land of the Negroes. Command was given on the part of Osiris to return me to earth; I came back as a seed until I met with Satmi, the son of Pharaoh, on the mountain of Heliopolis or Memphis. I grew in that plant of colocasia in order to enter a body and be born again on earth to make enchantments against that Ethiopian enemy who is there in the court of audience." Horus, son of Panishi, performed a deed of magic by written spells in the form of Senosiris against the plague of Ethiopia ; he surrounded him with a fire, which consumed him in the midst of the court, in the sight of Pharaoh, as well as of his nobles and the people of Egypt ; then Senosiris vanished as a shadow before Pharaoh and his father Satmi, so that they saw him no more.

From *Popular Stories of Ancient Egypt*
(Translated by SIR G. MASPERO)

FROM one Soul of the Universe are all those Souls which in all Worlds are tossed up and down as it were, and severally divided. Of these Souls there are many Changes, some into a more fortunate Estate, and some quite contrary. And they which are of Creeping Things are changed into those of Watery Things, and those of Things living in the Water to those of Things living on the Land ; and Airy ones into Men ; and Human Souls that lay hold of Immortality are changed into (holy) Demons. And so they go on into the Sphere of the Gods. . . . And this is the most perfect Glory of the Soul.

Human souls, not all of them, but only the pious ones, are daimonic and divine. Once separated from the body, and after the struggle to acquire piety, which consists in knowing God and injuring none, such a soul becomes all intelligence. The impious soul, however, remains in its own essence and punishes itself by seeking a human body to enter into, for no other body can receive a human soul ; it cannot enter the body of an animal devoid of reason. Divine law preserves the human soul from such infamy.

Hermes Trismegistus

(NOTE.—The so-called Hermetic Books are of unknown date, and are supposed by competent authorities to represent the esoteric doctrines of the Ancient Egyptian priesthood, which were inspired by the god Thoth, known also as Hermes Trismegistus.)

Pre-Christian Era

AND every God by his own proper power brought forth what was appointed him. Thus there arose four-footed beasts, and creeping things, and those that in the water dwell, and things with wings, and everything that beareth seed, and grass, and sport of every flower, all having in themselves seed of again-becoming.[1]

The Sole Ruler said to the souls: " You know that, as long as you were sinless, you dwelt in the places nigh to heaven ; but now that blame has come upon you, you have been condemned to imprisonment in the organs of mortal bodies, and must yourselves dwell in the regions assigned to them. And in that region, Desire and Necessity will be your masters ; for it is they that, after me, are masters and captains of all things below. Howbeit, not at random have I ordained the changes of your state ; but as your condition will be changed for the worse if you do aught unseemly, so will it be changed for the better if you resolve on action worthy of your origin. I myself will keep watch on you ; and if the charges against you shall be but slight, you shall be released from the deadly bondage of the flesh, and, freed from sorrow, shall greet again your home above. But if you shall be found guilty of any greater sins, in that case, when you quit your bodily frames, you shall not thereafter dwell in [heaven], nor yet in human bodies, but you shall be transferred into the bodies of beasts, and shall thenceforth continue to wander upon earth."

Having said this, my son Horus, God gave [bodies] to all the souls ; and thus he spoke again, and said, " . . . The destruction of your bodies then will be the starting point for a rebirth, and their dissolution a renewal of your former happiness."

[1] Or reincarnation

The Ring of Return

"Souls of the noblest kind, when they enter human bodies, become righteous kings, founders of cities and lawgivers, genuine philosophers, true diviners, trustworthy prophets, skilled musicians, sage astronomers, priests exact in the rites of sacrifice,[1] and all kinds of men that are of high worth in any sort of work. When such souls enter the bodies of birds, they become eagles; because eagles neither drive away other creatures of their kind, nor devour them, and do not seek to wrong any other sort of animal that is weaker than themselves, for eagles are most righteous by nature. When they enter the bodies of quadrupeds, they become lions; for the lion is a strong beast, and one that trains itself to imitate with its mortal body the immortal nature of the gods, inasmuch as lions are never tired, and never sleep. When they enter the bodies of reptiles, they become dragons; for the dragon is a powerful animal, and long-lived; and it is harmless, and so friendly to man that some dragons are even tamed by men; it has no venom; and it renews its youth when it has grown old, resembling the gods in this. And among the fishes[2] such souls are dolphins; for dolphins take pity on men who fall into the sea, they convey the man to land if he is still alive, and they never even touch him if he is dead, though the race of fishes is voracious beyond all others."

And, having thus spoken, God vanished from their sight.

Hermes Trismegistus
(Translated by G. R. S. MEAD)

THE Egyptians were the first who propounded the theory that the human soul is immortal and that, when the body of any one perishes, it enters into some other creature that may be born ready to receive

[1] Or possibly 'unerring herbalists'
[2] Or 'when they are in fish-bodies'

it, and that when it has gone the round of all created forms on land, in water and in air, then it once more enters a human body born for it ; and this cycle of existence for the soul takes place in three thousand years.

HERODOTUS (Book II)

The Ring of Return

HINDUISM AND BUDDHISM

LET him reflect on the transmigrations of men, caused by their sinful deeds, on their falling into hell, and on the torments in the world of Yama;

On the separation from their dear ones, on their union with hated men, on their being overpowered by age and being tormented with diseases;

On the departure of the individual soul from this body and its new birth in another womb, and on its wanderings through ten thousand millions of existences;

On the infliction of pain on embodied spirits, which is caused by demerit, and the gain of eternal bliss, which is caused by the attainment of their highest aim through spiritual merit.

Laws of Manu (Book V)

BUT they who conquer the worlds by sacrifice, charity and austerity go to smoke, from smoke to night, from night to the waning half of the moon, from the waning half of the moon to the six months when the sun moves South; from these months to the world of the Fathers, from the world of the Fathers to the moon. Having reached the moon, they become food, and the gods consume them there, as they consume Soma (moon) the King, saying, Wax and wane! But when this is over, they go back to the same ether, from ether to air, from air to rain, from rain to the earth. And when they have reached the earth, they become food, they are offered again in the fire which is man, and thence are born in the fire of woman. Then they rise upwards to the worlds, and go the same round as before. Those, however, who know neither of the two paths, become worms, insects, and creeping things.

Pre-Christian Era

As a goldsmith, having taken a piece of gold, makes another form, new and more beautiful, so, verily the Self, having cast off this body and having put away ignorance, makes another new and more beautiful form. . . . Having arrived at the end of that work—whatsoever he here doeth—he returns again from that world to this world of action.

Brhadāranyaka Upanishat

HAVING abandoned the former body, the incarnate Spirit, following the Law of Karma, obtains either heaven or hell according to his deeds. And having obtained a celestial body, or a body of suffering born of objects of desire, he experiences varied fruits in heaven or hell. At the end of the fruits, when the time for his rebirth arrives . . . then Time unites him again with activities selected from the accumulation of past activities.

Devi Bhagavata

DEVOTED to the fruits of acts, whatever kind of acts a person covetous of fruits accomplishes, the fruits, good or bad, that he actually enjoys, partake of their character. Like fishes going against a current of water, the acts of a past life are flung back on the actor. The embodied creature experiences happiness for his good acts, and misery for his evil ones.

Mahabharata, Shanti Parva

HE who forms desires in his mind is born again through his desires here and there.

Mundaka Upanishat

IN the source of all life, vast basis of all, in that wheel-sphere of Brahm, he is made to revolve, who comes and who goes; but if on the Self and Ordainer he dwells, as apart from the wheel, held by Him in honour thereafter, he goes to the state free of death.

Shvetashvatar Upanishat

The Ring of Return

PURIFIED, clarified in mind, the Bikkhu now directs his mind toward the recollection and recognition of previous modes of existence.

And he calls to mind his various lots in former lives; first one life, then two lives . . . up to fifty lives, then a thousand lives; then a hundred thousand.

Then he recalls the epochs of many a world-arising; then the epochs of many a world-destruction. . . . "There was I. That was my name. To that family I now belonged. This was my rank. This was my occupation.

"Such and such were the fresh weal and woe I underwent. Thus was now my life's ending. Departing once more, I came into existence again elsewhere." In such wise does the Bikkhu remember the characteristics and particulars of his varied lots in times past.

Sāmaññapala Sutta

AS the dweller in the body experienceth in the body childhood, youth, old age, so passeth he on to another body; the steadfast one grieveth not thereat. . . .

He who regardeth this as a slayer, or he who thinketh he is slain, both of them are ignorant. He slayeth not, nor is he slain.

He is not born, nor doth he die; nor having been, ceaseth he any more to be; unborn, perpetual, eternal and ancient, he is not slain when the body is slaughtered.

As a man, casting off worn-out garments, taketh new ones, so the dweller in the body, casting off worn-out bodies, entereth into others that are new.

Weapons cleave him not, nor fire burneth him, nor waters wet him, nor wind drieth him away.

Uncleavable he, incombustible he, and indeed neither to be wetted nor dried away; perpetual, all pervasive, stable, immovable, ancient.

Pre-Christian Era

Unmanifest, unthinkable, immutable, he is called; therefore, knowing him as such, thou shouldst not grieve.

Or if thou thinkest of him as being constantly born and constantly dying, even then, O mighty-armed, thou shouldst not grieve.

For certain is death for the born, and certain is birth for the dead; therefore over the inevitable thou shouldst not grieve.

Many births have been left behind by Me and by thee, O Arjuna. I know them all, but thou knowest not thine. . . .

Whenever there is decay of righteousness, O Bhârata, and there is exaltation of unrighteousness, then I myself come forth.

For the protection of the good, for the destruction of evil-doers, for the sake of firmly establishing righteousness, I am born from age to age.

He who thus knoweth My divine birth and action, in its essence, having abandoned the body, cometh not to birth again, but cometh unto me, O Arjuna.

Having attained to the worlds of the pure-doing, and having dwelt there for immemorial years, he who fell from yoga is reborn in a pure and blessed house.

Or he may even be born into a family of wise Yogis; but such a birth as that is most difficult to obtain in this world.

There he recovereth the characteristics belonging to his former body, and with these he again laboureth for perfection. . . .

Purified from sin, fully perfected through manifold births, he reacheth the supreme goal.

Bhagavad-Gîtâ
(Translated by ANNIE BESANT)

The Ring of Return

HE . . . who is without understanding, whose mind is uncontrolled and impure, does not reach the state [of Bliss] but enters into the circle of births and deaths.

He, however, who is gifted with understanding, who is steadfast in mind and [keeps himself] continually pure, verily he will never again lapse from that state [of Bliss] to be born again into the world.

He whose mind is guided by Intelligence and who can handle the reins of reason will reach the end of his journey [in safety], and attain to the exalted state of that All-pervading Spirit.

The Yoga of Yama
(Translated by W. GORN OLD)

THE Lord uttered the following stanzas:

With my Buddha-eye, monks, I see that the senior Kâsyapa here shall become a Buddha at a future Epoch, in an incalculable Æon, after he shall have paid homage to the most high of men.

This Kâsyapa shall see fully thirty thousand kotis of Ginas, under whom he shall lead a spiritual life for the sake of Buddha-knowledge.

After having paid homage to those highest of men and acquired that supreme knowledge, he shall in his last bodily existence be a Lord of the world, a matchless, great Seer.

And his field shall be magnificent, excellent, pure, goodly, beautiful, pretty, nice, even delightful, and set off with gold threads.

The Saddharma-Pundarika,
or The Lotus of the White Law
(Translated by H. KERN)

Pre-Christian Era

'And Ananda said: The monk Sālha has died, sir, at Nādika. Where has he been reborn, what is his destiny? The nun Nandā has there died. Where has she been reborn, what is her destiny? . . .

'The monk Sālha, Ananda, by the destruction of the cankers has, by himself and in this world, known, realised, attained to release of heart and mind. The nun Nandā has, by the destruction of the five fetters binding to the lower worlds, become reborn without parents, in higher worlds, there to become utterly well, thence never to return. The lay disciple Sudatta by the complete destruction of the three fetters, by the reducing to a minimum lust, ill-will and stupidity, has become a Once-returner, who on returning to this world will make an end of ill. The lay disciple the woman Sugatā, by the complete destruction of the three fetters has reached the stream (i.e. entered on the Way) is no longer liable to be reborn in an unhappy world, is assured of hereafter attaining enlightenment.' . . .

Dialogues of the Buddha
(Translated from the Pali of the *Dīgha Nīkaya*
by MRS. C. A. F. RHYS DAVIDS)

(I)

WHEN a *deva*[1] comes to decease from a world of *devas* there are five symptoms manifested: his garlands wilt, his robes are soiled, he sweats, he becomes weak, he takes no joy among his fellows. The *devas* seeing this, cheer him with three sayings: "Go hence to a happy bourne, sir; when you go, win a lucky state—enjoy!" And a monk said to the Lord: "What, sir, is reckoned a happy destiny for *devas*?" . . . "The state of man, monks! Then can he win faith in the *dhamma* and discipline taught by the Tathāgata."

[1] A word which in Buddhist scriptures frequently means not 'god' (as in the Vedas), but a *human being* in some happy, or heavenly world

The Ring of Return

(2)

When a *deva* from *deva*-world deceases from waning of life-span, three words of *devas* cheering him go forth : " Hence, sir, go to happy bourne, to fellowship of men ; become a man, win faith in the peerless teaching of the Better. That faith, for thee settled, become thy base, immovable while life lasts in the peerless teaching of the Better. Putting off bad ways in thought and word and deed, and all else that is corrupt, doing good in thought and word and deed, boundless, ungrasping, do well-based merit in giving, yea, much of it, and show other mortals the holy teaching of the Better." With this compassion the *devas*, when they know a *deva* is deceasing, cheer him, saying again and again : " Come, *deva* ! "

(1) *Prose passage,* (2) *Poem*
(Translated from the Pali by
MRS. C. A. F. RHYS DAVIDS)

FIVE in number are the destinies . . .—in purgatory, as an animal, as a *peta,*[1] as a human being, and as a *deva*[2]. Purgatory I know, the road thereto, the courses that lead to it, and what courses a man pursues to pass, at the body's dissolution after death, to rebirth in some unhappy state of misery or woe in purgatory. The animal world I know, and the worlds of *petas* and men, together with the roads to each. . . . *Devas* I know . . . and what courses a man pursues to pass, at the body's dissolution after death, to a state of blessedness in heaven. I know too Nirvana . . . and what courses a man pursues to dwell—here and now—by the extirpation of the Cankers, in that Deliverance of heart and mind which knows no Cankers, a Deliverance which he has, for and by himself, thought out and realised, so as to enter and abide therein.

There are two quests, Almsmen—the noble and the

[1] A man suffering penalty in an invisible body in this world

[2] See note on previous page

ignoble. First, what is the ignoble quest? Take the case of a man who, being in himself subject to rebirth, pursues what is no less subject thereto; who being in himself subject to decay, pursues what is no less subject thereto . . . wives and children, bondmen and bond-women, goats and sheep, fowls and swine, elephants, cattle, horses and mares, together with gold and coins of silver. . . . Secondly, what is the noble quest? Take the case of a man who, being himself subject to the round of rebirth—decay—disease—death—sorrow and impurity—sees peril in what is subject thereto, and so pursues after the consummate peace of Nirvana, which knows neither rebirth nor decay, neither disease nor death, neither sorrow nor impurity. This is the Noble Quest.

Just as a man who had passed from his own village to a second and thence to a third and finally back to his own village, might think how in his absence from home he had visited these other villages and how in each he had stood, sat, spoken, been silent—in just the same way does the Almsman call to mind his former existences . . . in all their details and features. . . .

Just as if there were two houses with doors and a man with eyes to see were to stand between those two houses and observe men going in and out and passing to and fro—in just the same way, with the Eye Celestial which is pure and far surpasses the human eye, does the Almsman see creatures in act of passing hence and reappearing elsewhere, creatures either lowly or debonair, fair or foul to view, happy or unhappy; and he is aware that they fare according to their deserts.

In the truth-finder all those Cankers which are of impurity, which lead to rebirth, entail suffering, ripen into sorrow, leaving behind a heritage of birth, decay, and death—all these have been grubbed up by the roots, like a bare cleaned site where once a palm tree grew, things which once have been and now can be no more.

Take the case of an Almsman who possesses faith and virtue, instruction, munificence, and understanding. The wish comes to him that, at the body's dissolution after death, he may be reborn a wealthy noble. On this he fixes and sets his heart, to this he trains his heart. The possession of the foregoing five plastic forces, coupled with this wish of his, conduce, with cultivation and development, to his being reborn accordingly. This is the road and way to such rebirth. . . .

Or in like manner, he forms the wish to be reborn a wealthy brahmin, or householder . . . or in communion with the Brāhma of one, two, three, four or five thousand worlds. . . . Or, possessing those same five qualities, the Almsman, hearing that the Brāhma of ten thousand worlds enjoys long life and beauty and abounds in well-being, forms the wish that he may be reborn in communion with that Brāhma. Now that Brāhma illuminates and pervades ten thousand worlds and all the creatures that are reborn there. . . . On this the Almsman fixes and sets his heart. . . . This is the road and way to such rebirth.

Further Dialogues of the Buddha
(Translated from the Pali of the
Majjhima Nīkaya
by Lord Chalmers)

THOSE who again and again go to the world with birth and death, to existence in this way or in that way—that is the state of ignorance. . . . The wise do not go to rebirth.

Dvayatānupassanasutta

Pre-Christian Era

IF a Bikkhu should desire, O brethren, to call to mind his various temporary states in days gone by—such as one birth, two births, three, four, five, ten, twenty, thirty, fifty, one hundred, or one thousand, or one hundred thousand births—in all their modes and all their details, let him be devoted to quietude of heart—let him look through things, let him be much alone.

Akankhayasutta

HE in whom there are no sins whatsoever originating in fear, which are the causes of coming back to this shore, that ascetic leaves this and the farther shore, as a snake its old worn-out skin.

Uragasutta

THE man who knows his previous birth-abodes, who sees both heaven and hell, who has reached the destruction of births, attained to insight, supreme, perfect in knowledge—him do I call a Brāhmana.

Vasetthasutta

THERE was a great god-sage called Nârada. . . . He travelled everywhere, and one day he was passing through a forest, and he saw a man who had been meditating until the white ants had built a huge mound round his body, so long had he been sitting in that position. He said to Nârada, " Where are you going? " Nârada replied, " I am going to heaven." " Then ask God when He will be merciful to me, when I shall attain freedom." Further on Nârada saw another man. He was jumping about, singing and dancing, and he said, " O Nârada, where are you going? " Nârada said, " I am going to heaven." " Then ask when I shall attain freedom." So Nârada went on. In the course of time he came again by the same road, and there was the man who had been meditating till the ant-hills had grown round him. He said, "O Nârada, did you ask the Lord about me?" "O yes." "What did He say?" "The Lord told me that you would attain freedom in four more births." Then the man began to weep and wail, and said, "I have meditated until an ant-hill has been raised around me, and I have to endure four more births yet!" Nârada went on to the other man. "Did you ask about me?" "O yes. Do you see this tamarind tree? I have to tell you that as many leaves as there are on that tree, so many times you will be born, and then you will attain freedom." Then the man began to dance for joy, and said, "After so short a time I shall be free!" A voice came, "My child, you shall have freedom this instant."

Kurma Purâna

WHAT now, Brothers, is the holy truth of the Cessation of Suffering? . . .

Released from Sensual Craving, released from the Craving for Existence, one does not return, one does not enter again into the world of Existence.

For it is even through the total extinction of this Craving that the Clinging to Existence ceases; with the cessation of the Clinging to Existence the Action-Process ceases; with the cessation of the Action-Process Rebirth is done away; through not being reborn, decay, death, sorrow, lamentation, suffering, grief, and despair cease.

The Word of the Buddha

AS a wayfarer takes a brief lodging, so he that is travelling through the way of existence finds in each birth but a passing rest.

Bodhicharyāvatāra

Pre-Christian Era

LONG ago, they say, when Kassapa the Buddha was promulgating the faith, there dwelt in one community near the Ganges a great company of members of the Order. Then the brethren, true to established rules and duties, rose early in the morning, and taking the long-handled brooms, would sweep out the courtyard and collect the rubbish into a heap, meditating the while on the virtues of the Buddha.

One day a brother told a novice to remove the heap of dust. But he, as if he heard not, went about his business; and on being called a second time, and a third, still went his way as if he had not heard. Then the brother, angry with so intractable a novice, dealt him a blow with the broomstick. This time, not daring to refuse, he set about the task, crying; and as he did so he muttered to himself this first aspiration: "May I, by reason of this meritorious act of throwing out the rubbish, in each successive condition in which I may be born up to the time when I attain Nirvana, be powerful and glorious as the mid-day sun!"

When he had finished his work, he went to the riverside to bathe, and on beholding the mighty billows of the Ganges seething and surging, he uttered this second aspiration: "May I, in each successive condition in which I may be born till I attain Nirvana, possess the power of saying the right thing, and saying it instantly, under any circumstances that may arise, carrying all before me like this mighty surge!"

Now that brother, after he had put the broom away in the broom closet, had likewise wandered down to the riverside to bathe, and as he walked he happened to overhear what the novice had said. Then thinking: "If this fellow, on the ground of such an act of merit, which after all was instigated by me, can harbour hopes like this, what may not I attain to?" He too made his wish, and it was thus: "In each successive condition in which I may be born till I attain Nirvana, may I too be ready in saying the right thing at once, and more especially may I have the power of unravelling and of solving each problem and each puzzling question this young man may put—carrying all before me like this mighty surge!"

Then for the whole period between one Buddha and the next those two people wandered from existence to existence among gods and men. And our Buddha saw them too, and just as he did to the son of Moggalî and to Tissa the Elder, so to them also did he foretell their future fate, saying: "Five hundred years after I have passed away will these two reappear, and the subtle Law and Doctrine taught by me will they two explain, unravelling and disentangling its difficulties by questions put and metaphors adduced."

(The novice and the brother were subsequently reborn as the King Milinda and the Sage Nagasena)

The king said: "Nagasena, is there any one who after death is not re-individualised?"

"Some say so, and some not."

"Who are they?"

"A sinful being is re-individualised, a sinless one is not."

"Will you be re-individualised?"

"If when I die, I die with craving for existence in my heart, yes; but if not, no."

"Very good, Nagasena."

The king said: "Nagasena, he who escapes re-individualisation, is it by reasoning that he escapes it?"

"Both by reasoning, your Majesty, and by wisdom, and by other good qualities."

"But are not reasoning and wisdom surely much the same?"

"Certainly not. Reasoning is one thing, wisdom is another. Sheep and goats, oxen and buffaloes, camels and asses have reasoning, but wisdom they have not."

"Well put, Nagasena."

The king said: "What is it, Nagasena, that is reborn?"

"Name-and-form is reborn."

"What, is it this same name-and-form that is re-born?"

"No, but by this name-and-form deeds are done, good or evil, and by these deeds (this Karma) another name-and-form is reborn."

"If that be so, sir, would not the new being be released from its evil Karma?"

The Elder replied: "Yes, if it were not reborn. But just because it is reborn, O king, it is therefore not released from its evil Karma."

"Give me an illustration."

"Suppose, O king, some man were to steal a mango from another man, and the owner of the mango were to seize him and bring him before the king, and charge him with the crime. And the thief were to say: 'Your Majesty, I have not taken away this man's mangoes. Those that he put in the ground are different from the ones I took. I do not deserve to be punished.' How then? Would he be guilty?"

"Certainly, sir. He would deserve to be punished."

"But on what ground?"

"Because, in spite of whatever he may say, he would be guilty in respect of the last mango which resulted from the first one (the owner set in the ground)."

"Just so, great king, deeds good or evil are done by this name-and-form and another is reborn. But that other is not thereby released from its deeds (its Karma)."

The Questions of King Milinda
(Translated by T. W. RHYS DAVIDS)

The Ring of Return

SUCH an one who does his duty is tolerant like the earth, or like a threshold ; he is like a lake without mud ; no new births are in store for him.

Many a birth have I traversed in this round of lives and deaths, vainly seeking the builder of the house. Wretched is birth again and again !

Builder of the house, now art thou seen ! Never again shalt thou build the house. Thy timbers all are broken, thy ridge-pole destroyed. Delivered is my mind ; achieved the conquest of craving.

Be free from the past, be free from the future, be free from the present, passing beyond them ! From all thus delivered in mind, no more shalt thou come to birth and to decay. . . .

Done with craving, unattached to aught, skilled in the meaning of the Teaching, knowing the arrangement of the words in order due—this is the final body of such an one !

Dhammapada
(*The Way of Truth*)

ALTHOUGH the Master was preaching, yet, of five laymen who sat there in His presence, one, being drowsy, fell asleep ; another sat grubbing in the ground with his finger ; the third idly shook a tree to and fro ; the fourth sat gazing at the sky and paid no heed to what was said ; while the fifth was the only one of them who gave heed to the teaching.

So the Elder Ananda, who stood there fanning the Master, observing the behaviour of these men, said to Him : " Lord, Thou art teaching the Truth to these men even as the voice of the thunder when the heavy rains are falling. Yet, behold ! they sit doing this and that, while Thou dost preach." . . .

Then said the Master to Ananda : " Of these five men, the one that sits asleep was reborn as a goblin-snake in many a birth, and, laying his head on his coils, would go to sleep. So now he sleeps, and no sound of mine can penetrate his ears. . . . Yonder man, who sits grubbing in the ground with his finger, took birth as an earthworm many a time and bored the earth. Now, too, he does the same and hears no word of mine. That one, who sits there and shakes a tree, was born many times successively as a monkey. It is his nature so to do—a habit engrained by countless former births. Thus no sound of mine can penetrate his ears. Next, yonder brāhmana, who sits gazing at the sky, was born for many times successively as an astrologer, a star-gazer. By dint of engrained habit even to-day he looks up at the sky, and no sound of mine can penetrate his ears. But this one, who, sitting, hears the Law attentively, for many, many times successively was a master of the Vedas three, a brāhmana who could repeat the Sacred Texts. So now also he pays good heed unto my words, just as if he were linking up a mantram."

" But, Lord," said Ananda, " Thy teaching cleaveth even through the skin and reacheth unto bones and marrow. How can it be that when Thou preachest the Law these men pay no heed thereto ? "

" Ananda, such things as The Buddha, or The Law, or The Order of Brethren, through countless hundred thousand cycles of time have never been heard of by these beings. Therefore they cannot listen to this Law. In this round of births and deaths, whose beginning is incalculable, these beings have come to birth hearing only the talk of divers animals. They spend their time in song and dance, in places where men drink and gamble and the like. Thus they cannot listen to the Law."

" But what, Lord, is the actual reason, the immediate cause why they cannot ? "

The Ring of Return

The Master replied : " Ananda, owing to hatred, owing to delusion, owing to lust, they cannot do so. There is no such fire as the fire of lust. It burns up creatures, nor even leaves an ash behind."

From the *Dhammapada Commentary*
(Translated by F. L. WOODWARD)

Pre-Christian Era

ANCIENT GREECE AND ROME

PYTHAGORAS was reported to have been the first of the Greeks to teach the doctrine that the soul, passing through the 'circle of necessity,' was bound at various times to various living bodies. . . . He was accustomed to speak of himself in this manner : that he had formerly been Æthalides, and had been accounted the son of Mercury ; and that Mercury had offered him any gift he pleased except immortality. Accordingly, he had requested that, whether living or dead, he might preserve the memory of what had happened to him. . . . At a subsequent period, he was reborn as Euphorbus, and was wounded by Menelaus at the siege of Troy, and so died. In that life he used to say that he had formerly been Æthalides; and that he had received as a gift from Mercury the memory of his soul's transmigrations, and of its temporary sojourns in the kingdoms of plants and animals ; also the gift of recollecting what his own soul and the souls of others had experienced between death and rebirth.

After Euphorbus died, he passed into Hermotimus ; and in that life he went into the territory of the Branchidæ, and, entering the temple of Apollo, he pointed out the shield which he had carried as Euphorbus, and which Menelaus had sent to the temple as a dedicatory offering. The shield had by that time rusted away until nothing remained but the carved ivory face on the boss of it. In his next birth he was a Delian fisherman ; and finally he reincarnated as Pythagoras.

DIOGENES LAERTIUS
(*Life of Pythagoras*)

MANY of his associates he reminded of the lives lived by their soul before it was bound to the body, and by irrefutable arguments demonstrated that he had been Euphorbus, the son of Panthus.

PORPHYRY
(*Life of Pythagoras*)

The Ring of Return

WHAT Pythagoras wished to indicate by all these particulars was that he knew the former lives he had lived, which enabled him to begin providential attention to others and remind them of their former existences.

IAMBLICHUS
(*Life of Pythagoras*)

HE who believes that he transmigrates, after death, into the body of a beast or a plant is grossly mistaken ; he is ignorant of the fact that the essential form of the soul cannot change, that it is and it remains human, and only metaphorically speaking does virtue make of it a god and vice an animal.

HIEROCLES
(*Commentary of the Golden Verses of Pythagoras*)

THERE is a word of Fate, an old decree
And everlasting, of the gods, made fast
With amplest oaths that whosoe'er of those
Far spirits, with their lot of age-long life,
Do foul their limbs with slaughter in offence,
Or swear foresworn, as failing of their pledge,
Shall wander thrice ten thousand weary years
Far from the Blessed, and be born through time
In various shapes of mortal kind, which change
Ever and ever troublous paths of life ;
For now Air hunts them onward to the Sea ;
Now the wild Sea disgorges them on Land ;
Now Earth will spue toward beams of radiant Sun ;
Whence he will toss them back to whirling Air—
Each gets from other what they all abhor,
And in that brood I too am numbered now,
A fugitive and vagabond from heaven,
As one obedient unto raving Strife.
Charis abhors intolerable Fate,
For I was once already boy and girl,
Thicket and bird, and mute fish in the waves.

Pre-Christian Era

All things doth Nature change, enwrapping souls
In unfamiliar tunics of the flesh.
The worthiest dwellings for the souls of men,
When 'tis their lot to live in form of brutes,
Are tawny lions, those great beasts that sleep
Couched on the black earth up the mountainside;
But when in forms of beautiful plumed trees
They live, the bays are worthiest for souls.

And seers at last and singers of high hymns,
Physicians sage, and chiefs o'er earth-born men
Shall they become, whence germinate the gods,
The excellent in honours.

EMPEDOCLES (*The Purifications*)
(Translated by WILLIAM ELLERY LEONARD)

THE souls of them from whom Persephone has accepted atonement for an ancient woe, she restoreth the ninth year to the light of the sun above the earth.

And from these souls come glorious kings and such as are strong and swift and excel in wisdom; and throughout all future time they are called holy heroes by mankind.

PINDAR

THEY who thrice on either side of death have refrained their souls from wickedness, travel on the road of Zeus to the tower of Cronus, where the ocean breezes blow around the island of the blest!

PINDAR

EVERY soul is immortal—for whatever is in perpetual motion is immortal. . . . All that is soul presides over all that is without soul and patrols all heaven, now appearing in one form and now in another. When it is perfect and fully feathered, it roams in upper air, and regulates the entire universe; but the soul that has lost its feathers is carried down till it finds some solid resting-place; and when it has settled there, when it has taken to itself, that is, an earthly body, which seems capable of self-motion, owing to the power of its new inmate, the name of animal is given to the whole; to this compound, I mean, of soul and body. . . . The natural efficacy of a wing is to lift up heavy substances and bear them aloft to those upper regions which are inhabited by the race of the Gods. . . . There are many ravishing views and opening paths within the bounds of heaven, whereon the family of the blessed Gods go to and fro . . . and they are followed by all who from time to time possess both will and power. . . . But whenever they go to feast and revel, they forthwith journey by an uphill path to the summit of the heavenly vault. Now the chariots of the Gods being of equal poise and obedient to the rein, move easily, but all others with difficulty; for they are burdened by the horse of vicious temper, which sways and sinks them towards the earth, if haply he has received no good training from his charioteer.[1] Whereupon there awaits the soul a crowning pain and agony. For those which we called immortal go outside when they are come to the topmost height, and stand on the outer surface of heaven, and as they stand they are borne round by its revolution and gaze on the external scene. . . . Real existence, colourless, formless and intangible, visible only to the intelligence which sits at the helm of the soul . . . has its abode in this region. . . . And the mind of every soul that is destined to receive its due inheritance is delighted at seeing the essence to which it has been so long a stranger, and by the light of truth is fostered and made to thrive, until, by the revolution of the heaven, it is brought round again to the same point. . . . And when in like manner it has seen all the

[1] The soul is compared throughout to a pair of winged steeds, with charioteer, one steed being 'of generous breed,' the other 'of opposite descent and opposite character'

rest of the world of essence, and feasted on the sight, it sinks down again into the interior of heaven and returns to its own home. . . . That [soul] which follows a God most closely and resembles him most nearly, succeeds in raising the head of its charioteer into the outer region and is carried round with the Immortals in their revolution, though sore encumbered by its horses and barely able to contemplate the real existences; while another rises and sinks by turns, his horses plunging so violently that he can discern no more than a part of these existences. . . . But the common herd follow at a distance . . . they make the revolution in the moisture of the lower element, trampling on one another. . . . There is an irrevocable decree that if any soul has followed a God in close companionship and discerned any of the true essences, it shall continue free from harm till the next revolution, and if it be ever thus successful, it shall be ever thus unharmed; but whenever, from inability to follow, it has missed that glorious sight, and, through some mishap it may have encountered, has become charged with forgetfulness and vice, and been thereby so burdened as to shed its feathers and fall to the earth, in that case there is a law that the soul thus fallen be not planted in any bestial nature during the first generation, but that if it has seen more than others of essential verity, it pass into the germ of a man who is to become a lover of wisdom or a lover of beauty.

[*Here follows the list of the various conditions of life for the various 'ranks' of soul; that of 'an absolute monarch' being ranked lowest of all*]

And in all these various conditions those who have lived justly receive afterwards a better lot; those who have lived unjustly a worse.

For to that same place from which each soul set out it does not return for ten thousand years; so long is it before it recovers its plumage, unless it has belonged to a guileless lover of philosophy. . . . On the termination of their first life . . . some go to the prison-houses beneath the earth, to suffer for their sins ; while others, by virtue of their trial, are borne lightly upward to some celestial spot, where they pass their days in a manner worthy of the life they have lived in their mortal form. But in the thousandth year both divisions come back again to share and choose their second life, and they select that which they severally please. . . .

And this is nothing more nor less than a recollection of those things which in time past our soul beheld when it travelled with a God, and, looking high over what we now call real, lifted up its head into the region of eternal essence. . . .

Every man's soul has by the law of his birth been a spectator of eternal truth, or it would never have passed into this our mortal frame, yet still it is no easy matter for all to be reminded of their past by their present existence. It is not easy either for those who, during that struggle I told you of, caught but a brief glimpse of upper glories, nor for those who, after their fall to this world, were so unfortunate as to be turned aside by evil associations into the paths of wickedness, and so made to forget that holy spectacle. . . .

PLATO
(*Phædrus*)
(Translated by J. WRIGHT)

WELL, I will tell you a tale, not like that of Odysseus to Alcinous, but of what once happened to a brave man, Er, the son of Armenius, a native of Pamphylia, who, according to story, was killed in battle. . . . On the twelfth day after his death, as he lay on the funeral pyre, he came to life again, and then proceeded to describe what he had seen in the other world. . . .

Each soul, as it arrived, wore a travel-stained appearance . . . and those who had descended from heaven were questioned about heaven by those who had risen out of the earth ; while the latter were questioned by the former about the earth. Those who were come from earth told their tale with lamentations and tears, as they bethought them of all the dreadful things they had seen and suffered in their subterranean journey, which they said had lasted a thousand years; while those who were come from heaven described enjoyments and sights of marvellous beauty. . . .

Now the souls were required to go to Lachesis. An interpreter first of all marshalled them in order, and then having taken from the lap of Lachesis a number of lots and plans of life, mounted a high pulpit, and spoke as follows: "Thus saith the maiden Lachesis, the daughter of Necessity. Ye short-lived souls, a new generation of men shall here begin the cycle of its mortal existence. Your destiny shall not be allotted to you, but you shall choose it for yourselves. Let him who draws the first lot be the first to choose a life, which shall be his irrevocably. Virtue owns no master. He who honours her shall have more of her, and he who slights her less. The responsibility lies with the chooser. Heaven is guiltless." Having said this, he threw the lots down upon the crowd; and each spirit took up the one which fell at his side, except Er himself, who was forbidden to do so. . . . This done, the plans of life, which far outnumbered the souls that were present, were laid before them on the ground. They were of every kind. There were lives of all living things, and among them every sort of human life. . . . The materials were very variously combined—wealth appearing here, and poverty there; disease here, and health there; and here again a mean between these extremes. This, my dear Glaucon, is apparently the moment when everything is at stake with a man; and for this reason, above all others, it is the duty of each of us diligently to investigate and study, to the neglect of every other subject, that science which may haply enable a man to learn and discover who will render him so instructed as to be able to discriminate between a good and an evil life, and according to his means to choose, always and everywhere, that better life, by carefully calculating the influence which the things just mentioned, in combination or in separation, have upon real excellence of life; and who will teach him to understand what evil or good is wrought by beauty tempered with poverty or wealth, and how the result is affected by the state of soul which enters into the combination . . . so as to be able to form a judgment from all these data combined, and, with an eye steadily fixed on the nature of the soul, to choose between the good and the evil life, giving the name of evil to the life which will draw the soul into becoming more unjust, and the name of good to the life which will lead it to become more just, and bidding farewell to every other consideration. . . .

It was a truly wonderful sight, he said, to watch how each soul selected its life—a sight at once melancholy, and ludicrous, and strange. The experience of their former life generally guided the choice. . . . It so happened that the soul of Odysseus had drawn the last lot of all. When he came up to choose, the memory of his former sufferings had so abated his ambition that he went about a long time looking for a quiet retired life, which with great trouble he discovered lying about, and thrown contemptuously aside by the others. As soon as he saw it, he chose it gladly, and said that he would have done the same if he had even drawn the first lot. . . .

Now, when all the souls had chosen their lives in the order of the lots . . . they all travelled into the plain of Forgetfulness . . . and took up their quarters by the bank of the river of Indifference, whose waters cannot be held in any vessel. All persons are compelled to drink a certain quantity of the water; but those who are not preserved by prudence drink more than the quantity; and each, as he drinks, forgets everything. When they had gone to rest, and it was now midnight, there was a clap of thunder and an earthquake; and in a moment the souls were carried up to their birth, this way and that, like shooting stars. Er himself was prevented from drinking any of the water; but how, and by what road, he reached his body, he knew not: only he knew that he suddenly opened his eyes at dawn, and found himself laid out upon the funeral pyre.

PLATO
(*The Republic*, Book X)

THE soul of the true philosopher . . . abstains as much as possible from pleasures and desires, griefs and fears . . . because each pleasure and pain, having a nail, as it were, nails the soul to the body, and fastens it to it, and causes it to become corporeal, deeming those things to be true whatever the body asserts to be so. For, in consequence of its forming the same opinions with the body, and delighting in the same things . . . it can never pass into Hades in a pure state, but must ever depart polluted by the body, and so quickly falls again into another body, and grows up as if it were sown, and consequently is deprived of all association with that which is divine, and pure, and uniform.

PLATO
(*Phædo*)
(Translated by HENRY CARY)

KNOW that if you become worse you will go to the worse souls, or if better to the better, and in every succession of life and death you will do and suffer what like may fitly suffer at the hands of like.

PLATO
(*Laws*, Book X)

THE mistakes and the sufferings of human life make me think sometimes that those ancient seers, or interpreters of the secrets of heaven and the counsels of the Divine Mind, had some glimpses of the truth, when they said that men are born in order to suffer the penalty for some sins committed in a former life.

CICERO
(*Treatise on Glory*)

The Ring of Return

ON the level bosom of this vale more thickly the tall trees
Grow, an' aneath quivering poplars and whispering alders
Lethe's dreamy river throu' peaceful scenery windeth.
Whereby now flitted in vast swarms many people of all lands,
As when in early summer honey-bees on a flowery pasture
Pill the blossoms, hurrying to an' fro,—innumerous are they,
Revisiting the ravish'd lily cups, while all the meadow hums.
Æneas was turn'd to the sight, and marvelling inquired,
" Say, sir, what the river that there i' the vale-bottom I see?
And who they that thickly along its bank have assembled? "
Then Lord Anchises, " The spirits for whom a second life
And body are destined ar' arriving thirsty to Lethe,
And here drink th' unmindful draught from wells of oblivyon.
My heart greatly desired of this very thing to acquaint thee,
Yea, and show thee the men to be born, our glory her'after,
So to gladden thine heart where now thy voyaging endeth."
" Must it then be believ'd, my sire, that a soul which attaineth
Elysium will again submit to her old body-burden?
Is this well? what hap can awake such dire longing in them? "
" I will tell thee, O son, nor keep thy wonder awaiting,"
Answereth Anchises, and all expoundeth in order.
" Know first that the heavens, and th' Earth, and space fluid or void,

Pre-Christian Era

Night's pallid orb, day's Sun, and all his starry coævals,
Are by one spirit inly quickened, and, mingling in each part,
Mind informs the matter, nature's complexity ruling.
Thence the living creatures, man, brute and ev'ry feathered fowl,
And what breedeth in Ocean aneath her surface of argent:
Their seed knoweth a fiery vigour, 'tis of airy divine birth,
In so far as unimpeded by an alien evil,
Nor dull'd by the body's framework condemn'd to corruption.
Hence the desires and vain tremblings that assail them, unable
Darkly prison'd to arise to celestial exaltation;
Nor when death summoneth them anon earth-life to relinquish,
Can they in all discard their stain, nor wholly away with
Mortality's plague-spots. It must be that, O, many wild graffs
Deeply at heart engrain'd have rooted strangely upon them:
Wherefore must sufferings purge them, yea, Justice atone them
With penalties heavy as their guilt: some purify exposed
Hung to the viewless winds, or others long watery searchings
Low i' the deep wash clean, some bathe in fiery renewal:
Each cometh unto his own retribution,—if after in ample
Elysium we attain, but a few, to the fair Happy Woodland,
Yet slow time still worketh on us to remove the defilement,
Till it hath eaten away the acquir'd dross, leaving again free

That first fiery vigour, the celestial virtue of our life.
All whom here thou seest, hav' accomplished purification:
Unto the stream of Lethe a god their company calleth,
That forgetful of old failure, pain and disappointment,
They may again into earthly bodies with glad courage enter."

VIRGIL (*Æneid*, Book VI.)
(A line for line paraphrase by ROBERT BRIDGES)

O RACE! stricken by the alarms of icy death, why do you dread Styx? . . . Souls are not subject to death; and having left their former abode, they ever inhabit new dwellings and, there received, live on . . .

The soul wanders about and comes from that spot to this, from this to that, and takes possession of any limbs whatever; it both passes from the beasts to human bodies, and so does our soul into the beasts; and in no lapse of time does it perish.

And as the pliable wax is moulded into new forms, and no longer abides as it was before, nor preserves the same shape, but yet is the same wax, so I tell you that the soul is ever the same, but passes into different forms.

OVID
(*Metamorphoses*)
(Translated by H. T. RILEY)

Pythagoras speaks:

THOSE I would teach; and by right reason bring
To think of death as but an idle thing.
Why thus affrighted at an empty name,
A dream of darkness, and fictitious flame?
Vain themes of wit, which but in poems pass,
And fables of a world that never was?
What feels the body when the soul expires,
By time corrupted, or consumed by fires?
Nor dies the spirit, but new life repeats
In other form, and only changes seats.

Pre-Christian Era

Ev'n I, who these mysterious truths declare,
Was once Euphorbus in the Trojan war;
My name and lineage I remember well,
And how in fight by Sparta's king I fell.
In Argive Juno's fane I late beheld
My buckler hung on high, and own'd my former shield.

Then death, so call'd, is but old matter dress'd
In some new figure, and a varied vest:
Thus all things are but alter'd, nothing dies;
And here and there the unbodied spirit flies,
By time, or force, or sickness dispossess'd,
And lodges, where it lights, in man or beast;
Or hunts without, till ready limbs it find,
And actuates those according to their kind;
From tenement to tenement though toss'd,
The soul is still the same, the figure only lost:
And, as the soften'd wax new seals receives,
This face assumes, and that impression leaves;
Now call'd by one, now by another name,
The form is only changed, the wax is still the same.
So death, so call'd, can but the form deface;
The immortal soul flies out in empty space,
To seek her fortune in some other place.

OVID
(*Metamorphoses*)
(Translated by JOHN DRYDEN)

III

EARLY CHRISTIAN AND OTHER WRITINGS OF THE FIRST FIVE CENTURIES A.D.

FOR all the prophets and the law prophesied until John. And if ye will receive it, this is Elias, which was for to come.

Matthew xi 13, 14

WHEN Jesus came into the coasts of Cæsarea Philippi, He asked His disciples, saying: Whom do men say that I, the Son of man, am? And they said: Some say that Thou art John the Baptist; some Elias; and others Jeremias, or one of the prophets.

Matthew xvi 13, 14

HIS disciples asked Him, saying, Why then say the scribes that Elias must first come? And Jesus answered and said unto them, Elias truly shall first come, and restore all things. But I say unto you, that Elias is come already, and they knew him not. . . . Then the disciples understood that He spake unto them of John the Baptist.

Matthew xvii 10–13

NOW Herod . . . was perplexed, because that it was said of some, that John had risen from the dead; and of some, that Elias had appeared: and of others, that one of the old prophets was risen again.

Luke ix 7, 8

AND as Jesus passed by, He saw a man which was blind from his birth. And His disciples asked Him, saying, Master, who did sin, this man, or his parents, that he was born blind? Jesus answered, Neither did this man sin nor his parents; but that the works of God should be made manifest in him.

John ix 1–4

The Ring of Return

THE company of disembodied souls is distributed in various orders. The law of some of them is to enter mortal bodies and after certain prescribed periods be again set free. But those possessed of a diviner structure are absolved from all local bonds of earth. . . . Some of these souls choose confinement in mortal bodies because they are earthly and corporeally inclined. Others depart, being released again according to supernaturally determined times and seasons. Therefore, all such as are wise, like Moses, are living abroad from home. For the souls of such formerly chose this expatriation from heaven, and through curiosity and the desire of acquiring knowledge they came to dwell abroad in earthly nature, and while they dwell in the body they look down on things visible and mortal around them and urge their way thitherward again whence they came originally: and call that heavenly region in which they have their citizenship, fatherland, but this earthly in which they live, foreign.

PHILO OF ALEXANDRIA

EVERY soul, whether without mind, or joined to mind, or departing from the body, is ordained to wander in the region lying between the moon and the earth for a term. . . .

In like manner there are deep places and gulfs—like in the moon . . . in which the souls either suffer or inflict punishment for the things which they have either done or endured when they have already been made genii. . . . The genii do not always pass their time upon her [the moon], but they come down hither or take charge of Oracles; they are present at, and assist in, the most advanced of the initiatory rites, as punishers and keepers of wrongdoers; they act, and shine as saviours in battle and at sea; and whatsoever thing in these capacities they do amiss . . . they are punished for it, for they are driven down again to earth and coupled with human bodies.

PLUTARCH
(*Morals*)

First Five Centuries A.D.

TO his [Apollonius's] mother, just before he was born there came an apparition of Proteus, who changes his form so much in Homer, in the guise of an Egyptian demon. She was in no way frightened, but asked him what sort of child she would bear. And he answered: "Myself." "And who are you?" she asked. "Proteus," answered he, "the god of Egypt."

Iarchas explained that his own soul had once been in the body of another man who was a king, and that in that state he had performed this and that exploit; while Apollonius told them that he had once been the pilot of a ship in Egypt, and had accomplished all sorts of exploits, which he enumerated to them.

"And you must not be surprised at my transformation from one Indian to another; for here is one"—and he [Iarchas] pointed to a stripling of about twenty years of age—"who in natural aptitude for philosophy excels everyone, and he enjoys good health, as you see, and is furnished with an excellent constitution; moreover, he can endure fire and all sorts of cutting and wounding, yet, in spite of all these advantages, he detests philosophy." "What, then," said Apollonius, "O Iarchas, is the matter with the youth? For it is a terrible thing to tell me, if one so well adapted by nature to the pursuit refuses to embrace philosophy, and has no love for learning, and that although he lives with you." "He does not live with us," replied the other, "but he has been caught like a lion against his will and confined here, but he looks askance at us when we try to domesticate him and caress him. The truth is this stripling was once Palamedes of Troy, and he found his bitterest enemies in Odysseus and Homer; for the one laid an ambush against him of people by whom he was stoned to death, while the other denied him any place in his Epic; and because neither the wisdom with which he was endowed was of any use to him nor did he meet with any praise from Homer, to whom, nevertheless, many people of no great importance owe their renown, and because he was outwitted by Odysseus in spite of his innocence, he has conceived an aversion to philosophy, and deplores his ill-luck. And he is Palamedes, for indeed he can write without having learned his letters."

The following incident of Apollonius's stay in Egypt was thought remarkable. There was a man led a tame lion about by a string, as if it had been a dog ; and the animal not only fawned upon him, but on anyone who approached it. It went collecting alms all round the towns, and was admitted even in the temples, being a pure animal ; for it never licked up the blood of the victims, nor pounced on them when they were being flayed and cut up, but lived upon honey-cakes and bread and dried fruits and cooked meat ; and you also came on it drinking wine without changing its character. One day it came up to Apollonius when he was sitting in the temples, and whined and fawned at his knees, and begged of him more earnestly than it had ever done of anybody. The bystanders imagined it wanted some solid reward, but Apollonius exclaimed : " This lion is begging me to make you understand that a human soul is within him, the soul namely of Amasis, the king of Egypt in the province of Sais." And when the lion heard that, he gave a piteous and plaintive roar, and, crouching down, began to lament, shedding tears. Thereupon Apollonius stroked him, and said : " I think the lion ought to be sent to Leontopolis and dedicated to the temple there, for I consider it wrong that a king who has been changed into the most kingly of beasts should go about begging, like any human mendicant." In consequence the priests met and offered sacrifice to Amasis, and, having decorated the animal with a collar and ribbons, they conveyed him up-country to Egypt, with pipings, hymns, and songs composed in his honour.

PHILOSTRATUS
(*Life of Apollonius of Tyana*)

First Five Centuries A.D.

HOW my spirit first proceeded from Apollo, and took flight to earth, and entered into a human form, and what was the nature of the crime thus expiated—all this would take too long to tell; nor is it fitting either for me to speak of such matters or for you to hear them. . . . When I was Euphorbus, I fought at Troy and was slain by Menelaus. Some time then elapsed before I entered into the body of Pythagoras. . . .

A king; then a pauper; and presently a satrap; and after that came horse, jackdaw, frog, and I know not how many more; there is no reckoning them up in detail.

LUCIAN
(*Dialogue of the Cock and the Cobbler*)

FIRST DEALER: Where do you come from?

Pythagoreanism: From Samos.

First Dealer: Where did you get your schooling?

Pythagoreanism: From the sophists of Egypt.

First Dealer: If I buy you, what will you teach me?

Pythagoreanism: Nothing. I will remind you. . . . You have to learn that you yourself are not the person you appear to be.

First Dealer: What, I am someone else; not the I who am speaking to you?

Pythagoreanism: You are that you now: but you have formerly inhabited another body and borne another name. And in course of time you will change once more.

First Dealer: Why, then I shall be immortal and take one shape after another? But enough of this. . . .

LUCIAN
(*The Sale of Creeds*)

EVERY soul . . . comes into this world strengthened by the victories or weakened by the defeats of its previous life. Its place in this world as a vessel appointed to honour or dishonour is determined by its previous merits or demerits. Its work in this world determines its place in the world which is to follow this.

The Ring of Return

I am indeed of the opinion that as the end and consummation of the saints will be in those [ages] which are not seen, and are eternal, we must conclude that rational creatures had also a similar beginning. . . . And if this is so, then there has been a descent from a higher to a lower condition, on the part not only of those souls who have deserved the change by the variety of their movements, but also on that of those who, in order to serve the whole world, were brought down from those higher and invisible spheres to these lower and visible ones, although against their will. . . . The hope of freedom is entertained by the whole of creation—of being liberated from the corruption of slavery—when the sons of God, who either fell away or were scattered abroad, shall be gathered into one, and when they shall have fulfilled their duties in this world.

ORIGEN
(*De Principiis*)

IS it not more in conformity with reason that every soul for certain mysterious reasons (I speak now according to the opinion of Pythagoras and Plato and Empedocles, whom Celsus frequently names) is introduced into a body, and introduced according to its deserts and former actions?

Is it not rational that souls should be introduced into bodies, in accordance with their merits and previous deeds, and that those who have used their bodies in doing the utmost possible good should have a right to bodies endowed with qualities superior to the bodies of others? . . .

The soul, which is immaterial and invisible in its nature, exists in no material place without having a body suited to the nature of that place; accordingly, it at one time puts off one body, which was necessary before, but which is no longer adequate in its changed state, and it exchanges it for a second.

ORIGEN
(*Contra Celsum*)

First Five Centuries A.D.

WE were in being long before the foundation of the world; we existed in the eye of God, for it is our destiny to live in Him. We are the reasonable creatures of the Divine Word; therefore we have existed from the beginning, for in the beginning was the Word. . . . Not for the first time does He show pity on us in our wanderings; He pitied us from the very beginning.

St. Clement of Alexandria
(*Exhortations to the Pagans*)

IT is a dogma recognised throughout antiquity that the soul expiates its sins in the darkness of the infernal regions, and that afterwards it passes into new bodies, there to undergo new trials.

When we have gone astray in multiplicity, we are first punished by our wandering away from the path, and afterwards by less favourable conditions, when we take on new bodies.

The gods are ever looking down upon us in this world. No reproach we bring against them can be justifiable, for their providence is never-ending; they allot to each individual his appropriate destiny, one that is in harmony with his past conduct, in conformity with his successive existences.

Plotinus
(*Second Ennead*)

THOSE who have exercised human faculties are born again as men. Those who have used only their senses go into the bodies of brutes, and especially into those of ferocious beasts, if they have yielded to bursts of anger; so that even in this case, the difference between the bodies that they animate conforms to the difference of their propensities. Those who have sought only to gratify their lust and appetite pass into the bodies of lascivious and gluttonous animals. Finally, those who have degraded their senses by disuse, are compelled to vegetate in the plants. Those who have loved music to excess and yet have lived pure lives, go into the bodies of melodious birds. Those who have ruled tyrannically become eagles. Those who have spoken lightly of heavenly things, keeping their eyes always turned toward heaven, are changed into birds which always fly toward the upper air. He who has acquired civic virtues becomes a man ; if he has not these virtues, he is transformed into a domestic animal, like the bee.

PLOTINUS
(Translated by THOMAS TAYLOR)

THE soul therefore, falling from on high, suffers captivity, is loaded with fetters, and employs the energies of sense. . . . She is reported also to be buried and to be concealed in a cave ; but when she converts herself to intelligence she then breaks her fetters and ascends on high, receiving first of all from reminiscence the ability of contemplating real beings ; at the same time possessing something super-eminent and ever abiding in the intelligible world. Souls therefore are necessarily of an amphibious nature, and alternately experience a superior and inferior condition of being ; such as are able to enjoy a more intimate converse with Intellect abiding for a longer period in the higher world, and such to whom the contrary happens, either through nature or fortune, continuing longer connected with these inferior concerns. . . .

Thus the soul, though of divine origin, and proceeding from the regions on high, becomes merged in the dark receptacle of body, and, being naturally a posterior god, it descends hither through a certain voluntary inclination, for the sake of power, and of adorning inferior concerns. . . . By this means it receives a knowledge of evil, unfolds its latent powers, and exhibits a variety of operations peculiar to its nature, which, by perpetually abiding in an incorporeal habit, and never proceeding into energy, would have been bestowed in vain. . . .

Through an abundance of sensible desire it becomes profoundly merged in matter, and no longer totally abides with universal soul. Yet our souls are able alternately to rise from hence, carrying back with them an experience of what they have known and suffered in their fallen state ; from whence they will learn how blessed it is to abide in the intelligible world, and by a comparison, as it were, of contraries, will more plainly perceive the excellence of a superior state. For the experience of evil produces a clearer knowledge of good. . . . This is accomplished in our souls according to the circulations of time, in which a conversion takes place from subordinate to more exalted natures. . . .

Indeed, if it is proper to speak clearly what appears to me to be the truth, contrary to the opinions of others, the whole of our soul does not enter into body, but something belonging to it always abides in the intelligible and something different from this in the sensible world : and that which abides in the world of sense, if it conquers —or rather if it is vanquished and disturbed—does not permit us to perceive that which the supreme part of the soul contemplates. . . . For every soul possesses something which inclines towards the body, and something which tends upwards towards intellect . . . but the superior part of the soul is never influenced by fraudulent delights, and lives a life always uniform and divine.

PLOTINUS
(*The Descent of the Soul*)
(Translated by THOMAS TAYLOR)

PHILOSOPHY speaks of souls being prepared by a course of transmigrations, the imagination being made light in weight or being polluted by the good or bad disposition. . . . In the region beneath the earth is the place where moist spirits are punished by spending an unhappy life. By several lives of this kind the soul may be purified and arise again. When first it comes down to earth, it embarks on this animal spirit as on a boat, and through it is brought into contact with matter. The soul's object is to take this spirit back with her; for if she were to abandon it and leave it behind on earth . . . the manner of her return would bring disgrace on her. . . .

The soul which did not quickly return to the heavenly region from which it was sent down to earth had to go through many lives of wandering.

SYNESIUS
(*On Dreams*)

FATHER, grant that my soul may merge into Light and be no more thrust back into the illusion of earth.

SYNESIUS

SAY, Lord, to me . . . say, did my infancy succeed another age of mine that died before it? Was it that which I spent within my mother's womb? . . . and what before that life again, O God my joy, was I anywhere or in any body? For this I have none to tell me, neither father nor mother, nor experience of others, nor mine own memory.

The Confessions of Saint Augustine

THE message of Plato, the purest and most luminous in all philosophy, has at last scattered the darkness of error, and now shines forth mainly in Plotinus, a Platonist so like his master that one would think they lived together, or rather—since so long a period of time separates them—that Plato is born again in Plotinus.

SAINT AUGUSTINE
(*Contra Academicos*)

First Five Centuries A.D.

THE souls that are not destined for the tortures of hell, and those that have passed through this expiation, are born again, and divine Justice gives them a new body, in accordance with their merits and demerits.

PORPHYRY
(*Concerning Abstinence*)

WHAT appears to us to be an accurate definition of justice does not also appear to be so to the Gods. For we, looking at that which is most brief, direct our attention to things present, and to this momentary life, and the manner in which it subsists. But the powers that are superior to us know the whole life of the Soul, and all its former lives ; and in consequence of this, if they inflict a certain punishment in obedience to the entreaties of those that invoke them, they do not inflict it without justice, but looking at the offences committed by souls in former lives : which men, not perceiving, think that they unjustly fall into the calamities which they suffer.

IAMBLICHUS
(*Egyptian Mysteries*, Book IV)

THEY [the great ones of the emanations of the Light] indeed have not at all suffered and have not at all changed themselves in the regions, nor at all torn themselves asunder, nor poured themselves into bodies of different kinds and from one into another, nor have they been in any affliction at all. . . . And ye are in great suffering and great afflictions in your being poured from one into another of different kinds of bodies of the world.

Now, therefore, all men, sinners or better who are no sinners, not only if ye desire that they be taken out of the judgments and violent chastisements, but that they be removed into a righteous body which will find the mysteries of the Godhead, so that it goeth on high and inheriteth the Light-Kingdom—then perform the third mystery of the Ineffable and say: Carry ye the soul of this and this man of whom we think in our hearts, carry him out of all the chastisements of the rulers and haste ye quickly to lead him before the Virgin of Light; and in every month let the Virgin of Light seal him with a higher seal, and in every month let the Virgin of Light cast him into a body which will be righteous and good, so that it goeth on high and inheriteth the Light-Kingdom.

And the Virgin of Light sealeth that [the sinful] soul and handeth it over to one of her receivers, and will have it cast into a body which is suitable to the sins which it hath committed.

And amen, I say unto you: They will not discharge that soul from the changes of the body until it hath yielded its last circuit according to its merit.

Blessed indeed are the souls which shall receive of those mysteries; but if they turn and transgress and come out of the body before they have repented, the judgment of those men is sorer than all the judgments and it is exceedingly violent, even if those souls are new and it is their first time for coming into the world. They will not return to the changes of the bodies from that hour onwards and will not be able to do anything, but they will be cast out into the outer darkness and perish and be non-existent for ever.

The Saviour answered and said unto his disciples: "Herald unto the whole world and say unto men: Strive thereafter that ye may receive the mysteries of the Light in this time of affliction and enter into the Light-Kingdom. Join not one day to another, or one circuit to another, hoping that ye may succeed in receiving the mysteries if ye come into the world in another circuit."

But the rulers of the Fate, when an old soul is about to come down through them . . . give the old soul a cup of forgetfulness out of the seed of wickedness, filled with all the different desires and all forgetfulness. And straightway, when that soul shall drink out of the cup, it forgetteth all the regions to which it hath gone and all the chastisements through which it hath travelled.

And when I came to the regions of the æons, I have turned Elias and sent him into the body of John the Baptiser, and the rest also I turned into righteous bodies.

And then cometh Yaluham, the receiver of Sabaoth, the Adamas, who handeth the souls the cup of forgetfulness, and he bringeth a cup filled with the water of forgetfulness and handeth it to the soul, and it drinketh it and forgetteth all things and all the regions to which it hath gone. And they cast it down into a body which will spend its time continually troubled in its heart.
This is the chastisement of the curser.

Thereafter cometh Yaluham, the receiver of Sabaoth, the Adamas, who bringeth the cup of forgetfulness and handeth it unto the soul; and it drinketh it and forgetteth all things and all the regions to which it had gone. And they cast it into a lame, halt, and blind body.
This is the chastisement of the thief.

And Yaluham, the receiver of Sabaoth, the Adamas,

cometh and bringeth the cup with the water of forgetfulness and handeth it to the soul, and it drinketh and forgetteth all things and all the regions to which it had gone. And they cast it up into a lame and deformed body, so that all despise it persistently.

This is the chastisement of the arrogant and overweening man.

[To] a man who hath committed no sin but done good persistently, but hath not found the mysteries . . . there cometh a receiver of the little Sabaoth, the Good, him of the Midst. He himself bringeth a cup filled with thought and wisdom, and soberness is in it; and he handeth it to the soul. And they cast it into a body which can neither sleep nor forget because of the cup of soberness that hath been handed unto it; but it will whip its heart persistently to question about the mysteries of the Light until it find them, through the decision of the Virgin of Light, and inherit the Light for ever.

Jesus said unto his disciples: "When the sphere turneth itself, and Kronos and Ares come behind the Virgin of Light and Zeus and Aphrodite come in face of the Virgin, they being in their own æons, then the veils of the Virgin draw themselves aside and she falleth into joy in that hour when she seeth these two light-stars before her. And all the souls which she shall cast at that hour into the circuit of the æons of the sphere, that they may come into the world, will be righteous and good and find at this time the mysteries of the Light; she sendeth them anew that they may find the mysteries of the Light.

From the *Pistis Sophia*: a Gnostic Gospel translated from Greek into Coptic in the third or fourth century. (English version by G. R. S. Mead)

First Five Centuries A.D.

BEING born from out the state of birth-and-death that giveth birth to mortal life, I now, set free, pass to the state transcending birth, as Thou hast stablished it, according as Thou hast ordained and made the mystery.

From *A Mithraic Ritual*
(Fourth century)

IV

MISCELLANEOUS SOURCES (BEFORE A.D. 1700)

JEWISH

NOW I was a child good by nature, and a good soul fell to my lot. Nay, rather, being good, I came into a body undefiled.

The Book of Wisdom viii 19, 20

THEN Job arose and rent his mantle, and shaved his head, and fell down upon the ground, and worshipped. And said, Naked came I out of my mother's womb, and naked shall I return thither.

Job i 20, 21

LORD, Thou hast been our dwelling-place in all generations. . . . Thou turnest man to destruction: and sayest, Return, ye children of men. For a thousand years in Thy sight are but as yesterday when it is past. . . . The days of our years are threescore years and ten.

Psalm xc

DO ye not remember that all pure Spirits who are in conformity with the divine dispensation live on in the lowliest of heavenly places, and in course of time they are again sent down to inhabit sinless bodies; but the souls of those who have committed self-destruction are doomed to a region in the darkness of the underworld?

(From an address of Josephus to some Jewish soldiers who desired to kill themselves rather than be captured by the Romans)

The Ring of Return

THEY say that all souls are incorruptible; but that the souls of good men are removed into other bodies, while the souls of bad men are subject to eternal punishment.

JOSEPHUS
(*De Bello Judaico*)

KNOW that Cain's essential soul passed into Jethro, but his spirit into Korah, and his animal soul into the Egyptian. . . . Samson the hero was possessed by the soul of Japhet, and Job by that of Terah.

If a man be niggardly either in a financial or a spiritual regard, giving nothing of his money to the poor, or not imparting of his knowledge to the ignorant, he shall be punished by transmigration into a woman. . . . Know thou that Sarah, Hannah, the Shunamite, and the widow of Zarepta, were each in turn possessed by the soul of Eve. . . . The soul of Rahab transmigrated into Heber the Kenite, and afterwards into Hannah; and this is the mystery of her words: " I am a woman of a sorrowful spirit "—for there still lingered in her soul a sorrowful sense of inherited defilement. . . . Eli possessed the soul of Jael, the wife of Heber the Kenite. . . . Sometimes the souls of pious Jews pass by metempsychosis into Gentiles, in order that they may plead on behalf of Israel and treat them kindly.

For one form of uncleanness the soul will be invested with the body of a Gentile, who will [eventually] become a proselyte; for another, the soul will pass into the body of a mule; for others it transmigrates into an ass, a woman of Ashdod, a bat, a rabbit or a hare, a she-mule or a camel. Ishmael transmigrated first into the ass of Balaam, and subsequently into the ass of Rabbi Pinchas ben Nair.

Miscellaneous Sources

Sometimes the soul of a righteous man may be found in the body of a clean animal or fowl.

The soul of a slanderer is transmigrated into a silent stone.

Rabbi Isaac Zuria was once passing the great academy of Rabbi Jochanan in Tiberias, when he showed his disciples a stone in the wall, remarking, " In this stone there is a transmigrated soul, and it cries that I should pray on its behalf. And this is the mystic meaning of 'The stone shall cry out of the wall' " (Hab. ii. 11).

The murderer is transmigrated into water. The mystical sign of this is indicated in " Ye shall pour it upon the earth as water " (Deut. xii. 16); and the meaning is, he is continually rolling on and on without any rest. Therefore let no man drink [direct] from a running tap or spout, but from the hollow of his hands, lest a soul pass into him, and that the soul of a wicked sinner.

One who sins with a married woman is, after undergoing the penalty of wandering about as a fugitive and vagabond, transmigrated, together with his accomplice, into the millstone of a water-mill, according to the mystery of " Let my wife grind unto another " (Job xxxi. 10).

The sages of truth have written, " He who does not wash his hands before eating, as the Rabbis of blessed memory have ordained, will be transmigrated into a cataract, where he will have no rest, even as a murderer, who is also transmigrated into water."

From *A Talmudic Miscellany*
(Translated by Paul Isaac Hershon)

The Ring of Return

IN the house of Rabbi Elazar a filly was born which killed everybody who came near it. He presented it to the king. There it only permitted Jews to attend it. It was used by the king in battle, and helped him to victory, but was unmanageable afterwards. He therefore returned it to Rabbi Elazar. The horse suddenly spoke with a human voice and told its story. It was possessed of the soul of a certain Abiathar, a priest who had led a wicked life. He had died through a fiery snake coming out of his body and killing him. After death, he had suffered all kinds of punishment in Hell, and had been reborn as a hare, and after death had again been punished in Hell. While there he witnessed the triumphant progress of the pious to Paradise, hoping that they might rescue him. The soul of Abiathar was then again sent up to the world and entered the body of a young man. It was exorcised by Rabbi Nathan Jerushalmi, and then entered the horse. It was exorcised again by Nathan Jerushalmi, and the spirit came out like a fiery flame, destroying everything.

From *Exempla of the Rabbis*: A Collection
of Tales from rare Hebrew books and MSS
(Edited by DR. MOSES GASTER)

ALL souls are subjected to the tests of transmigration; men know not the designs of the Most High with regard to them; they know not how they are being at all times judged, both before coming into this world and when they leave it; they have no knowledge of the mysterious transformations and sufferings they must undergo; . . . they are ignorant of the revolutions to which they are subjected, revolutions similar to those of a stone when it is being hurled from a sling. And now the time has come when the veil shall be removed from all these mysteries. . . . Souls must in the end be plunged back into the substance from which they came. But before this happens, they must have developed all the perfections the germs of which are implanted within them ; if these conditions are not realised in one existence, they must be born again until they reach the stage that makes possible their absorption in God. At the time when the soul is to descend, the Lord calls it and says, " Go to such and such a place ! " The soul replies, " Let me remain here and not be defiled in that other world." The Lord answers, " From the beginning thou hast been created for the purpose of getting into this world." Then the soul submits, and descends against its will. The Law which helps the soul, says to it, " See how the Lord had mercy on you. He has given you his precious pearl [the Law] to help you in this world, so that ye may remain pure." But, if laden with sin, the soul must obtain purification so as not to be delivered to Gehinnom ; for two rows of angels and demons are waiting for the soul ; the good to lead to Eden and the evil spirits to Gehinnom ; and to be saved from punishment the soul migrates from body to body.

The Zohar (*Book of the Splendour of God*)
(A Cabbalistic classic of the
fourteenth century)

The Ring of Return

PERSIAN

O BROTHER, know for certain that this work has been before thee and me in bygone ages, and that each man has already reached a certain stage. No one has begun this work for the first time.

SHARF-U'D-DÍN-MANERÍ
(A Sufi Teacher)

A STONE I died and rose again a plant,
A plant I died and rose an animal ;
I died an animal and was born a man.
Why should I fear ? What have I lost by death ?
As man, death sweeps me from this world of men
That I may wear an angel's wings in heaven :
Yet e'en as angel may I not abide,
For nought abideth save the face of God.
Thus o'er the angels' world I wing my way
Onwards and upwards, unto boundless lights ;
Then let me be as nought, for in my heart
Rings as a harp-song that we must return to Him.

JALÁLU'D-DÍN RÚMÍ
(Persian Mystic ; thirteenth century)

FIRST man appeared in the class of inorganic things,
Next he passed therefrom into that of plants.
For years he lived as one of the plants,
Remembering naught of his inorganic state so different ;
And when he passed from the vegetive to the animal state
He had no remembrance of his state as a plant,
Except the inclination he felt to the world of plants,
Especially at the time of spring and sweet flowers ;
Like the inclination of infants towards their mothers,
Which know not the cause of their inclination to the breast.
Again the Creator, as you know,
Drew men out of the animal into the human state.

Miscellaneous Sources

Thus man passed from one order of nature to another,
Till he became wise and knowing and strong as he is now.
Of his first states he has now no remembrance,
And he will be again changed from his present state.

JALÁLU'D-DÍN RÚMÍ
(*Masnavi*, Book IV)

THOSE who, in the season of prosperity, experience pain and grief, suffer them on account of their words or deeds in a former body, for which the Most Just now punisheth them.

The Desatir
(The Book of the Prophet Zoroaster)

The Ring of Return

MOHAMMEDAN

THEY shall say: Our Lord! twice didst Thou make us subject to death, and twice hast Thou given us life, so we do confess our faults: is there then a way to get out?

How is it that ye believe not in God? Since ye were dead, and He gave you life, He will hereafter cause you to die, and will again restore you to life; then shall ye return unto Him.

God generates beings, and sends them back over and over again, till they return to Him.

Or the like of him who passed by a town, and it had fallen down upon its roofs. He said: When will Allah give it life after its death? So Allah caused him to remain in a state of death for a hundred years, then roused him. He said: How long have you tarried? He said: I have tarried a day, or part of a day. Said He: Nay! You have tarried a hundred years; then look at your food and drink—years have not passed over it; and look at your ass: and that We may make you a sign to men, look at the bones, how We set them together, then clothe them with flesh. So when it became clear to him, he said: I know that Allah has power over all things.

They say, What! when we have become bones and rubbish are we to be raised up a new creature? Say, Be ye stones or iron, or a creature, the greatest your breasts can conceive! Then they shall say, Who is to restore us? Say, We who originated you at first. And they will wag their heads and say, When will that be? Say, It may perhaps be nigh. *The Koran*

Miscellaneous Sources

AND when his body falleth off altogether, as an old fish-shell, his soul doeth well by the releasing, and formeth a new one instead.

The disembodied spirits of man and beast return as the clouds to renew the young streamlets of infancy. . . .

When a man dieth or leaveth his body, he wendeth through the gate of oblivion and goeth to God, and when he is born again, he cometh from God and in a new body maketh his dwelling ; hence is this saying :

The body to the tomb and the spirit to the womb. . . .

The soul of the lower beast goeth to the body of the higher, and the soul of the higher beast to the body of the savage, and the soul of the savage to the man. . . .

Ye who now lament to go out of this body wept also when ye were born into it. . . .

The person of man is only a mask which the soul putteth on for a season ; it weareth its proper time and then is cast off, and another is worn in its stead. . . .

I tell you, of a truth, that the spirits which now have affinity shall be kindred together, although they all meet in new persons and names.

The New Koran

YOU were an apple, friend of mine,
And apples upon you shall dine,
Varied the lanterns where the flame is lit,
In varied ways of dance the shadows flit.

ABUL ALA, THE SYRIAN

The Ring of Return

CHINESE

ONCE upon a time, I, Chuang Tzu, dreamt I was a butterfly, fluttering hither and thither, to all intents and purposes a butterfly. I was conscious only of following my fancies as a butterfly, and was unconscious of my individuality as a man. Suddenly I awaked, and there I lay, myself again. Now I do not know whether I was then a man dreaming I was a butterfly, or whether I am now a butterfly dreaming I am a man. Between a man and a butterfly there is necessarily a barrier. The transition is called metempsychosis.

To have attained to the human form must be always a source of joy. And then, to undergo countless transitions, with only the infinite to look forward to—what incomparable bliss is that! Therefore it is that the truly wise rejoice in that which can never be lost, but endures alway.

The Master came, because it was his time to be born; he went, because it was his time to die. For those who accept the phenomena of birth and death in this sense, lamentation and sorrow have no place. . . . The fuel is consumed, but the fire may be transmitted, and we know not that it comes to an end.

Birth is not a beginning; death is not an end.

CHUANG TZU, *c.* 450 B.C.
(From *Musings of a Chinese Mystic*)
(Translated by LIONEL GILES)

IF I depart, I cast no look behind
Still wed to life, I still am free from care.
Since life and death in cycles come and go,
Of little moment are the days to spare.

Miscellaneous Sources

Thus strong in faith I wait, and long to be
One with the pulsings of Eternity.

Po Chu-I, *c.* A.D. 800
(*Peaceful Old Age*)
(Translated by Lionel Giles)

A PRIEST of Tao, one of the Hung-tu school,
Was able by his magic to compel
The spirits of the dead. So to relieve
The sorrows of his king, the man of Tao
Receives an urgent summons. Borne aloft
Upon the clouds, on ether charioted,
He flies with speed of lightning [till] . . .
. . . knocking at the jade door
At the western gate of the golden house, he bids
A fair maid breathe his name to one more fair
Than all. She, hearing of this embassy
Sent by the Son of Heaven, starts from her dreams
Among the tapestry curtains. Gathering
Her robes around her. . . . begins to deck herself
With pearls and gems. . . .
Then raising from their lacquered gloom
Old keepsakes, tokens of undying love,
A golden hair-pin, an enamel brooch,
She bids him bear them to her lord. One half
The hair-pin still she keeps, one half the brooch,
Breaking with her dim hands the yellow gold,
Sundering the enamel. " Tell my lord,"
She murmured, " to be firm of heart as this
Gold and enamel ; then, in heaven or earth
Below, we twain may meet once more."

Po Chu-I
(*The Never-Ending Wrong*)
(Translated by L. Cranmer Byng)

YEARS since We last forgathered, O Man-ch'ing !
Methinks I see thee now,
Lord of the noble brow,
And courage from thy glances challenging.

The Ring of Return

Ah! when thy tired limbs were fain to keep
The purple cerements of sleep,
Thy dim beloved form
Passed from the sunshine warm,
From the corrupting earth, that sought to hold
Its beauty, to the essence of pure gold.
Or haply art thou some far-towering pine,
Some rare and wondrous flower?

Ah! that a song could bring
Peace to thy dust, Man-ch'ing!

OU-YANG HSIU OF LU-LING, *c.* A.D. 1050
(Translated by L. CRANMER BYNG)

MOTHER of Pity, hear my prayer
That in the endless round of birth
No more may break my heart on earth,
Nor by the windless waters of the Blest
Weary of rest:
That, drifting, drifting, I abide not anywhere.
Yet if by Karma's law I must
Resume this mantle of the dust,
Grant me, I pray,
One dewdrop from thy willow-spray,
And in the double lotus keep
My hidden heart asleep.

Lines from the Tomb of an Unknown Woman in the Mountain District of So-Chan in the Province of Kiangsu
(Translated by L. CRANMER BYNG)

Miscellaneous Sources

JAPANESE

WHEN he who is born into the land of Pure Peace returneth again into this sinful world, even like unto that Buddha made flesh in India, he wearieth not in asking the welfare of all men. . . .

The Srāvakas, the Bodhisattvas, the Heavenly Beings and Souls in Paradise, they in whom wisdom is made equal unto beauty, declare their attributes in order, according to their former birth. . . .

Whoso would be born into Paradise shall in this life be made one with those men that return no more unto birth and death. . . .

Go forward, O Valiant Souls, seeking the Law though all the world fall into flame and ruin, for ye shall have passed beyond birth and death.

Teaching all that have life in the Ten Regions, that they might, with sincerity, faith, and hope, be born again into Paradise, He set forth that promise infinite and divine—the true seed of birth within the Kingdom of Truth.

Whoso attaineth unto the True Faith is in unity with them that return no more to birth and death, for, having thus attained, they pass onward into Nirvana, their lives being ended. . . .

Seek refuge in the Sole Vehicle of His merciful promise. For the transitory teachings have let and hindered men in the Way of Enlightenment so that they must needs pass through the long weariness of birth and death.

At that moment when faith in the Enlightened One is perfected, pure and lasting as the diamond, then shall the Spiritual Light shine upon us and guard us, the light which for ever guideth us from rebirth and death. . . .

The Ring of Return

Throughout the long, long Kalpa of my lives that are overpast could I never find the way of Deliverance, and if Hōnen Shōnin, the Great Teacher, had not arisen in this world, vainly had I spent the precious hours of my life.

The people passed it from mouth to mouth that this Hōnen Shōnin was the living incarnation of Doshaku Zenji, or yet again of Zendo Daishi. . . .

And now, his time being at hand, Hōnen Shōnin spake:

" Thrice have I taken birth in the Land of Purity, and of these three times the last hath given unto me the fullness of peace."

Once did Hōnen Shōnin speak, saying:

" In the glorious day of our Lord was I among the holy Assemblage on the Peak of Vultures, and my Spirit was rapt in self-instruction and in the doctrine of salvation."

Having taken birth in that small and remote island, Hōnen Shōnin spread abroad the doctrine of the Holy Name for the sake of all men's salvation. And thus had he done not only then, but many times in ages gone by.

No hope is there that the men now living in these last days shall escape the fetters of birth and death if they refuse the merciful promise of the Blessed One. . . .

He that receiveth the true Faith, and is one with them that return no more to birth and death, shall receive the Perfected Wisdom even as that Bodhisattva Maitreya that is called " He that shall come." . . .

Our Father hath perfected His mercy by uttering the Divine Promise that giveth all His merit unto man, that He might save them that are fast bound unto birth and death. . . .

If we accept not the two divine gifts, the gift of entering the Promised Kingdom, and the gift of return into this evil world, then shall the wheel of birth and death turn with us for ever.

Japanese Buddhist Psalms
(Translated by S. YAMAKE
and L. ADAMS BECK)

EXALTED One, to Thee I pray
Whose beams the regions ten illume.
In Thee, Tathāgata, I trust,
Grant me Thine ever-ready aid.
O give me birth in Thy Pure Land,
Which now in vision I behold. . . .
O may we all be born again
With Thee ; like Thee, the Truth proclaim !
I pray that I may see Thee, Lord,
That I and all men by Thy grace
May to Thy Land of Bliss attain.

AMITAYUS SUTROPADESA
(Fourth or fifth century A.D.)

OLD scrolls of Scripture, row on row,
Five score, a hundred score, we know !
Profound, profound past human ken,
Their teachings manifold we pen.
What boots this toil of scribe and sage
While wisdom hides within the page ?
Self yet unknowable remains :
It thinks and thinks, nor wisdom gains.
Mad, mad are beings here forlorn,
Yet know they not their madness :
Blind, blind are sentient creatures all,
Yet know they not their blindness.
Again, again, they are reborn
To darkness and to sadness :
Again, again they pass and die
Blinded by sense eternally !

Japanese Buddhist Hymn
(Eighth century A.D.)

The Ring of Return

INDIAN

DUSHMANTA (Emperor of India): " Ah, what makes me so melancholy at hearing a mere song on absence, when I am not in fact separated from any real object of my affection? Perhaps the sadness of men otherwise happy, on seeing beautiful forms and listening to sweet melody, arises from some faint remembrance of past joys and the traces of connexions in a former state of existence."

Kasyapa: " What other favours can I bestow on thee? "

Dushmanta: " Can any favours exceed those already bestowed? Let every king apply himself to the attainment of happiness for his people; let Sereswati, the goddess of liberal arts, be adored by all readers of the Veda; and may Siva, of the azure neck and red locks, eternally potent and self-existing, avert from me the pain of another birth in this particular world, the seat of crimes and of punishment.

KALIDASA
(*Sakuntala:* an old Indian drama of uncertain date; probably about A.D. 300. From an anonymous translation published in 1789)

I WAS in immobile and mobile creatures, in worms and in moths;
I passed through many births of various kinds.
In this way I occupied many bodies;
But when, O God, I assumed *human* birth,
I was a Jogi, a Jati, a penitent, a Brahmachāri;
Sometimes a king, an emperor, and sometimes a beggar.
Saith Kabir, " O God, have mercy on us;
We have grown weary; make us now whole."

Miscellaneous Sources

. . . Through error I have wandered among human and lower births; I am now weary and over-spent with travel.

KABIR
(Indian mystic and reformer of the fifteenth century)
(Translated by MAX ARTHUR MACAULIFFE)

TUKA to Iswara saith:
"We shall take, if so Thou will,
Birth, and learn of life and death;
But we ask that Thou shalt fill
All our life-ways, dark and long
With remembrance of Thy Face
And with comrades rich in song,
Mindful of our heavenly place.
So in frailty of the flesh
We may travel free from stain,
Miss the snaring senses' mesh,
Yea, and freedom's subtle chain."

From the *Marathi of Tukaram*
(Seventeenth century)
(Paraphrased by JAMES COUSINS)

GERMAN

DO not think that mankind hath such a beginning, as we must say of ourselves, according to the creation: no, the image hath appeared in God from eternity in the virgin of wisdom. . . .

The living Word, which dwelleth in the eternal virgin, attracted to it the flesh of Mary. . . . And thus the perished soul of Adam, in the body of Mary, was again set in the eternal humanity, for the Word dwelt in Christ's flesh and assumed the soul in him. . . .

The soul is out of the centre of nature, generated out of the essences, and it belongeth to the body; for it goeth forth from the essences of the body, and it attracteth corporeity to it.

JACOB BOEHME
(*Threefold Life of Man*)

SPANISH (Dutch)

IT is impossible for us to remember that we had existence prior to the body, since the body can have no vestige of it, and eternity cannot be defined in terms of time or have any relation of time. But, nevertheless, we have in our experience a perception that we are eternal. For the mind is sensible no less of what it understands than of what it remembers. . . .

Although, therefore, we do not remember that we existed before the body, yet we perceive that our mind is eternal, in so far as it involves the body's essence under the category of eternity, and that this its existence cannot be defined by time or interpreted by duration.

SPINOZA
(*Ethics*, Book V)

Miscellaneous Sources

ITALIAN

IF, in man, the immortal nature is united for an instant to the mortal nature, only to abandon it for the rest of the time, no permanent bond would be made between these two mortal and immortal elements, but a temporary union which, the mortal element once removed, would immediately dissolve, and dissolve with it the general harmony. It remains to be said that the union of these two natures exists partially, temporarily, and that whenever the body is destroyed each returns to its respective independence, and this process is renewed indefinitely throughout eternity.

As to ourselves, our soul, partaking of the divine nature, remains immortal and eternal in the precincts which are the limit of our world. Attached to a mortal envelope, it is sent by the gods now into one body, now into another, in view of the universal harmony, in order that the union of the mortal and immortal elements in human nature may contribute to the unity of the Whole.

GEORGE GEMISTUS: the 'Sage of Miziterra'
(Fourteenth century)

THERE is an eternal Principle or Substance which is truly the man and no accident derived from Composition. This is the Deity, the hero, the particular God, the intelligence in, from, and through whom different Complexes and bodies are formed and form themselves, so that it continually reappears in different species, names, and fortunes.

I have reasoned deeply, and, speaking as a philosopher, since the soul is not found without body, and yet is not body, it may be in one body or in another, and pass from body to body.

The Ring of Return

If not to be believed, it is gravely to be pondered whether a vile life be not disposed of by fatal justice, interwoven in a prison-house suited to its failure or crime, with organs and instruments suitable for such a workman or craftsman. . . . Let us supplicate the Divinity to bestow happy geniuses upon us in our transfusion, passage, or metempsychosis ; since, however inexorable He be, we must attend Him with wishes, to be either preserved in our present state, or to enter into a better or a like, or one but a little worse. . . . He that is favoured by the Gods must obtain this by means of good desires and good actions.

GIORDANO BRUNO (sixteenth century)
(*The Expulsion of the Triumphant Beast*)

I FEAR that by my death the human race
Would gain no vantage. Thus I do not die.
So wide is this vast cage of misery
That flight and change lead to no happier place.
Shifting our pains, we risk a sorrier case :
All worlds, like ours, are sunk in agony :
Go where we will, we feel ; and this my cry
I may forget like many an old disgrace.
Who knows what doom is mine ? The Omnipotent
Keeps silence ; nay, I know not whether strife
Or peace was with me in some earlier life.
Philip in a worse prison has me pent
These three days past—but not without God's will.
Stay we as God decrees : God doth no ill.

T. CAMPANELLA (sixteenth century)
(*A Sonnet on Caucasus*)

Miscellaneous Sources

DRUIDIC AND CELTIC

AS one of their leading dogmas they [the Druids] inculcate this : that souls are not annihilated, but pass after death from one body to another, and they hold that by this teaching men are much encouraged to valour, through disregarding the fear of death.

CÆSAR
(*De Bello Gallico*, Book VI)

AMONG them [the Druids] the doctrine of Pythagoras had force, namely, that the souls of men are undying, and that after a fixed number of years they begin to live again, the soul passing into another body.

DIODORUS OF SICILY

[THE Druids] would fain have us believe that the souls of men are immortal. I should be tempted to call these breeches-wearing gentry, fools, were not their doctrine the same as that of the mantle-clad Pythagoras.

DALERIUS MAXIMUS

FROM you [the Druids] we learn that the destination of man's spirit is not the grave, nor the Kingdom of the Shades. The same spirit in another world animates a body and, if your teaching be true, death is the centre, not the finish, of a long life [= a round of lives]. Happy the folk upon whom the Bear looks down, happy in this error, whom of fears, the greatest moves not, the dread of death. . . . For who were coward enough to grudge a life sure of its return?

LUCAN
(*The Pharsalia*)

The Ring of Return

THREE necessities of Transmigration—the least of all things, whence a beginning; the substance of all things, whence progress; and the formation of all things, whence individuality.

A Druidic Triad

HE will be in the shape of every beast,
Both in the azure sea and on land.
He will be a dragon before hosts at the onset,
He will be a wolf of every great forest.
He will be a stag with horns of silver
In the land where chariots are driven,
He will be a speckled salmon in a full pool,
He will be a seal, he will be a fair white swan.

From *The Voyage of Bran*
(Translated by ALFRED NUTT)

I HAVE been in many shapes before I attained a congenial form. I have been a narrow blade of a sword; I have been a drop in the air; I have been a shining star; I have been a word in a book; I have been a book in the beginning; I have been a light in a lantern a year and a half; I have been a bridge for passing over three score rivers; I have journeyed as an eagle; I have been a boat on the sea; I have been a director in battle; I have been a sword in the hand; I have been a shield in fight; I have been the string of a harp; I have been enchanted for a year in the foam of water. There is nothing in which I have not been.

TALIESIN
(Welsh bard; sixth century, A.D.)

PRIMARY chief bard am I to Elphin,
And my original country is the region of the summer stars;
Idno and Heinin called me Merddin,
At length every king will call me Taliesin.

Miscellaneous Sources

I was with my Lord in the highest sphere
On the fall of Lucifer into the depth of hell;
I have borne a banner before Alexander;
I know the names of the stars from north to south;
I have been on the galaxy at the throne of the Distributor;
I was in Canaan when Absalom was slain;
I conveyed the Divine Spirit to the level of the vale of Hebron;
I was in the court of Don before the birth of Gwydion.
I was instructor to Eli and Enoc;
I have been winged by the genius of the splendid crosier;
I have been loquacious prior to being gifted with speech;
I was at the place of the crucifixion of the merciful Son of God;
I have been three periods in the prison of Arianrod;
I have been the chief director of the work of the tower of Nimrod;
I am a wonder whose origin is not known.
I have been in Asia with Noah in the ark,
I have seen the destruction of Sodom and Gomorra;
I have been in India when Roma was built,
I am now come here to the remnant of Troia.
I have been with my Lord in the manger of the ass;
I have strengthened Moses through the water of Jordan;
I have been in the firmament with Mary Magdalene;
I have obtained the muse from the cauldron of Caridwen;
I have been bard of the harp to Lleon of Lochlin.
I have been on the White Hill, in the court of Cynvelyn,
For a day and a year in stocks and fetters,
I have suffered hunger for the Son of the Virgin,
I have been fostered in the land of the Deity,
I have been teacher to all intelligences,
I am able to instruct the whole universe.

The Ring of Return

I shall be until the day of doom on the face of the
earth ;
And it is not known whether my body is flesh or fish.

Then I was for nine months
In the womb of the hag Caridwen ;
I was originally little Gwion,
And at length I am Taliesin.

TALIESIN
(Translated by DR. OWEN PUGHE)

I AM a grey-cowled minstrel.
I believe in illusion.
I was for a time in the sky.
I was observing the stars.

I went travelling : I was an eagle ;
I was a coracle on the seas,
I was the attraction in good,
I was a drop in a shower.

I am not one who does not sing ;
I sang, though I was little,
At the battle of the Scrub-shoots,
Against Britain's ruler,
And the *Irish* ships,
A rich-laden fleet.

'Twas not of father and mother, whence I was born.
'Tis after a new fashion I was created from nine
constituents :
From the essence of fruits
did God begin :
from primrose flowers :
from the pollen of shrubs,
the pollen of Oak and Nettle,
of Meadow-sweet and Broom ;

from the Mould of the earth;
from the Water of the ninth wave;
from the Fire of the lightning—
from these things was I made.

I was a speckled snake on the hill;
I was a dragon in the lake;
I was the slave of Kynbyn;
I was a herdsman besides.

Thin and white are my fingers:
It is long since I was a herdsman.
I wandered on the earth
Or ever I touched literature,
I slept in a hundred mansions,
A hundred inhabited forts.

TALIESIN
(*The Battle of the Scrub*)

DECHTIRE, sister of Conchobor, fled one day, and with her fifty damsels. . . . Track nor trace of them was not found for three years, nor was aught heard of them. Then they came in bird-guise to the plain of Emania and they devoured everything and left no blade of grass standing. . . . Full of beauty was the bird-flock and their song. They sang as they were flying . . . preceding the hunters to the end of the land. Night fell upon the men of Ulster and thick snow fell. . . . Hardly were they in the house with their chariots and their horses and their arms, but there came to them all manner of good things, meats known and unknown, so that they never had a better night. The master of the house then told the men of Ulster that his wife was in travail. Dechtire went to her and she gave birth to a son. . . . The men of Ulster took the child . . . Dechtire brought him up. . . . The child grew up and, falling ill, died. Great was Dechtire's grief.

The Ring of Return

On her return from burying him she asked for drink in a vessel of brass. Drink was brought to her. As she raised the vessel to her lips she felt a little beast come with it, and she drank it in. She slept afterwards, and at night she saw somewhat ; a man neared her and spake unto her, telling her she was with child by him.

He it was who had carried her off with her companions, he had led them in the shape of birds. He was the child she had reared ; now he was about to enter her womb, and would take the name of Setanta. He was Lug, son of Ethne.

> Fragments of the ancient Irish folk-tale of the *Birth of Cuchulinn* ; preserved in *The Book of the Dun Cow* ; eleventh century.

ON the morrow early in the morning there came to them[1] a venerable cleric, who bade them welcome. . . . Finnen asked him to tell his name. Said he to them, " Of the men of Ulster am I. Tuan, son of Cairell, son of Muredach Red-neck, am I. I have taken this hermitage in which thou art upon the hereditary land of my father." . . . Finnen said they would not eat with him until he told them the stories of Ireland. . . .

" Five times verily," said he, " Ireland was taken after the Flood, and it was not taken after the Flood until three hundred and twelve years had gone. Then Partholon, son of Sera, took it. He had gone upon a voyage with twenty-four couples . . . They settled in Ireland until there were five thousand of their race. Between two Sundays a mortality came upon them, so that all died, save one man only . . . That man am I," said he. " Then I was from hill to hill and from cliff to cliff, guarding myself from wolves. . . . At last old age came upon me. . . . Then as I was asleep one night I saw myself passing into the shape of a stag. In

[1] Finnen of Moville and his men who had come with the Gospel into Ireland

that shape I was, and I young and glad of heart. . . . In that way I spent my life during the time of Nemed and his offspring. . . . Then at last old age came upon me and I fled from men and wolves. Once as I was in front of my cave—I still remember it—I knew that I was passing from one shape to another. Then I passed into the shape of a wild boar. . . . In the same place I changed into all these shapes. Therefore I always visited that place to await the renewal. . . . I went to my own dwelling always. I remembered every shape in which I had been before. . . . I went into the shape of a large hawk. . . . Beothach, the son of Iarbonel the prophet, seized this island from the races that dwelt in it. From them are the Tuatha Dè and Andè whose origin the learned do not know. . . . I was for a long time in the shape of that hawk, so that I outlived all the races who had invaded Ireland. However, the sons of Mil took this island by force from the Tuatha Dè Danann. Then I was in the shape of that hawk in which I had been, and was in the hollow of a tree on a river. There I fasted for three days and three nights, when sleep fell upon us, and I passed into the shape of a river salmon. . . . Once more I felt happy and my swimming was good, and I used to escape from every danger and every snare. . . . Once, however, when God, my help, deemed it time . . . the fisherman of Cairell, the king of that land, caught me and took me to Cairell's wife. . . . And the Queen desired me and ate me by herself, so that I was in her womb. Again I remember the time I was in her womb and what each one said to her in the house and what was done in Ireland during that time. I also remember when speech came to me, as it comes to any man, and I knew all that was being done in Ireland and I was a seer ; and a name was given to me—to wit, Tuan, son of Cairell. Thereupon Patrick came with the Faith to Ireland. Then I was of great age ; and I was baptised, and alone believed in the King of all things with His elements.

From *The Book of the Dun Cow*

The Ring of Return

. . . MONGAN was in Rathmore of Moylinny in his kingship. To him went Forgoll the poet. . . . One day Mongan asked his poet what was the death of Fothad Airgthech. Forgoll said he was slain at Duffry in Leinster. Mongan said it was false. The poet said he would satirise his father and his mother and his grandfather and he would sing (spells) upon their waters, so that fish should not be caught in their river-mouths. He would sing upon their woods, so that they should not give fruit, upon their plains so that they should be barren for ever. . . . Mongan promised him his will in precious things. . . . At last (anything) save his own liberty with that of his wife Briothigemd, unless he were redeemed before the end of three days. The poet refused all except as regards the woman. For the sake of his honour Mongan consented. Thereat the woman was sorrowful. . . . Mongan told her not to be sorrowful, help would certainly come to them. . . . When night came to them, Mongan was on his couch in his palace, and his wife at his right hand. . . . The poet was summoning them by their sureties and their bonds. While they were there, a man is announced, approaching the earth from the south. . . . "What is the matter here?" said he. "I and the poet yonder," said Mongan, "have made a wager about the death of Fothad Airgthech. He said it was false." The warrior said the poet was wrong. . . . "It shall be proved. We were with thee with Find," said the warrior. "Hush!" said Mongan, "that is not fair." "We were with Find then," said he. "We came from Scotland. We met with Fothad Airgthech here yonder on the Larne river. There we fought a battle. I made a cast at him, so that it passed through him and went into the earth beyond him and left its iron head in the earth. This here is the shaft that was in that spear. The bare stone from which I made that cast will be found, and the iron head will be found in the earth, and the tomb of Fothad Airgthech will be found a little to the east of it. . . . And by his tomb there is a stone pillar. . . ." They went with the warrior. Everything was found thus. It was Caille, Find's foster-son, that had come to them. . . . Mongan, however, was Find, though he would not let it be known.

Story from which it is inferred that Mongan was a reincarnation of Find na Cumaill, and the cause of the death of Fothad Airgthech.
(From *The Book of the Dun Cow*)

The Ring of Return

ENGLISH

IF there be nothing new, but that which is
Hath been before, how are our brains beguiled,
Which, labouring for invention, bear amiss
The second burthen of a former child!
O, that record could with a backward look,
Even of five hundred courses of the sun,
Show me your image in some antique book,
Since mind at first in character was done.
That I might see what the old world could say
To this composèd wonder of your frame;
Whether we are mended, or whether better they,
Or whether revolution be the same.
O, sure I am, the wits of former days
To subjects worse have given admiring praise.

SHAKESPEARE
(*Sonnet LIX*)

ROSALIND: I was never so be-rhymed since Pythagoras' time, that I was an Irish rat, which I can hardly remember.

SHAKESPEARE
(*As you Like It,* III ii)

GRATIANO: Thou almost makest me waver in my faith
To hold opinion with Pythagoras,
That souls of animals infuse themselves
Into the trunks of men; thy currish spirit
Govern'd a wolf, who, hang'd for human slaughter,
Even from the gallows did his fell soul fleet,
And, whilst thou lay'st in thy unhallow'd dam,
Infused itself in thee: for thy desires
Are wolvish, bloody, starved and ravenous.

SHAKESPEARE
(*The Merchant of Venice,* IV i)

Miscellaneous Sources

CLOWN: What is the opinion of Pythagoras concerning wild fowl?

Malvolio: That the soul of our grandam might haply inhabit a bird.

Clown: What thinkest thou of his opinion?

Malvolio: I think nobly of the soul, and no way approve his opinion.

Clown: Fare thee well. Remain thou still in darkness: thou shalt hold the opinion of Pythogoras ere I will allow of thy wits, and fear to kill a woodcock, lest thou dispossess the soul of thy grandam. Fare thee well.

SHAKESPEARE
(*Twelfth Night,* IV ii)

ALL which I will bid you remember . . . is, that the Pythagorean doctrine doth not only carry one soul from man to man, nor man to beast, but indifferently to plants also: and therefore you must not grudge to find the same soul in an Emperor, in a Post-horse, and in a Macaron. . . . And therefore though this soul could not move when it was a Melon, yet it may remember, and can now tell me, at what luxurious banquet it was served. And though it could not speak when it was a Spider, yet it can remember, and now tell me, who used it for poison to attain dignity. However the bodies have dulled her other faculties, her memory hath ever been her own. . . .

JOHN DONNE
(From the Foreword to his satirical poem,
The Progress of the Soul)

I SING the progress of a deathless soul,
Whom fate, which God made, but doth not control,
Placed in most shapes; all times, before the law
Yoked us, and when, and since, in this I sing. . . .

For though through many straits and lands I roam,
I launch at Paradise, and I sail towards home;

The Ring of Return

The course I there began shall here be stay'd,
Sails hoisted there, struck here, and anchors laid
In Thames, which were at Tigris and Euphrates weigh'd.

For the great soul which here amongst us now
Doth dwell, and moves that head, and tongue, and brow,
Which, as the moon the sea, moves us ; to hear
Whose story with long patience you will long—
For 'tis the crown and last strain of my song—
This soul, to whom Luther and Mahomet were
Prisons of flesh ; this soul, which oft did tear
And mend the wracks of th' Empire, and late Rome,
And lived when every great change did come,
Had first in Paradise a low, but fatal room.

JOHN DONNE
(*The Progress of the Soul*)

THE Pythagoreans defend Metempsychosis; and Palingenesia, that souls go from one body to another, *epotâ prius Lethes undâ*, as men into wolves, bears, dogs, hogs, as they were inclined in their lives. . . . Julian the Apostate thought Alexander's soul was descended into his body : Plato in Timæo and in his Phædon (for aught I can perceive) differs not much from this opinion, that it was from God first and knew all, but being inclosed in the body, it forgets, and learns anew, which he calls *reminiscentia* or recalling, and that it was put into the body for a punishment ; and thence it goes into a beast's or man's . . . and after ten thousand years is to return into the former body again.

ROBERT BURTON
(*The Anatomy of Melancholy*)

WERT thou some Starr which from the ruin'd roofe
Of shak't Olympus by mischance did fall ;
Which carefull Jove in nature's true behoofe
Took up, and in fit place did reinstall ?

Or did of late Earth's Sonnes besiege the wall.
Of sheenie Heav'n, and thou some goddess fled
Amongst us here below to hide thy nectar'd head?

Or wert thou that just Maid who once before
Forsook the hated earth, O tell me sooth,
And cam'st again to visit us once more?
Or wert thou that sweet-smiling Youth?
Or that crown'd Matron, sage white-robèd Truth?
Or any other of that heav'nly brood
Let down in clowdie throne to do the world some good?

Or wert thou of the golden-wingèd hoast,
Who having clad thyself in humane weed,
To earth from thy præfixèd seat didst poast,
And after short abode flie back with speed,
As if to show what creatures Heav'n doth breed,
Thereby to set the hearts of men on fire
To scorn the sordid world, and unto Heav'n aspire?

JOHN MILTON
(*On the Death of a Fair Infant*)

TO see ourselves again we need not look for Plato's year; every man is not only himself; there hath been many Diogenes, and as many Timons, though but few of that name; men are liv'd over again; the world is now as it was in Ages past; there was none then, but there hath been someone since that parallels him, and is, as it were, his revived self.

SIR THOMAS BROWNE
(*Religio Medici*)

A SPARK or ray of the Divinity,
Clouded in earthly fogs, yclad in clay,
A precious drop sunk from Eternity,
Spilt on the ground or rather slunk away.
For then we fell when we 'gan first t'assay
By stealth, of our own selves something to bear,
Uncentring our selves from our great stay.

The Ring of Return

So we as stranger Infants elsewhere born
Can not divine from what spring we did flow,
Nor dare these base alliances to scorn,
Nor lift ourselves a whit from hence below,
Nor strive our Parentage again to know.

Thus may the souls in long succession
Leap out into distinct activity. . . .
What may engage them to descend so low,
Removed far from the steam of earthly mire?
My wits be here too scant and faith too slow,
Nor longer lists my wearied thought to tire.
Let bolder spirits to such heights aspire,
But well I wrote, if there admitted were
A pre-existency of souls entire,
And due Returns in courses circular,
This course all difficulties with ease away
    would bear.

HENRY MORE
(*The Song of the Soul*)

I LOOK on this life as the progress of an essence royal: the soul but quits her court to see the country. . . . Thus her descent speaks her original. God in love with His own beauty frames a glass, to view it by reflection. But the frailty of the matter excluding eternity, the composure was subject to dissolution. Ignorance gave this release the name of death, but properly it is the soul's birth and a charter that makes for her liberty. . . . The magicians tell me that the soul passes out of one mode and enters another.

I speak of that most secret and silent lapse of the spirit 'through the degrees of natural forms'; and this is a mystery not easily apprehended. It is a Kabalistic maxim that 'no spiritual being descending here below can operate without a garment.' . . . The soul of man, whiles she is in the body, is like a candle shut up in a dark lanthorn, or a fire that is almost stifled for want of air. Spirits—say the Platonics—when they are 'in their own country' are like the inhabitants of green fields who live perpetually amongst flowers, in a spicy, odorous air: but here below 'in the circle of generation,' they mourn because of darkness and solitude, like people locked up in a pest-house. This is it makes the soul subject to so many passions, to such a Proteus of humours. Now she flourishes, now she withers—now a smile, now a tear; and when she hath played out her stock, then comes a repetition of the same fancies, till at last she cries out with Seneca: "How long this self-same round?" . . .

Now will the Peripatetics brand me with their *contra principia*, and the school divines with a *tradatur Satanæ*. I know I shall be hated of most for my pains, and perhaps scoffed at like Pythagoras in Lucian: 'Who buyeth Eugenius? Who seeketh to be more than a man, or to know the harmony of the world and be born again?'

THOMAS VAUGHAN ('EUGENIUS PHILALETHES')

CHRIST and His Apostles spoke and writ as the condition of the persons, with whom they dealt, administered occasion. . . . Therefore doubtless there were many noble theories which they could have made the world acquainted with. . . . Few speculative truths are delivered in Scripture but such as were called forth by the controversies of those times; and Pre-existence was none of them, it being the constant opinion of the Jews, as appears by that question, "Master, was it for this man's sin or his father's that he was born blind?" . . . And the author of the Book of Wisdom, who certainly was a Jew, probably Philo, plainly supposeth the same doctrine in that speech, "For I was a witty child and had a good spirit, wherefore the rather, being good, I came into a body undefiled." As also did the disciples in their forementioned question to our Saviour ; for except they supposed that he might have sinned before he was born, the question had been senseless and impertinent. Again when Christ asked them whom men said He was they answered, that some said John the Baptist, others, Elias, others, Jeremias or one of the Prophets, which sayings of theirs suppose their belief of a Metempsychosis and consequently of Pre-existence. These, one would think, were very proper occasions for our Saviour to have rectified His mistaken followers had their supposition been an error. . . .

Every soul brings a kind of sense with it into the world, whereby it tastes and relisheth what is suitable to its peculiar temper. . . . What can we conclude but that the soul itself is the immediate subject of all this variety and that it came prejudiced and prepossessed into this body with some implicit notions that it had learnt in another? To say that all this variety proceeds primarily from the mere temper of our bodies is methinks a very poor and unsatisfying account. For those that are the most like in the temper, air, and complexion of their bodies, are yet of a vastly differing genius. . . . Besides, there are all kind of makes, forms, dispositions, tempers and complexions of body, that are addicted by their natures to the same exercise and employments. . . . And to say all these inclinations are from custom or education, is the way not to be believed, since all experience testifies to the contrary.

What then can we conjecture is the cause of all this diversity, but that we had taken a great delight and pleasure in some things like and analogous unto these in a former condition?

JOSEPH GLANVILL
(*Lux Orientalis*)

IF thy pre-existing soul
Was form'd at first with myriads more,
It did through all the mighty poets roll
Who Greek or Latin laurels wore,

Miscellaneous Sources

And was that Sappho last, which once it was before.
  If so, then cease thy flight, O heaven-born mind!
Thou hast no dross to purge from thy rich ore:
  Nor can thy soul a fairer mansion find,
Than was the beauteous frame she left behind:
  Return to fill or mend the choir of thy celestial kind.

DRYDEN
(*Ode to the Memory of Mrs. Anne Killigrew*)

V

A.D. 1700-1900

GERMAN

THE soul of man
Is like water:
From heaven it cometh,
To heaven it mounteth,
And thence again
It must back to earth,
Forever changing.

WOLFGANG VON GOETHE
(*Faust*)

TELL me what destiny has in store for us? Wherefore has it bound us so closely to each other? Ah! in bygone times thou must have been my sister or my wife . . . and there remains, from the whole of those past ages, only one memory, hovering like a doubt above my heart, a memory of that truth of old that is ever present in me.

WOLFGANG VON GOETHE
(From a letter to Frau von Stein)

THE very same way by which the race reaches its perfection must every individual man—one sooner, another later—have travelled over. Have travelled over in one and the same life? . . . Surely not that: but why should not every individual man have existed more than once upon this world? Is this hypothesis so laughable merely because it is the oldest? Because the human understanding, before the sophistries of the schools had dissipated and debilitated it, lighted upon it at once? Why may not even I have already performed those steps of my perfecting which bring to men only temporal punishments and rewards? And, once more, why not another time all those steps to perform which the views of eternal rewards so powerfully assist us? Why should I not come back as often as I am capable of acquiring fresh knowledge, fresh expertness? Do I bring away so much from once that there is nothing to repay the trouble of coming back? Is this a reason against it? Or, because I forget that I have been here already? Happy is it for me that I do forget. The recollection of my former condition would permit me to make only a bad use of the present. And that which even I must forget *now*, is that necessarily forgotten for ever?

LESSING
(*The Divine Education of the Human Race*)
(Translated by REV. F. W. ROBERTSON)

DO you not know great and rare men who cannot have become what they are at once, in a single human existence? Who must often have existed before in order to have attained that purity of feeling, that instinctive impulse for all that is true, beautiful, and good—in short, that elevation and natural supremacy over all around them? . . .

Have you never had remembrances of a former state, which you could find no place for in this life? . . . Have you not seen persons, been in places, of which you were ready to swear that you had seen those persons, or had been in those places before? . . . And such are *we*; we who, from a hundred causes, have sunk so deep and are so wedded to matter, that but few reminiscences of so pure a character remain to us. The nobler class of men who, separated from wine and meat, lived in perfect simplicity according to the order of nature, carried it further, no doubt, than others, as we learn from the example of Pythagoras, of Iarchas, of Apollonius, and others, who remembered distinctly what and how many times they had been in the world before.

A.D. 1700-1900

If we are blind, or can see but two steps beyond our noses, ought we therefore to deny that others may see a hundred or a thousand degrees farther, even to the bottom of time, into the deep, cool well of the foreworld, and there discern everything, plain and bright and clear? . . .

You know the law of economy which rules throughout nature. Is it not probable that the Deity is guided by it in the propagation and progress of human souls? He who has not become ripe in one form of humanity is put into the experience again, and, some time or other, must be perfected. I am not ashamed of my half-brothers, the brutes; on the contrary, as far as they are concerned, I am a great advocate of metempsychosis. I believe, for a certainty, that they will ascend to a higher grade of being, and am unable to understand how anyone can object to this hypothesis, which seems to have the analogy of the whole creation in its favour. . . .

When you stand before the statue of a high-hearted Apollo, do you not feel what you lack of being that form? Can you ever attain to it here below, though you should return ten times? And yet that was only the idea of an artist. . . . Has the almighty Father no nobler forms for us than those in which our heart now heaves and groans? The soul lies captive in its dungeon, bound as with a sevenfold chain, and only through a strong grating, and only through a pair of light and air-holes, can it breathe and see. . . . That restless discontent shall some time finally release us from our repeated sojourns on earth, through which the Father is training us for a complete divorce from sense-life.

J. G. von Herder
(*Dialogues on Metempsychosis*)
(Translated by F. H. Hedge)

In this tumultuous world of misery and sin
From one belief alone I hope and comfort win:
That the One God, who sees us with the Sun for Eye,

The Ring of Return

When help is needed sends us helpers from on high:
And, when men think that evil can ne'er be overthrown,
That He Himself in form of Human Love comes down.
So more than once hath He already blessed the earth,
And plans, methinks, e'en now where He shall next have birth.

FRIEDRICH RÜCKERT
(*The Brahman's Wisdom*)
(Translated by EVA MARTIN)

THESE two systems, the purely spiritual and the sensuous—which last may consist of an immeasurable series of particular lives—exist in me from the moment when my active reason is developed, and pursue their parallel course. The former alone gives to the latter meaning and purpose and value.

I *am* immortal, imperishable, eternal, so soon as I form the resolution to obey the law of reason. After an existence of myriad lives the super-sensuous world cannot be more present than at this moment. Other conditions of my sensuous existence are to come, but these are no more the true life than the present condition is.

Man is not a production of the world of sense; and the end of his existence can never be attained in that world. His destination lies beyond time and space and all that pertains to sense. . . . Even because Nature puts me to death she must quicken me anew. It can only be my higher life, unfolding itself in her, before which my present life disappears; and that which mortals call death is the visible appearing of another vivification.

J. G. FICHTE
(*The Destiny of Man*)

THE individuality disappears at death, but we lose nothing thereby; for it is only the manifestation of quite a different Being—a Being ignorant of time, and, consequently, knowing neither life nor death. The loss of intellect is the Lethe but for which the Will would remember the various manifestations it has caused. When we die, we throw off our individuality, like a worn-out garment, and rejoice because we are about to receive a new and better one.

Were an Asiatic to ask me for a definition of Europe, I should be forced to answer him : It is that part of the world which is haunted by the incredible delusion that man was created out of nothing, and that his present birth is his first entrance into life.

SCHOPENHAUER
(*Parerga and Paralipomena*)

WHAT sleep is for the individual, death is for the will. It would not endure to continue the same actions and sufferings throughout an eternity, without true gain, if memory and individuality remained to it. It flings them off, and this is Lethe; and through the sleep of death it reappears refreshed and fitted out with another intellect, as a new being—'a new day tempts to new shores.' These constant new births, then, constitute the recession of the life-dreams of a will which in itself is indestructible. . . . Every new-born being comes fresh and blithe into the new existence, and enjoys it as a free gift : but there is, and can be, nothing freely given. Its fresh existence is paid for by the old age and death of a worn-out existence which has perished, but which contained the indestructible seed out of which the new existence has arisen : they are *one* being. To show the bridge between the two would certainly be the solution of a great riddle. . . . We find the doctrine of metempsychosis springing from the earliest and noblest ages of the human race, always spread abroad in the earth as the belief of the great majority of mankind ; nay, really as the teaching of all religions, with the exception of that of the Jews and the two which have proceeded from it : in the most subtle form, however, and coming nearest to the truth, in Buddhism. Accordingly, while Christians console themselves with the thought of meeting again in another world . . . in those other religions the meeting again is going on now, only *incognito*. In the succession of births . . . the persons who now stand in close connection or contact with us will also be born again with us at the next birth, and will have the same or analagous relations and sentiments towards us as now, whether these are of a friendly or a hostile description.

SCHOPENHAUER
(*The World as Will and Idea*)

OUR duty is present with us every instant.

My doctrine is: Live so that thou mayest desire to live again—that is thy duty; for, in any case, thou wilt live again!

And in every one of these cycles of human life there will be one hour where for the first time one man, and then many, will perceive the mighty thought of the eternal recurrence of all things—and for mankind this is always the hour of noon.

FRIEDRICH NIETZSCHE

TO those who think like us, things all dance themselves: they come and hold out the hand, and laugh, and flee—and return.

Everything goeth, everything returneth; eternally rolleth the wheel of existence. Everything dieth, everything blossometh forth again; eternally runneth on the year of existence.

Everything breaketh, everything is integrated anew; eternally buildeth itself the same house of existence.

All things separate, all things again greet one another; eternally true to itself remaineth the ring of existence.

Behold, we know what thou teachest, that all things eternally return, and ourselves with them, and that we have already existed times without number, and all things with us. . . .

The plexus of causes returneth in which I am intertwined—it will again create me! I myself pertain to the causes of the eternal return.

If I be a diviner and full of the divining spirit, which wandereth on high mountain-ridges, 'twixt two seas:—

Wandereth 'twixt the past and the future as a heavy cloud—hostile to sultry plains, and to all that is weary and can neither die nor live:

Ready for lightning in its dark bosom and for the redeeming flash of light, charged with lightnings which say Yea! which laugh Yea! ready for divining flashes of lightning:—

Blessed, however, is he who is thus charged! And verily, long must he hang like a heavy tempest on the mountain, who shall one day kindle the light of the future!—

Oh, how could I not be ardent for Eternity, and for the marriage-ring of rings—the ring of the return?

If ever a breath hath come to me of the creative breath, and of the heavenly necessity which compelleth even chances to dance star-dances:

If ever I have laughed with the laughter of the creative lightning, to which the long thunder of the deed followeth, grumblingly, but obediently:

If ever I have played dice with the Gods at the divine table of the earth . . .

Oh, how could I not be ardent for Eternity, and for the marriage-ring of rings—the ring of the return?

If my virtue be a dancer's virtue, and if I have often sprung with both feet into golden-emerald rapture:

If my wickedness be a laughing wickedness, at home among rose-banks and hedges of lilies:

The Ring of Return

For in laughter is all evil present, but it is sanctified and absolved by its own bliss:

And if it be my Alpha and Omega that everything heavy shall become light, every body a dancer, and every spirit a bird: and verily, that is my Alpha and Omega!—

Oh, how could I not be ardent for Eternity and for the marriage-ring of rings—the ring of the return?

If ever I have spread out a tranquil heaven above me, and have flown into mine own heaven with mine own pinions:

If I have swum playfully in profound luminous distances, and if my freedom's avian wisdom hath come to me:—

Thus however speaketh avian wisdom: "Lo, there is no above and no below! Throw thyself about—outward, backward, thou light one! Sing! Speak no more!

"Are not all words made for the heavy? Do not all words lie to the light ones? Sing! Speak no more!"—

Oh, how could I not be ardent for Eternity, and for the marriage-ring of rings—the ring of the return?

Never yet have I found the woman by whom I should like to have children, unless it be this woman whom I love: for I love thee, O Eternity!

For I love thee, O Eternity!

FRIEDRICH NIETZSCHE
(*Thus Spake Zarathustra*)
(Translated by THOMAS COMMON)

NOW, if the real heir of our attainments in the world of sense—of all, that is, which in Darwinism is thrown to the Unconscious—is the transcendental Subject . . . and inasmuch as this Subject possesses essentially the same physical powers as its projection, the man of the senses, the capacity of the transcendental Subject for development cannot be limited to the single case of the earthly existence, but the marked individuality which we already bring with us into this existence must have been acquired in a similar way to that in which it is augmented in this life. . . . From the strength of the impulse to incarnation . . . is to be inferred a great advantage from immersion into the world of sense, and the consequent desirability in the interest of the Subject of the repetition of this mode of existence, so that the unconscious attainments of one existence may be transmitted to the next. The hypothesis of a transcendental consciousness, which many followers of Darwin might repudiate, is therefore completely compatible with Darwinism. . . .

According to Darwin, habits are transmitted to the germ-cells, and so to all later generations, species, and kinds; according to the transcendental psychologist, habits pass as predispositions to the transcendental Subject, and so determine its later phenomenal forms, which these later generations just are. These two views are not opposed to each other. . . .

Those who think the metaphysical Darwinism, tending to Palingenesis, a crude explanation of individuality, should consider that the alternative explanations offered by materialism and pantheism are by no means less crude. They do not simplify the problem of life, if only because they do not seek in it unity; it returns with every birth; and becomes permanent when in every birth they see a new creation. . . .

Our transcendental Subject not only introduces us into life and determines our particular individuality, but also leads us through life; but it cares only for our transcendental good, and is regardless of our wishes, just as in dreams we, the secret directors, are regardless of our wishes in the dream. . . .

Whoever recognises the transcendental Subject in us will see that the earthly misery is for our transcendental advantage, and that this earthly existence is our own act. . . .

Man is his own heir, the Subject inherits from the

person, and what I have acquired morally and intellectually remains with me. The law of the Conservation of Energy . . . avails also for the psychical world.

So should we again arrive at the oldest of philosophical conceptions of man, the migration of souls; but this old theory would be revived in a new and incomparably higher form, which could only be described as Palingenesis. . . .

As our earthly phenomenal form is the product of our intelligible character, so also after stripping off this phenomenal form we shall be that which we have made ourselves through the earthly existence, whether we have thereby advanced or injured our Subject. This is the transcendental justification, before which all human complaint of terrestrial injustice is dumb.

CARL DU PREL
(*The Philosophy of Mysticism*)
(Translated by C. C. MASSEY)

A.D. 1700-1900

SWEDISH

MAXIMUS: "Must I remind you how fortune has borne you, as on mighty pinions, through an agitated and perilous life? Who are you, sire? Are you Alexander born again, not, as before, in immaturity, but perfectly equipped for the fulfilment of the task?

Julian: "Maximus!"

Maximus: There is One who ever reappears, at certain intervals, in the course of human history. He is like a rider taming a wild horse in the arena. Again and yet again it throws him. A moment, and he is in the saddle again, each time more secure and more expert; but off he has had to go, in all his varying incarnations, until this day. Off he had to go as the god-created man in Eden's grove; off he had to go as the founder of the world-empire; off he *must* go as the prince of the empire of God. Who knows how often he has wandered among us when none have recognised him? How know you, Julian, that you were not in him whom you now persecute?

Julian (looking far away): "Oh, unfathomable riddle——!"

HENRIK IBSEN
(*Emperor and Galilean*)
(Translated by WILLIAM ARCHER)

The Ring of Return

FRENCH

IT is not more surprising to be born twice than once; everything in Nature is resurrection.

VOLTAIRE

WHERE is there an old man who would not like to feel certain that he would be born again and bring back into another life the experience he has gained in the present one? . . . We must recognise that we have already lived before being what we now are, and that many other lives await us, some in this world, and the rest in a higher sphere, with a finer body and more delicate senses.

FRANÇOIS FOURIER
(*Theory of Universal Unity*)

EACH of us is a reincarnating being, ignorant both of his present and of his former transformations. . . . This life we spend on earth, shut in between an apparent birth and an equally apparent death is, in reality, only a portion of our existence, one manifestation of man in time.

Animals are without individuality, but nevertheless the immaterial principle which is in them cannot be destroyed. Can there be an eternal cosmic law whereby the Being at the head of a hierarchy unceasingly recalls, and by continuous action makes his own, the immaterial principle of the whole Sphere ruled by him? The law of an intelligent being is to perfect himself, for without that he would be like the animals whose instincts remain unaltered, unless, through domesticity, they enter the magnetic Sphere of man. One can conceive that the essence of all the species gravitates gradually towards the essence of domestic animals.

There are men in advance of their century; there are even some in advance of this actual existence, who participate in the future existence. . . . There are men sustained by divine goodness to hasten the accomplishment of its designs, who voluntarily take up the burden in order to lighten it for others.

PIERRE BALLANCHE
(Translated by EVA MARTIN)

IN philosophic mood, last night, as idly I was lying,
That souls may transmigrate methought there could be no denying:
So, just to know to what I owe propensities so strong,
I drew my soul into a chat—our gossip lasted long.
" A votive offering," she observed, " well might I claim from thee;
For thou in being hadst remained a cipher, but for me:
Yet not a virgin soul was I when first in thee enshrined."
Ah! I suspected, little soul, thus much that I should find!

" Yes," she continued, " yes, of old—I recollect it now—
In humble ivy I was wreathed round many a joyous brow.
More subtle next the essence was that I essayed to warm,
A bird's, that could salute the skies—a little bird's my form:
Where thickets made a pleasant shade, where shepherdesses strolled,
I fluttered round, hopped on the ground, my simple lays I trolled;
My pinions grew whilst still I flew in freedom on the wind."
Ah! I suspected, little soul, thus much that I should find!

" Médor my name, I next became a dog of wondrous tact,
The guardian of a poor blind man, his sole support, in fact ;
The trick of holding in my mouth a wooden bowl I knew—
I led my master through the streets, and begged his living, too.
Devoted to the poor, to please the wealthy was my care,
Gleaning as sustenance for one, what others well could spare ;
Thus did I good, since to good deeds so many I inclined."
Ah ! I suspected, little soul, thus much that I should find !

" Next, to breathe life into her charms, in a young girl I dwelt ;
There, in soft prison, snugly housed, what happiness I felt !
Till to my hiding-place a swarm of Cupids entrance gained,
And, after pillaging it well, in garrison remained.
Like old campaigners there the rogues all sorts of mischief did ;
And night and day, whilst still I lay in little corner hid,
How oft I saw the house on fire I scarce can call to mind."
Ah ! I suspected, little soul, thus much that I should find.

" Some light on thy propensities may now upon thee break ;
But prithee, hark ! one more remark I still," said she, " would make.
'Tis this—that having dared one day with Heaven to make too free,
God for my punishment resolved to shut me up in thee.

And what with sittings up at night, with work and
woman's art,
Tears and despair—for I forbear some secrets to impart—
A poet is a very hell for soul thereto consigned!"
Ah! I suspected, little soul, thus much that I should
find.

PIERRE JEAN DE BÉRANGER
(*La Métempsycose*)
(Translated by WILLIAM YOUNG)

IN proportion as the soul is developed by successive lives, the body to which it is to be united will necessarily be superior to those it has worn out, otherwise there would be no harmony between these two elements of human existence. . . .

Man's work will be a continuation of his past work. . . . He will again have a life of toil; he will participate, to the extent God has permitted him, in the endless creations produced by divine omnipotence; he will again love; he will never cease to love; he will continue his eternal progress, because the distance between himself and God is infinite.

CONSTANT SAVY

IF this [law of reincarnation] had not been instituted by God and if it had not been the essential reality, then man would have shown himself greater and better than God by the mere fact of having imagined it.

CHARLES LANCELIN

"HOW is it that in thy short life thou hast found the time to learn so many things?" said the young girl.

"I remember," he replied.

"Farewell," she said, "farewell, home of Earth,

warmed by the fires of love ; where all things press with ardent force from the centre to the extremities. . . . Farewell, all ye who have descended into the sphere of Instinct that you may suffer there for others ! . . . Farewell, ye granite rocks that shall bloom a flower ; farewell, flower that becomes a dove ; farewell, dove that shalt be woman ; farewell, woman, who art Suffering, man who art Belief ! Farewell, you who shall be all love, all prayer ! "

All human beings go through a previous life in the sphere of Instinct, where they are brought to see the worthlessness of earthly treasures, to amass which they gave themselves such untold pains ! Who can tell how many times the human being lives in the sphere of Instinct before he is prepared to enter the sphere of Abstraction, where thought expends itself on erring science, where mind wearies at last of human language ? For, when Matter is exhausted, Spirit enters. Who knows how many fleshly forms the heir of heaven occupies before he can be brought to understand the value of that silence and solitude whose starry plains are but the vestibule of Spiritual Worlds ? He feels his way amid the void, makes trial of nothingness, and then at last his eyes revert upon the Path. Then follow other existences—all to be lived to reach the place where Light effulgent shines. Death is the post-house of the journey. A lifetime may be needed merely to gain the virtues which annul the errors of man's preceding life. . . .

The virtues we acquire, which develop slowly within us, are the invisible links which bind each one of our existences to the others—existences which the spirit alone remembers, for Matter has no memory for spiritual things. Thought alone holds the tradition of the bygone life. The endless legacy of the past to the present is the secret source of human genius. . . .

When a human soul draws its first furrow straight,

the rest will follow surely. . . . All ends in God; and many are the ways to find Him by walking straight before us. . . .

The final life, the fruition of all other lives, to which the powers of the soul have tended, and whose merits open the Sacred Portals to perfected man, is the life of Prayer. . . . Cast yourself on the breast of the stream in Prayer! Silence and meditation are the means of following the Way. God reveals Himself, unfailingly, to the solitary, thoughtful seeker.

It is thus that the separation takes place between Matter, which so long has wrapped its darkness round you, and Spirit, which was in you from the beginning, the light which lighted you and now brings noon-day to your soul.

HONORÉ DE BALZAC
(*Seraphita*)
(Translated by K. P. WORMELEY)

IN this doctrine, so evidently based on reason, everything is linked and held together: the fore-knowledge of God and the agreement thereof with man's free-will. This problem, hitherto impossible to solve, no longer offers any difficulty, if by it is meant that God, knowing before birth, by reason of his previous deeds, what there is in the heart of man, brings man to life and removes him from it in circumstances that best fit in with the accomplishment of his purposes. . . .

And so there falls away and disappears the greatest difficulty in the doctrine of grace, which consisted in explaining how it came about that God made some men pitiful and others hard-hearted, without there being in him either justice or acceptance of persons . . . since evidently according to this theory it is not (as Origen has already said) apart from previous merit that some are formed for vessels of honour, and others for vessels of shame and wrath. . . .

Consequently the most sublime mysteries of religion,

the most wonderful facts regarding the destiny of the soul, find their natural explanation in a clear understanding of the doctrine of metempsychosis, however strange and extraordinary it may at first appear.

D'ORIENT
(*The Soul's Destinies*)

IF we regard the world as a series of successive lives for each creature, we see very well how it comes about that God, to whom there is neither time nor space, and who perceives the final goal of all things, permits evil and suffering as being necessary phases through which creatures must pass, in order to reach a state of happiness which the creature does not see, and consequently cannot enjoy in so far as it is a creature, but which God sees, and which, therefore, the creature virtually enjoys in him, for the time will come when it will partake of that happiness.

PIERRE LEROUX
(*Concerning Humanity*)

THE question may well be asked whether the talents, the good and evil tendencies man brings with him at birth, may not be the fruit of acquired intelligence, of qualities and vices gained in one or many former existences. Is there a previous life the elements of which have prepared the conditions of the life now being lived by each of us? People in ancient times thought so. Inborn dispositions, so different in children, caused them to believe in impressions left by previous existences in the imperishable germ of man. From the time when intelligence begins to show itself in children, we faintly discern a general attitude towards things, which is very like a memory thereof. . . . Rebirth in humanity constitutes no more than an initial circle of tests. . . . The limit to the progress man must have attained to, before entering upon another circle of tests in another sphere, is at present unknown to us ; science and philosophy will doubtless succeed in determining this limit later on.

I affirm the perpetual union of the soul to organic bodies ; these bodies succeed each other, being born from one another, and fitting themselves for the constitutive forms of the worlds traversed by the immortal ego in its successive existences. . . . Let us not forget that the soul always carries off a material germ from one existence to the next, making itself anew, so to speak, several times, in that endless ascent of lives through the worlds.

ALPHONSE ESQUIROS

"ALBERT had persuaded himself, and would have persuaded us, that he was the same Wratislaw, the son of Withold, who was the first to bear the maternal name of Rudolstadt. He recounted all the events of his childhood ; his memories of the execution of Count Withold (for which he blamed the Jesuit Dithmar, whom he declared to be none other than the Abbé, his present tutor) ; the deep hatred he had felt during his childhood for this Dithmar, for Austria, and for all Imperialists and Catholics. Then his recollections seemed to become confused, and he uttered a thousand incomprehensible statements about eternal and perpetual life, asserting the reappearances of men on earth . . . all with such a show of conviction, with such precise and interesting details of what he claimed to have seen, not only as Wratislaw, but again as John Ziska, and I know not how many other dead persons whom he maintained to have been previous incarnations of himself in the past, that we listened with open mouths, incapable either of interrupting or contradicting him."

" If one asks him how he has been able to learn so many different languages, he replies that he knew them before he was born, and that he only has to recall them to memory—one that he spoke twelve hundred years ago, another during the Crusades—alas, how can I tell? You will hear many strange accounts of what he calls his former existences."

"Albert," she said, "for your name is no longer John, as mine is no longer Wanda, look at me well, and understand that I am changed in face and in character, even as you are. . . . God commands us to pardon and to forget. These wild and detailed recollections of former lives, this determination to exercise a faculty not given to other men, this fatal memory is an offence to God, and He withdraws it from you because you have abused it. . . . It is God who has made you to live again under new conditions and with new duties. These duties you do not know, Albert—or you despise them. You retrace the course of ages with an impious pride; you aspire to penetrate the secrets of destiny; you think to attain equality with God, embracing in a glance the present and the past. This retrograde thought is rash and criminal. . . . Renounce in your own soul, renounce firmly and once for all, the wish to know yourself beyond this transitory life that is imposed on you. . . . Without losing faith in your immortality, without doubting the divine goodness which pardons the past and protects the future, concentrate on rendering humane and fruitful this present life that you despise, when you ought to respect it and give yourself up to it entirely, with all your strength, and abnegation, and charity."

"Consuelo," he said to her. . . . "I am going to leave you for a time, and then I shall return to earth by means of a new birth. I shall return accursed and despairing if you abandon me now, in my last hour. You know that the crimes of John Ziska are not fully expiated, and only you, my sister Wanda, can accomplish the act of purification in this phase of my life. We are brethren ; ere we become lovers, death must once more separate us. But we must be united by the marriage-vow, that I may be re-born calm and strong, and free, like other men, from the memory of past lives which has been my torment and my punishment for so many centuries. Consent to this vow. It will not bind you to me in this life, which I am about to leave, but it will reunite us in eternity. It will be as a seal to help us to recognise one another when the shades of death have effaced the clearness of our memories."

George Sand
(*Consuelo*)
(Translated by Eva Martin)

I AM a soul. I know well that what I shall render up to the grave is not myself. That which is myself will go elsewhere.

Earth, thou art not my abyss !

The whole creation is a perpetual ascension, from brute to man, from man to God. To divest ourselves more and more of matter, to be clothed more and more with spirit, such is the law. Each time we die we gain more of life.

Souls pass from one sphere to another without loss of personality, become more and more bright, unceasingly approach nearer to God.

A man sleeps. He dreams. He dreams that he is a wild beast, a lion, a wolf, and he experiences all the adventures of the wilds. On awakening he recovers himself. The dream has vanished. He is what he was before. He is a man and not a lion.

The next night he has another dream. He is a bird or a serpent. He awakes and finds himself a man.

So it is with life. So with all the terrestrial lives that we may be compelled to traverse. . . .

The Ring of Return

The I which persists after the awakening is the I anterior and external to the dream. The I which persists after death is the I anterior and external to life.

VICTOR HUGO
(*Life and Death*: From *Victor Hugo's Intellectual Autobiography*)
(Translated by LORENZO O'ROURKE)

OUR efforts must be free, voluntary, sheltered from the influences of the past; the field of strife must be seemingly untrodden, so that the athlete shall show and exercise his virtue. Previously gained experience, the energies which he has acquired, help him in the new strife, but in a latent way of which he is unconscious. . . . Lethe, like free-will, is a law of the world as it is.

Original sin does not account for the particular fate of individuals, as it is the same for all. . . .

Once accept the theory of pre-existence, and a glorious light is thrown on the dogma of sin, for it becomes the result of personal faults from which the guilty soul must be purified.

Pre-existence, once admitted as regards the past, logically implies a succession of future existences for all souls that have not yet attained to the goal, and that have imperfections and defilements from which to be cleansed. In order to enter the *circle of happiness* and leave the *circle of wanderings*, one must be pure.

ANDRÉ PEZZANI
(*The Plurality of the Soul's Existences*)

ALL are destined to attain perfection by passing through the different degrees of the spirit-hierarchy. . . . Material life is a trial which they have to undergo many times until they have attained to absolute perfection ; it is a sort of filter, or alembic, from which they issue more or less purified after each new incarnation. . . .

The incarnation of spirits always takes place in the human race ; it would be an error to suppose that the soul or spirit could be incarnated in the body of an animal. . . .

The soul possessed its own individuality before its incarnation ; it possesses that individuality after its separation from the body.

On its re-entrance into the spirit-world, the soul finds there all those whom it has known upon the earth, and all its former existences eventually come back to its memory, with the remembrance of all the good and of all the evil which it has done in them.

He who is conscious of his own inferiority derives a consoling hope from the doctrine of reincarnation. If he believes in the justice of God, he cannot hope to be placed, at once and for all eternity, on a level with those who have made a better use of life than he has done ; but the knowledge that his inferiority will not exclude him for ever from the supreme felicity, and that he will be able to conquer this felicity through new efforts, revives his courage and sustains his energy. Who does not regret, at the end of his career, that the experience he has acquired should have come too late to allow of his turning it to useful account ? This tardily acquired experience will not be lost for him ; he will profit by it in a new corporeal life.

Just as in a human lifetime there are days which bear no fruit, so in the life of a spirit there are corporeal existences which are barren of profitable result, because he has failed to make a right use of them.

The possibilities of the future are open to all, without

exception, and without favour to any. Those who are the last to arrive have only themselves to blame for the delay.

A philosopher has said that 'if God did not exist, it would be necessary to invent Him for the happiness of the human race'; the same might be said in regard to the plurality of existences.

We assert that the doctrine of the plurality of existences is the only one which explains what, without this doctrine, is inexplicable; that it is at once eminently consolatory and strictly conformable with the most rigorous justice; and that it is the anchor of safety which God in His mercy has provided for mankind.

ALLAN KARDEC
(*The Spirit's Book*)
(Translated by A. BLACKWELL)

HOW glorious the light that would be cast on the present order of things by a knowledge of our former existences! And yet, not only is our memory helpless regarding the times that preceded birth, it is not even conscious of the whole of the intervening period, often playing us false in the course of a lifetime. . . . We die, and everything is dark around us; we are born again, and the light begins to appear, like a star through the mist; we live, and it develops and grows, suddenly disappears again, and reappears once more; from one eclipse to another we continue our way, and this way, interrupted by periods of darkness, is a continuous one, whose elements, only apparently separated, are linked to each other by the closest of bonds; we always bear within ourselves the principle of what we shall be later on; we are always rising higher. . . . And who knows but what our soul, in the unknown secret of its essence, has power some day to throw light on its successive journeyings. . . . There are strong reasons for thinking that such is the case, since the entire restoration of memory appears, with good reason, to be one of the main conditions of our future happiness.

We cannot fully enjoy life until we become, like Janus, kings of time; until we know how to concentrate in ourselves, not only the sentiment of the present, but that of the future and the past. Then, if perfect life be one day given to us, perfect memory must also be given to us. Let us try to conceive the infinite treasures of a mind enriched by the recollections of an innumerable series of existences, entirely different from each other, and yet admirably linked together by a continual dependence. . . . Let us banish the idea of disorder from the earth, by opening the gates of time beyond our birth, as we have banished the idea of injustice by opening other gates beyond the tomb.

JEAN REYNAUD
(*Earth and Heaven*)

DESCARTES and Leibnitz have demonstrated that the human understanding possesses ideas called *innate*, that is to say, ideas which we bring with us to our birth. This fact is certain. In our time, the Scotch philosopher Dugald Stewart, has put Descartes' theory into a more precise form, by proving that the only really *innate* idea, that which has universal existence in the human mind after birth, is the idea or the *principle of causality*, a principle that makes us say and think that there is no effect without cause, which is the beginning of reason. . . .

Innate ideas and the principle of causality are explained very simply by the doctrine of the plurality of existences; they are, indeed, merely deductions from that doctrine. A man's soul, having already existed, either in the body of an animal or that of another man, has preserved the trace of the impressions received during that existence. It has lost, it is true, the recollection of actions performed during its former incarnation, but the abstract principle of causality, being independent of the particular facts . . . must remain in the soul in its second incarnation.

We are endeavouring to prove that the soul of the man remains always the same, in spite of its numerous peregrinations, notwithstanding the variety of form of the bodies in which it is successively lodged. . . . We are endeavouring to establish that the soul, notwithstanding all its journeys, throughout all its incarnations and metamorphoses, remains always identical with itself, doing nothing more in each metamorphosis . . . than perfect and purify itself, growing in power and in intellectual capacity. We are endeavouring to prove that, notwithstanding the shadows of death, our individuality is never destroyed. . . .

Natural aptitudes, special faculties, vocations, are the traces of impressions formerly received, of knowledge already acquired, and, being revealed from the cradle, cannot be explained otherwise than by a life gone by. We have lost the remembrance of the facts, but there remains the moral consequence, the *resultant* . . . and thus the *innate ideas* indicated by Descartes, which exist in the soul from its birth, and also the *principle of causality*, which teaches us that every effect has a cause, are explained.

LOUIS FIGUIER
(*The Day After Death*)

THE degrees of initiation are innumerable. Watch, then, disciple of life, watch and labour towards the development of the angel within thee! For the divine Odyssey is but a series of more and more ethereal metamorphoses, in which each form, the result of what goes before, is the condition of those which follow.

All that we are, desire, do, and know, is more or less superficial, and below the rays and lightnings of our periphery there remains the darkness of unfathomable substance . . . the abyss of the Unrevealed, the Virtual, pledge of an infinite future—the obscure self, the pure subjectivity which is incapable of realising itself in mind, conscience, or reason, in the soul, the heart, the imagination, or the life of the senses, and which makes for itself attributes and conditions out of all these forms of its own life.

Life is only a document to be interpreted, matter to be spiritualised. Such is the life of the thinker. Every day he strips himself more and more of personality. . . . He does not even believe his body his own ; he feels the vital whirlwind passing through him—lent to him, as it were, for a moment, in order that he may perceive the cosmic vibrations. . . . He asks nothing from life but wisdom.

I possess myself only as Monad and as Ego, and I feel my faculties themselves reabsorbed into the substance which they have individualised. . . . The whole rainbow is withdrawn within the dewdrop ; consequences return to the principle, effects to the cause, the bird to the egg, the organism to its germ. This psychological reinvolution is an anticipation of death ; it represents the life beyond the grave ; . . . it implies the simplication of the individual who, allowing all the accidents of personality to evaporate, exists henceforward only in the indivisible state, the state of point, of potentiality, of pregnant nothingness. . . . What is the acorn but the oak which has lost its leaves, its branches, its trunk, and its roots—that is to say, all its apparatus, its forms, its particularities—but which is still present in concentration, in essence, in a form which contains the possibility of complete revival? . . . To be reduced to those elements in one which are eternal is indeed to die, but not to be annihilated.

Amiel's Journal
(Translated by MRS. HUMPHRY WARD)

TO every awakened soul the question comes: Why does evil exist?

So long as the enigma remains unsolved, Suffering remains a threatening sphinx, opposing God and ready to devour mankind.

The Key to the secret lies in Evolution, which can be accomplished only by means of the continual return of souls to earth.

When once man learns that suffering is the necessary result of divine manifestation; that inequalities of condition are due to the different stages which beings have reached and the changeable action of their will; that the painful phase lasts only a moment in Eternity, and that we have it in our power to hasten its disappearance; that, though slaves of the past, we are masters of the future; that, finally, the same glorious goal awaits all beings—then despair will be at an end; hatred, envy, and rebellion will have fled away; and peace will reign over a humanity made wise by knowledge.

Inequality of condition arises, above all else, from the continuity of what might be called creation. . . . Souls ascend slowly from one kingdom to another, whilst the places they leave are filled by new-comers, by younger souls.

A second cause of human inequality is the difference in effort and deed accomplished by the will of human beings who have reached a certain point in evolution.

As soon as this will is guided by intelligence and the moral sense, it hastens or delays individual evolution, makes it easy when it acts in harmony with divine Law —by doing what is called 'good'—or disturbs evolution by pain, when it opposes this Law, by doing 'evil.' . . . These effects of the will influence to a noticeable degree the life during which they have originated; they are preserved in a latent condition after death, and appear again in future returns to earth.

Thus are men born laden with the result of their past, and in possession of the capacities they have developed in the course of their evolution. . . . Men are philosophers or mathematicians, artists or *savants*, from the very cradle.

But if we are the slaves of the past, if fate compels us to reap what we have sown, we yet have the future in our hands, for we can tear up the weeds, and in their place sow useful plants. Just as, by means of physical hygiene, we can change within a few years the nature of the constituents that make up our bodies, so also, by a process of moral hygiene, we can purify our passions and then turn their strength in the direction of good.

Another fact strikes the observer: the cyclic march of evolution. After action comes reaction; after activity, rest; after winter, summer; after day, night. . . . Ideas also have their successive cycles of glory and decadence. . . . Races are born and grow up, die and are born again; pass through a state of childhood, of youth, of maturity, and of old age. . . . Continents submit to the same law; history and science show how they pass through a series of immersions and emersions. . . . The very planets, too, come under this law. . . .

Everything, then, in appearance is born and dies. In reality, each thing springs from its germ, makes an effort—the effort of the divine Will incarnated in this germ—develops its potentialities up to a certain step in the ladder of evolution, then garners the acquired qualities and again returns to activity in continuous cycles of life until its full development is reached.

DR. THÉOPHILE PASCAL
(*Reincarnation: A Study in Human Evolution*)
(Translated by FRED ROTHWELL)

A.D. 1700-1900

AMERICAN

WHEN I see nothing annihilated (in the works of God) and not a drop of water wasted, I cannot suspect the annihilation of souls, or believe that He will suffer the daily waste of millions of minds ready made that now exist, and put Himself to the continual trouble of making new ones. Thus, finding myself to exist in the world, I believe I shall, in some shape or other, always exist; and, with all the inconveniences human life is liable to, I shall not object to a new edition of mine, hoping, however, that the *errata* of the last may be corrected.

BENJAMIN FRANKLIN

The Body
of
BENJAMIN FRANKLIN
Printer,
Like the cover of an old book,
Its contents worn out,
And stripped of its lettering and gilding,
Lies here, food for worms.
But the work shall not be lost,
For it will, as he believed, appear once more,
In a new and more elegant edition,
Revised and corrected
by
The Author

(*Epitaph written for himself by* BENJAMIN FRANKLIN *when he was twenty-three years of age*)

THUS the seer, with vision clear,
Sees forms appear and disappear
In the perpetual round of strange
Mysterious change

The Ring of Return

From birth to death, from death to birth,
From earth to heaven, from heaven to earth ;
Till glimpses more sublime
Of things, unseen before,
Unto his wondering eyes reveal
The Universe, as an immeasurable wheel
Turning for evermore
In the rapid and rushing river of Time.

H. W. Longfellow
(*Rain in Summer*)

WHERE do we find ourselves? In a series, of which we do not know the extremes, and believe that it has none. We wake, and find ourselves on a stair: there are stairs below us, which we seem to have ascended ; there are stairs above us, many a one, which go upward and out of sight. But the Genius which, according to the old belief, stands at the door by which we enter, and gives us the lethe to drink, that we may tell no tales, mixed the cup too strongly, and we cannot shake off the lethargy now at noon-day. Sleep lingers all our lifetime about our eyes, as night hovers all day in the boughs of the fir-tree.

Ralph Waldo Emerson

WE must infer our destiny from the preparation. We are driven by instinct to hive innumerable experiences which are of no visible value, and we may revolve through many lives before we shall assimilate or exhaust them. Now there is nothing in nature capricious, or whimsical, or accidental, or unsupported. Nature never moves by jumps, but always in steady and supported advances. . . . If there is the desire to live, and in larger sphere, with more knowledge and power, it is because life and power are good for us, and we are the natural depositaries of these gifts. The love of life is out of all proportion to the value set on a single day, and seems to indicate a conviction of immense resources and possibilities proper to us, on which we have never drawn. All the comfort I have found teaches me to confide that I shall not have less in times and places that I do not yet know.

RALPH WALDO EMERSON

PERCHANCE not he but Nature ailed,
The world and not the infant failed.
It was not ripe yet to sustain
A genius of so fine a strain,
Who gazed upon the sun and moon
As if he came unto his own,
And, pregnant with his grander thought,
Brought the old order into doubt.
His beauty once their beauty tried;
They could not feed him, and he died,
And wandered backward as in scorn
To wait an æon to be born.

RALPH WALDO EMERSON
(*Threnody*)

AS when the haze of some wan moonlight makes
Familiar fields a land of mystery,
Where, chill and strange, a ghostly presence wakes
In flower or bush or tree,

Another life the life of day o'erwhelms,
The past from present consciousness takes hue,
As we remember vast and cloudy realms
Our feet have wandered through:

So, oft, some moonlight of the mind makes dumb
The stir of outer thought, wide open seems
The gate wherethrough strange sympathies have come,
The secret of our dreams. . . .

All outward vision yields to that within,
Whereof nor creed nor canon holds the key;

The Ring of Return

We only feel that we have ever been
And evermore shall be.

And thus I know, by memories unfurled
In rarer moods, and many a nameless sign,
That once in Time and somewhere in the world
I was a towering pine. . . .

Some blind harmonic instinct pierced the rind
Of that slow life which made me straight and high,
And I became a harp for every wind,
A voice for every sky. . . .

And if some wild, full-gathered harmony
Rolls its unbroken music through my line,
There lives and murmurs, faintly though it be,
The spirit of the pine.

BAYARD TAYLOR
(*The Metempsychosis of the Pine*)

THE river hemmed with leaving trees
Wound through the meadows green,
A low blue line of mountain showed
The open pines between.

One sharp tall peak above them all
Clear into sunlight sprang,
I saw the river of my dreams,
The mountain that I sang.

No clue of memory led me on,
But well the ways I knew;
A feeling of familiar things
With every footstep grew.

Yet ne'er before that river's rim
Was pressed by feet of mine,
Never before mine eyes had crossed
That broken mountain line.

A.D. 1700-1900

A presence strange at once and known
  Walked with me as my guide,
The skirts of some forgotten life
  Trailed noiseless at my side.

Was it a dim-remembered dream
  Or glimpse through æons old?
The secret which the mountains kept,
  The river never told.

J. G. WHITTIER
(*A Mystery*)

I KNOW I am deathless,
  I know this orbit of mine cannot be swept by a carpenter's compass. . . .
And whether I come to my own to-day or in ten thousand or ten million years,
I can cheerfully take it now, or with equal cheerfulness I can wait.
My foothold is tenon'd and mortis'd in granite,
I laugh at what you call dissolution,
And I know the amplitude of time. . . .

To be in any form, what is that?
(Round and round we go, all of us, and ever come back thither.) . . .
I troop forth replenish'd with supreme power, one of an average unending procession,
Inland and sea-coast we go, and pass all boundary lines,
Our swift ordinances on their way over the whole earth,
The blossoms we wear in our hats the growth of thousands of years. . . .

I do not despise you priests, all time, all the world over,
My faith is the greatest of faiths and the least of faiths,
Enclosing worship ancient and modern and all between ancient and modern,

The Ring of Return

Believing I shall come again upon the earth after five
thousand years. . . .

The clock indicates the moment—but what does eternity
indicate?
We have thus far exhausted billions of winters and
summers,
There are trillions ahead, and trillions ahead of them.
Births have brought us richness and variety,
And other births will bring us richness and variety. . . .
I am an acme of things accomplished, and I an encloser
of things to be.

My feet strike an apex of the apices of the stairs,
On every step bunches of ages, and larger bunches
between the steps,
All below duly travell'd, and still I mount and mount.

Rise after rise bow the phantoms behind me,
Afar down I see the huge first nothing, I know I was
even there,
I waited unseen and always, and slept through the
lethargic mist,
And took my time, and took no hurt from the fœtid
carbon.
Long I was hugg'd close—long and long.

Immense have been the preparations for me,
Faithful and friendly the arms that have help'd me.

Cycles ferried my cradle, rowing and rowing like cheerful
boatmen,
For room to me stars kept aside in their own rings,
They sent influences to look after what was to hold
me. . . .

All forces have been steadily employ'd to complete and
delight me,

A.D. 1700-1900

Now on this spot I stand with my robust soul.

I tramp a perpetual journey (come listen all!) . .
This day before dawn I ascended a hill and look'd at
the crowded heaven,
And I said to my spirit, *When we become the enfolders of those orbs, and the pleasure and knowledge of everything in them, shall we be fill'd and satisfied then?*
And my spirit said, *No, we but level that lift to pass and continue beyond.*

And as to you, Life, I reckon you are the leavings of
many deaths.
(No doubt I have died myself ten thousand times before.)

WALT WHITMAN
(*Song of Myself*)

TO the garden the world anew ascending,
Potent mates, daughters, sons, preluding,
The love, the life of their bodies, meaning and
being,
Curious here behold my resurrection after slumber,
The revolving cycles in their wide sweep having brought
me again,
Amorous, mature, all beautiful to me, all wondrous,
My limbs and the quivering fire that ever plays through
them, for reasons most wondrous,
Existing I peer and penetrate still,
Content with the present, content with the past,
By my side or back of me, Eve following,
Or in front, and I following her just the same.

WALT WHITMAN

YEAR after year beheld the silent toil
That spread his lustrous coil;
Still, as the spiral grew,
He left the past year's dwelling for the new,

Stole with soft step its shining archway through,
Built up its idle door,
Stretched in his last-found home, and knew the old no
    more.

Build thee more stately mansions, O my soul!
As the swift seasons roll!
Leave thy low-vaulted past!
Let each new temple, nobler than the last,
Shut thee from heaven with a dome more vast,
Till thou at length art free,
Leaving thine outgrown shell by life's unresting sea!

OLIVER WENDELL HOLMES
(*The Chambered Nautilus*)

I KNOW my own creation was divine.
    Strewn on the breezy continents I see
    The veinèd shells and burnished scales which once
Enclosed my being—husks that had their use;
I brood on all the shapes I must attain
Before I reach the perfect, which is God,
And dream my dream, and let the rabble go;
For I am of the mountains and the sea,
The deserts and the caverns in the earth,
The catacombs and fragments of old worlds.
    I was a spirit on the mountain-top,
A perfume in the valleys, a simoon
On arid deserts, a nomadic wind
Roaming the universe, a tireless Voice.
I was ere Romulus and Remus were;
I was ere Nineveh and Babylon;
I was and am and evermore shall be,
Progressing, never reaching to the end.
    A hundred years I trembled in the grass,
The delicate trefoil that muffled warm
A slope on Ida; for a hundred years

A.D. 1700-1900

Moved in the purple gyre of those dark flowers
The Grecian women strew upon the dead.
Under the earth, in fragrant glooms, I dwelt;
Then in the veins and sinews of a pine
On a lone island . . .
till the hand of God
Let down the lightning from a sultry sky,
Splintered the pine, and split the iron rock;
And from my odorous prison-house, a bird,
I in its bosom, darted. . . .
A century was as a single day.
What is a day to an immortal soul?
A breath, no more. . . .
So was it destined; and thus came I here
To walk the earth and wear the form of Man,
To suffer bravely as becomes my state,
One step, one grade, one cycle nearer God.

T. B. Aldrich
(*The Metempsychosis*)

We do not all start fair in the race that is set before us, and therefore all cannot be expected, at the close of our brief mortal pilgrimage, to reach the same goal. . . . The commonest observation assures us that one child is born with limited capacities and perhaps a wayward disposition, strong passions, and a sullen temper. . . . Another, on the contrary, seems happily endowed from the start . . . a child of many hopes. . . . The differences of external conditions also are so vast and obvious that they seem to detract much from the merit of a well-spent life and from the guilt of vice and crime. . . . How can such frightful inequalities be made to appear consistent with the infinite wisdom and goodness of God?

If metempsychosis is included in the scheme of the divine government of the world, this difficulty disappears altogether. Considered from this point of view, everyone is born into the state which he has fairly earned by his own previous history. He carries with him from one stage of existence to another the habits or tendencies which he has formed, the dispositions which he has indulged, the passions which he has not chastised. . . .

We can easily imagine and believe that every person now living is a *re*-presentation of some one who lived perhaps centuries ago under another name in another country. . . . His surroundings are changed ; the old house of flesh has been torn down and rebuilt ; but the tenant is still the same. He has come down from some former generation, bringing with him what may be either a help or a hindrance—namely, the character and tendencies which he there formed and nurtured. And herein is retribution ; he has entered upon a new stage of probation, and in it he has now to learn what the character which he there formed naturally leads to when tried upon a new and perhaps broader theatre. . . . [Men] bring with them no recollection of the incidents of their former life, as such memory would unfit them for the new part which they have to play. But they are still the same in the principles and modes of conduct, in the inmost spring of action, which the forgotten incidents of their former life have developed and strengthened. . . .

The transmigration of souls may be regarded also in another light, as that portion of the divine government of this world's affairs which maintains distributive justice, since, through its agency, in the long run, all inequalities of condition and favouring or unfavouring circumstances may be compensated, and each person may have his or her equitable share of opportunities for good and of the requisite means for discipline and improvement.

PROFESSOR FRANCIS BOWEN
(From an article on 'Christian Metempsychosis' in the *Princeton Review*, May 1881)

A.D. 1700-1900

REINCARNATED we have all been many times. Regeneration is a step beyond reincarnation. Reincarnation means the total loss of one physical body and the getting of a new one through the aid of another organisation. . . .

A spiritualising and refining power has ever been and will ever be working on this planet. It has through innumerable ages changed all forms of being, whether mineral, animal, or vegetable, from coarse to finer types. It works with man as with all other organisations. It is ever changing him gradually from a material to a more spiritual being. It is carrying him through his many physical existences from one degree of perfection to another. It has in store for him new powers, new lives, and new methods of existence. . . .

Regeneration may supersede reincarnation, because of our coming into a higher order of life, or receiving and being built of a higher order of thoughts. The spirit will then be ever changing its physical body for one still finer and more spiritualised. This is the process referred to by Christ as being ' born again.'

Life is an eternal series of regenerations. . . . The spirit is regenerated when it shakes off the old physical body. It shakes off an old body because it is tired of carrying an instrument through which it cannot express itself.

The spirit of a mammoth living countless ages ago may now exist in the elephant, deer, or wild horse. It is the refined spirit, using a body lesser in size, finer in quality, more graceful, and more agile. It is the result of the unconscious tendency in all forms of life to the finer and better. . . .

The true evolution, then, is that of spirit, taking on itself through successive ages many re-embodiments and adding to itself some new quality with each re-embodiment.

PRENTICE MULFORD
(*The Gift of the Spirit*)

The Ring of Return

A BOY went to school. He was very little. All that he knew he had drawn in with his mother's milk. His teacher (who was God) placed him in the lowest class, and gave him these lessons to learn: Thou shalt not kill. Thou shalt do no hurt to any living thing. Thou shalt not steal. So the man did not kill; but he was cruel, and he stole. At the end of the day (when his beard was grey; when the night was come) his teacher (who was God) said: "Thou hast learned not to kill. But the other lessons thou hast not learned. Come back to-morrow."

On the morrow he came back, a little boy. And his teacher (who was God) put him in a class a little higher, and gave him these lessons to learn: Thou shalt do no hurt to any living thing. Thou shalt not steal. Thou shalt not cheat. So the man did no hurt to any living thing; but he stole and he cheated. And at the end of the day (when his beard was grey; when the night was come) his teacher (who was God) said: "Thou hast learned to be merciful. But the other lessons thou hast not learned. Come back to-morrow."

Again, on the morrow, he came back, a little boy. And his teacher (who was God) put him in a class yet a little higher, and gave him these lessons to learn: Thou shalt not steal. Thou shalt not cheat. Thou shalt not covet. So the man did not steal; but he cheated, and he coveted. And at the end of the day (when his beard was grey; when the night was come) his teacher (who was God) said: "Thou hast learned not to steal. But the other lessons thou hast not learned. Come back, my child, to-morrow."

This is what I have read in the faces of men and women, in the book of the world, and in the scroll of the heavens which is writ with stars.

BERRY BENSON
(*The Century Magazine*, May 1894)

A.D. 1700-1900

ENGLISH

WHAT is incorruptible must also be ungenerable. The soul, therefore, if immortal, existed before our birth. . . . The metempsychosis is therefore the only system of this kind that philosophy can hearken to.

DAVID HUME
(*The Immortality of the Soul*)

OFT o'er my brain does that strange fancy roll
Which makes the present (while the flash doth last)
Seem a mere semblance of some unknown past,
Mix'd with such feelings as perplex the soul
Self-question'd in her sleep : and some have said
We liv'd ere yet this fleshy robe we wore.
O my sweet Baby ! when I reach my door,
If heavy looks should tell me thou wert dead
(As sometimes, thro' excess of hope, I fear)
I think that I should struggle to believe
Thou wert a Spirit to this nether sphere
Sentenc'd for some more venial crime to grieve ;
Didst scream, then spring to meet Heaven's quick reprieve,
While we wept idly o'er thy little bier.

SAMUEL TAYLOR COLERIDGE
(*Sonnet composed on a journey homeward, after hearing of the birth of his son ; September* 1796)

AND as the seed waits eagerly watching for its flower and fruit,
Anxious its little soul looks out into the clear expanse
To see if hungry winds are abroad with their invisible array ;

The Ring of Return

So Man looks out in tree, and herb, and fish, and bird, and beast,
Collecting up the scattered portions of his immortal body
Into the elemental forms of everything that grows. . . .
He stores his thoughts
As in store-houses in his memory. He regulates the forms
Of all beneath and all above, and in the gentle West
Reposes where the sun's heat dwells. He rises to the sun,
And to the planets of the night, and to the stars that gild
The zodiacs, and the stars that sullen stand to North and South ;
He touches the remotest pole, and in the centre weeps
That man should labour and sorrow, and learn and forget, and return
To the dark valley whence he came, and begin his labours anew.
In pain he sighs, in pain he labours in his universe. . . .
And in cries of birth and in the groans of death his voice
Is heard throughout the universe. Wherever a grass grows,
Or a leaf buds, the Eternal Man is seen, is heard, is felt,
And all his sorrows, till he reassumes his ancient bliss.

William Blake
(*Vala*)

THEN Milton rose up from the Heavens of Albion ardorous :
The whole Assembly wept prophetic, seeing in Milton's face
And in his lineaments divine the shades of Death and Ulro ;
He took off the robe of the Promise, and ungirded himself from the oath of God.
And Milton said : " I go to Eternal Death ! The nations still

Follow after the detestable Gods of Priam, in pomp
Of warlike Selfhood, contradicting and blaspheming. . . .
My soul lies at the gates of death. . . .
I will go down to self-annihilation and Eternal Death;
Lest the Last Judgment come and find me unannihilate,
And I be seiz'd and giv'n into the hands of my own Selfhood." . . .

And Milton said: "I go to Eternal Death!" Eternity shudder'd;
For he took the outside course, among the graves of the dead,
A mournful Shade. Eternity shudder'd at the image of Eternal Death.

Then on the verge of Beulah he beheld his own Shadow,
A mournful form, double, hermaphroditic, male and female
In one wonderful body, and he enter'd into it
In direful pain. . . . Milton bent down
To the bosom of Death: what was underneath soon seem'd above,
A cloudy heaven mingled with stormy seas in loudest ruin;
But as a wintry globe descends precipitant, thro' Beulah bursting,
With thunders loud and terrible, so Milton's Shadow fell
Precipitant, loud thund'ring, into the Sea of Time and Space.

WILLIAM BLAKE
(*Milton*)

WHY is it that some scenes awaken thoughts which belong, as it were, to dreams of early and shadowy recollections, such as old Brahmin moonshine would have ascribed to a state of previous existence? How often do we find ourselves in society which we have never before met, and yet feel impressed with a mysterious and ill-defined consciousness that neither the scene nor the speakers nor the subject are entirely new ; nay, feel as if we could anticipate that part of the conversation which has not yet taken place.

SIR WALTER SCOTT
(*Guy Mannering*)

YESTERDAY at dinner-time, I was strangely haunted by what I would call the sense of pre-existence—viz. a confused idea that nothing that passed was said for the first time—that the same topics had been discussed, and the same persons had stated the same opinions on them. . . . The sensation was so strong as to resemble what is called a *mirage* in the desert.

SIR WALTER SCOTT, February 17, 1828

STRANGER, though new the frame
Thy soul inhabits now, I've traced its flame
For many an age, in every chance and change
Of that Existence, through whose varied range—
As through a torch-race, where, from hand to hand
The flying youths transmit their shining brand—
From frame to frame the unextinguished soul
Rapidly passes, till it reach the goal !

THOMAS MOORE
(*Lalla Rookh*)

WORLDS on worlds are rolling ever
From creation to decay,
Like the bubbles on a river,
Sparkling, bursting, borne away.
But they are still immortal
Who, through birth's orient portal
And death's dark chasm hurrying to and fro,
Clothe their unceasing flight
In the brief dust and light
Gathered around their chariots as they go ;

A.D. 1700-1900

New shapes they still may weave,
New gods, new laws receive:
Bright or dim are they as the robes they last
On Death's bare ribs had cast.

PERCY BYSSHE SHELLEY
(*Hellas*)

O HAPPY Earth! reality of Heaven!
To which those restless souls that ceaselessly
Throng through the human universe, aspire. . . .
Thou art the end of all desire and will,
The product of all action: and the souls
That by the paths of an aspiring change
Have reached thy haven of perpetual peace,
There rest from the eternity of toil
That framed the fabric of thy perfectness.

Yet, human Spirit, bravely hold thy course,
Let virtue teach thee firmly to pursue
The gradual paths of an aspiring change:
For birth and life and death and that strange state
Before the naked soul has found its home,
All tend to perfect happiness, and urge
The restless wheels of being on their way.

PERCY BYSSHE SHELLEY
(*Queen Mab*)

ARIEL to Miranda: Take
This slave of music for the sake
Of him, who is the slave of thee. . . .
Poor Ariel sends this silent token
Of more than ever can be spoken;
Your guardian spirit, Ariel, who
From life to life must still pursue
Your happiness, for thus alone
Can Ariel ever find his own. . . .
When you die, the silent moon,

In her interlunar swoon,
Is not sadder in her cell
Than deserted Ariel;
When you live again on earth,
Like an unseen star of birth
Ariel guides you o'er the sea
Of life from your nativity.
Many changes have been run
Since Ferdinand and you begun
Your course of love, and Ariel still
Has tracked your steps and served your will.
Now in humbler, happier lot
This is all remembered not;
And now, alas! the poor sprite is
Imprisoned for some fault of his
In a body like a grave—
From you he only dares to crave,
For his service and his sorrow,
A smile to-day, a song to-morrow.
The artist who this idol wrought,
To echo all harmonious thought,
Felled a tree, while on the steep
The woods were in their winter sleep . . .
and so this tree—
O that such our death may be!—
Died in sleep and felt no pain
To live in happier form again;
From which, beneath Heaven's fairest star,
The artist wrought this loved Guitar.

PERCY BYSSHE SHELLEY
(*Ariel to Miranda: with a Guitar*)

SHELLEY sighed as we walked on. "How provokingly close are these new-born babes!" he ejaculated; "but it is not the less certain, notwithstanding the cunning attempts to conceal the truth, that all knowledge is reminiscence. The doctrine is far more ancient than the times of Plato, and as old as the venerable allegory that the Muses are the daughters of memory ; not one of the Muses was ever said to be the child of invention."

From DOWDEN'S *Life of Shelley*

IT does not appear improbable to me that some of the more refined machinery of thought may adhere, even in another state, to the sentient principle, for though the organs of gross sensation, the nerves and brain, are destroyed by death, yet something of the more ethereal value may be less destructible, and I sometimes imagine that many of those powers which have been called distinctive belong to the more refined clothing of the spirit. Conscience, indeed, seems to have some indefined source, and may bear relations to a former state of being.

SIR HUMPHREY DAVY
(*Consolations in Travel,* Dialogue IV)

THE power that dwelleth in sweet sounds to waken
Vague yearnings like the sailor's for the shore,
And dim remembrances whose views seem taken
From some bright former state, our own no more :
Is not this all a mystery ? Who shall say
Whence are these thoughts and whither tends their way ?

The sudden images of vanished things
That o'er the spirit flash, we know not why ;
Tones from some broken harp's deserted strings,
Warm sunset hues of summers long gone by,
A rippling wave, the dashing of an oar,
A flower scent floating past our parent's door !

Darkly we move, we press upon the brink
Haply of viewless worlds, and know it not,
Yes ! it may be that nearer than we think
Are those whom death has parted from our lot !
Fearfully, wonderfully our souls are made.
Let us walk humbly on, but undismayed.

FELICIA HEMANS

The Ring of Return

DETACHED, separated! I say there is no such separation: nothing hitherto was ever stranded, cast aside; but all, were it only a withered leaf, works together with all; is borne forward on the bottomless, shoreless flood of Action, and lives through perpetual metamorphoses.

Nay, if you consider it, what is Man himself, and his whole terrestrial Life, but an Emblem; a Clothing or visible Garment for that divine life of his, cast hither, like a light-particle down from Heaven?

Are we not Spirits, that are shaped into a body, into an Appearance; and that fade away again into air and Invisibility? . . . Ghosts! There are nigh a thousand-million walking the Earth openly at noontide. . . . These Limbs, whence had we them; this stormy Force; this life-blood with its burning Passion? They are dust and shadow; a Shadow-system gathered round our life; wherein, through some moments or years, the Divine Essence is to be revealed in the Flesh. . . . Thus, like some wild-flaming, wild-thundering train of Heaven's Artillery, does this mysterious Mankind thunder and flame, in long-drawn, quick-succeeding grandeur, through the unknown Deep. . . . Can the Earth, which is but dead and a vision, resist Spirits which have reality and are alive? On the hardest adamant some footprint of us is stamped-in; the last Rear of the host will read traces of the earliest Van. But whence? O Heaven, whither? Sense knows not; Faith knows not; only that it is through Mystery to Mystery, from God and to God.

THOMAS CARLYLE
(*Sartor Resartus*)

ETERNITY may be but an endless series of those migrations which men call deaths, abandonments of home after home, ever to fairer scenes and loftier heights. Age after age the spirit may shift its tent, fated not to rest in the dull Elysium of the heathen, but carrying with it evermore its two elements, activity and desire.

BULWER LYTTON

AS when with downcast eyes we muse and brood
And ebb into a former life, or seem
To lapse far back in a confusèd dream
To states of mystical similitude,
If one but speaks or hems or stirs a chair
Ever the wonder waxeth more and more,
So that we say, all this hath been before,
All this *hath* been, I know not when or where :—
So, friend, when first I looked upon your face,
Our thoughts gave answer, each to each, so true,
Opposèd mirrors each reflecting each—
Although I knew not in what time or place,
Methought that I had often met with you,
And each had lived in other's mind and speech.

ALFRED, LORD TENNYSON

O DEAR spirit half-lost
In thine own shadow and this fleshly sign
That thou art thou—who wailest being born. . . .
Live thou. . . .
From death to death, thro' life and life, and find
Nearer and ever nearer Him, who wrought
Not Matter, nor the finite Infinite,
But this main miracle that thou art thou,
With power on thine own act and on the world.

ALFRED, LORD TENNYSON
(*De Profundis*)

YET oft when sundown skirts the moor
An inner trouble I behold,
A spectral doubt which makes me cold,
That I shall be thy mate no more,

The Ring of Return

Tho' following with an upward mind
  The wonders that have come to thee,
  Thro' all the secular to-be,
But evermore a life behind.

I vex my heart with fancies dim:
  He still outstript me in the race;
  It was but unity of place
That made me dream I ranked with him.

And so may Place retain us still,
  And he, the much-beloved again,
  A lord of large experience, train
To riper growth the mind and will.

ALFRED, LORD TENNYSON
(*In Memoriam*)

AS old mythologies relate,
  Some draught of Lethe might await
  The slipping thro' from state to state.

As here we find in trances, men
Forget the dream that happens then,
Until they fall in trance again.

So might we, if our state were such
As one before, remember much,
For those two likes might meet and touch.

But, if I lapsed from nobler place,
Some legend of a fallen race
Alone might hint of my disgrace;

Or if thro' lower lives I came—
Tho' all experience past became
Consolidate in mind and frame—

I might forget my weaker lot;
For is not our first year forgot?
The haunts of memory echo not.

Moreover, something is or seems
That touches me with mystic gleams,
Like glimpses of forgotten dreams—

Of something felt, like something here;
Of something done, I know not where;
Such as no language may declare.

ALFRED, LORD TENNYSON
(*The Two Voices*)

AT times I almost dream
I too have spent a life the sages' way,
And tread once more familiar paths. Perchance
I perished in an arrogant self-reliance
Ages ago; and in that act, a prayer
For one more chance went up so earnest, so
Instinct with better light let in by death,
That life was blotted out—not so completely
But scattered wrecks enough of it remain,
Dim memories, as now, when once more seems
The goal in sight again.

ROBERT BROWNING
(*Paracelsus*)

I SHALL never, in the years remaining,
Paint you pictures, no, nor carve you statues,
Make you music that should all-express me;
So it seems: I stand on my attainment.
This of verse alone, one life allows me;
Verse and nothing else have I to give you.
Other heights in other lives, God willing:
All the gifts from all the heights, your own, Love!

ROBERT BROWNING
(*One Word More*)

IS it too late then, Evelyn Hope?
What, your soul was pure and true,
The good stars met in your horoscope,
Made you of spirit, fire and dew—

And, just because I was thrice as old,
And our paths in the world diverged so wide,
Each was nought to each, must I be told?
We were fellow-mortals, nought beside?

No, indeed! for God above
Is great to grant, as mighty to make,
And creates the love to reward the love:
I claim you still, for my own love's sake!
Delayed it may be for more lives yet,
Through worlds I shall traverse not a few:
Much is to learn and much to forget
Ere the time be come for taking you.

But the time will come—at last it will,
When, Evelyn Hope, what meant (I shall say)
In the lower earth, in the years long still,
That body and soul so pure and gay?
Why your hair was amber, I shall divine,
And your mouth of your own geranium's red—
And what you would do with me, in fine,
In the new life come in the old one's stead.

ROBERT BROWNING
(*Evelyn Hope*)

THEREFORE I summon age
To grant youth's heritage,
Life's struggle having so far reached its term:
Hence shall I pass, approved
A man, for aye removed
From the developed brute; a god though in the germ.

And I shall thereupon
Take rest, ere I be gone
Once more on my adventure brave and new:
Fearless and unperplexed,
When I wage battle next,
What weapons to select, what armour to indue.

ROBERT BROWNING
(*Rabbi Ben Ezra*)

A.D. 1700-1900

BE ye my judges, imaginative minds, full-fledged to soar into the sun,
Whose grosser natural thoughts the chemistry of wisdom hath sublimed,
Have ye not confessed to a feeling, a consciousness strange and vague,
That ye have gone this way before, and walk again your daily life,
Tracking an old routine, and on some foreign strand,
Where bodily ye have never stood, finding your own footsteps?
Hath not at times some recent friend looked out, an old familiar,
Some newest circumstance or place teemed as with ancient memories?
A startling sudden flash lighteth up all for an instant,
And then it is quenched, as in darkness, and leaveth the cold spirit trembling.

MARTIN TUPPER
(*Proverbial Philosophy: On Memory*)

WHO taught this pleading to unpractis'd eyes?
Who hid such import in an infant's gloom?
Who lent thee, child, this meditative guise?
Who mass'd, round that slight brow, these clouds of doom?

What mood wears like complexion to thy woe?
His, who in mountain glens, at noon of day,
Sits rapt, and hears the battle break below?
Ah! thine was not the shelter, but the fray.

What exile's, changing bitter thoughts with glad?
What seraph's, in some alien planet born?
No exile's dream was ever half so sad,
Nor any angel's sorrow so forlorn.

The Ring of Return

Is the calm thine of stoic souls, who weigh
  Life well, and find it wanting, nor deplore:
But in disdainful silence turn away,
  Stand mute, self-centred, stern, and dream no more?

Or do I wait to hear some grey-hair'd king
  Unravel all his many-coloured lore:
Whose mind hath known all arts of governing,
  Mused much, lov'd life a little, loath'd it more?

Down the pale cheek long lines of shadow slope,
  Which years, and curious thought, and suffering give—
Thou hast foreknown the vanity of hope,
  Foreseen thy harvest—yet proceed'st to live.

The Guide of our dark steps a triple veil
  Betwixt our senses and our sorrow keeps:
Hath sown, with cloudless passages, the tale
  Of grief, and eased us with a thousand sleeps.

Ah! not the nectarous poppy lovers use,
  Not daily labour's dull, Lethean spring,
Oblivion in lost angels can infuse
  Of the soil'd glory, and the trailing wing. . . .

MATTHEW ARNOLD
(*To a Gipsy Child by the Sea-shore*)

AND then we shall unwillingly return
  Back to this meadow of calamity,
  This uncongenial place, this human life;
And in our individual human state
Go through the sad probation all again,
To see if we will poise our life at last,
To see if we will now at last be true
To our own only true deep-buried selves,
Being one with which we are one with the whole world;

Or whether we will once more fall away
Into some bondage of the flesh or mind,
Some slough of sense, or some fantastic maze
Forg'd by the imperious lonely Thinking-Power . . .
Slave of Sense
I have in no wise been: but slave of thought—?
And who can say—I have been always free,
Liv'd ever in the light of my own soul?
I cannot: I have lived in wrath and gloom,
Fierce, disputatious, ever at war with man,
Far from my own soul, far from warmth and light.
But I have not grown easy in these bonds—
But I have not denied what bonds these were. . . .
And therefore, O ye Elements, I know—
Ye know it too—it hath been granted me
Not to die wholly, not to be all enslav'd.
I feel it in this hour. The numbing cloud
Mounts off my soul: I feel it, I breathe free.

MATTHEW ARNOLD
(*Empedocles on Etna*)

OUR present lack of recollection of past lives is no disproof of their actuality. Every night we lose all knowledge of the past, but every day we reawaken to a memory of the whole series of days and nights. So in one life we may forget and dream, and in another recover the whole thread of experience from the beginning.

In every event, it must be confessed that of all the thoughtful and refined forms of the belief in a future life, none has had so extensive and prolonged a prevalence as this. It has the vote of the majority, having for ages on ages been held by half the human race with an intensity of conviction almost without a parallel. Indeed, the most striking fact about the doctrine of the repeated incarnations of the soul, its form and experience in each successive embodiment being determined by its merits and demerits in the preceding ones, is the constant reappearance of that faith in all parts of the world, and its permanent hold on certain great nations.

REV. WILLIAM ALGER
(*A Critical History of the Doctrine of a Future Life*)

THERE is an end
Of Wrong and Death and Hell! When the long wear
Of Time and Suffering has effaced the stain
Ingrown upon the soul, and the cleansed spirit,
Long ages floating on the wandering winds
Or rolling deeps of Space, renews itself
And doth regain its dwelling, and, once more
Blent with the general order, floats anew
Upon the stream of Things, and comes at length,
After new deaths, to that dim waiting-place
Thou next shalt see, and with the justified
White souls awaits the End.

Time calls and Change
Commands both men and gods, and speeds us on
We know not whither; but the old earth smiles
Spring after Spring, and the seed bursts again
Out of its prison mould, and the dead lives
Renew themselves, and rise aloft and soar
And are transformed, clothing themselves with change
Till the last change be done.

SIR LEWIS MORRIS
(*The Epic of Hades*)

LIKE all the higher forms of inward life this character is a subtle blending and interpenetration of intellectual, moral, and spiritual elements. . . . It is a mind of taste lighted up by some spiritual ray within. . . . A magnificent intellectual force is latent within it. It is like the reminiscence of a forgotten culture that once adorned the mind; as if the mind of one φιλοσοφήσας ποτε μετ' ἔρωτος fallen into a new cycle, were beginning its spiritual progress over again, but with a certain power of anticipating its stages.

WALTER PATER
(*Diaphaneitè*)

PERHAPS I lived before
In some strange world where first my soul was shaped,
And all this passionate love, and joy, and pain,
That come, I know not whence, and sway my deeds,
Are old imperious memories, blind yet strong,
That this world stirs within me.

GEORGE ELIOT
(*The Spanish Gypsy*)

THE absence of memory of any actions done in a previous state cannot be a conclusive argument against our having lived through it. Forgetfulness of the past may be one of the conditions of an entrance upon a new stage of existence. The body, which is the organ of self-perception, may be quite as much a hindrance as a help to remembrance. In that case, casual gleams of memory, giving us sudden abrupt and momentary revelations of the past, are precisely the phenomena we would expect to meet with. If the soul has pre-existed, what we would *a priori* anticipate are only some faint traces of recollecion surviving in the crypts of memory.

PROFESSOR WILLIAM KNIGHT
(From an article in *The Fortnightly Review*, September 1878)

WHO toiled a slave may come anew a Prince
For gentle worthiness and merit won;
Who ruled a King may wander earth in rags
For things done and undone.

The Ring of Return

Before beginning and without an end,
  As space eternal and as surety sure,
Is fixed a Power divine which moves to good;
  Only its laws endure.

It slayeth and it saveth, nowise moved
  Except unto the working out of doom;
Its threads are Love and Life, and Death and Pain
  The shuttles of its loom.

It will not be contemned of anyone;
  Who thwarts it loses, and who serves it gains;
The hidden good it pays with peace and bliss,
  The hidden ill with pains.

That which ye sow ye reap. See yonder fields!
  The sesamum was sesamum, the corn
Was corn. The Silence and the Darkness knew!
  So a man's fate is born.

He cometh, reaper of the things he sowed,
  Sesamum, corn, so much cast in past birth;
And so much weed and poison-stuff, which mar
  Him and the aching earth.

If he shall labour rightly, rooting these,
  And planting wholesome seedlings where they grew,
Fruitful and fair and clean the ground shall be,
  And rich the harvest due.

If he shall day by day be merciful,
  Holy and just and kind and true; and rend
Desire from where it clings with bleeding roots,
  Till love of life shall end:

He, dying, leaveth as the sum of him
  A life-count closed, whose ills are dead and quit,
Whose good is quick and mighty, far and near,
  So that fruits follow it.

SIR EDWIN ARNOLD
(*The Light of Asia*)

A.D. 1700-1900

I HAVE been here before,
But when or how I cannot tell;
I know the grass beyond the door,
The sweet keen smell,
The sighing sound, the lights around the shore.

You have been mine before—
How long ago I may not know:
But just when at that swallow's soar
Your neck turned so,
Some veil did fall—I knew it all of yore.

Then, now, perchance again!
O, round mine eyes your tresses shake!
Shall we not lie as we have lain
Thus for Love's sake,
And sleep, and wake, yet never break the chain?

D. G. ROSSETTI
(*Sudden Light*)

CREATION thou dost work by faint degrees,
By shade and shadow from unseen beginning;
Far, far apart, in unthought mysteries
Of thy own dark, unfathomable seas,
Thou will'st thy will; and thence, upon the earth—
Slow travelling, his way through centuries winning—
A child at length arrives at never-ending birth.

GEORGE MACDONALD
(*The Diary of an Old Soul*)

BUT who believeth he shall not make haste,
Even passing through the water and the fire,
Or sad with memories of a better lot! . . .
Who knows love all, time nothing, he shall feel
No anxious heart, shall lift no trembling hand;
Tender as air, but clothed in triple steel,
He for his kind, in every age and land,
Hoping, will live; and, to his labour bent,
The Father's will shall, doing, understand.

GEORGE MACDONALD
(*Somnium Mystici*)

The Ring of Return

IT may be centuries of ages before a man comes to see a truth—ages of strife, of effort, of aspiration.

[God] regards men not as they are merely, but as they shall be. . . . Therefore a thousand stages, each in itself all but valueless, are of inestimable worth as the necessary and connected gradations of an infinite progress.

We cannot yet have learned all that we are meant to learn through the body. How much of the teaching even of this world can the most diligent and most favoured man have exhausted before he is called upon to leave it ! Is all that remains to be lost ?

GEORGE MACDONALD
(*Unspoken Sermons*)

NOR are recognitions of the doctrine [of reincarnation] wanting in the Old and New Testaments. Thus the writer of the Book of Wisdom says of himself : ' Being good, I came into a body undefiled.' The prophets Daniel and John are told by their inspiring angels that they shall stand again on the earth in the last days of the Dispensation. And of John it was also intimated by Jesus that he should tarry within reach of the earth-life, either for reincarnation or metempsychosis when the appointed time should come. . . .

The opening chapters of the Book of Genesis imply the like doctrine. For they represent creation as occurring through a gradual evolution from the lowest types upwards . . . they represent the animal as the younger self of the man, namely, as man rudimentary. All this is involved in the fact that the term applied to the genesis of living things below man, signifies *soul*, and is so translated when applied to man ; whereas when applied to beasts it is rendered ' living creature.' Thus, had the Bible been accurately translated, the doctrine that all creatures whatsoever represent incarnations, though in different conditions, of one and the same universal soul, would not now need to be re-declared, or when re-declared would not be received with repugnance. . . . Animals appeared first on earth, not, as is vainly supposed, to minister to man's physical wants, but as an essential preliminary to humanity itself. On no other hypothesis is their existence intelligible for the long ages which elapsed before the appearance of man.

When Psyche has once gathered force sufficient to burn centrally, her flame is not quenched by the disintegration of the physical elements. These, indeed, fall asunder and desquamate many times during life; yet the consciousness and memory remain the same. We have not in our physical bodies a single particle which we had some few years ago, and yet our ego is the same and our thought continuous. The Psyche in us, therefore, has grown up out of many elements; and their interior egos are perpetuated in our interior ego, because their psychic force is centralised in our individuality. And when our Psyche is disengaged from the disintegrating particles of our systems, she will—after due purgation—go forth to new affinities, and the reversion of matter to substance will still continue.

ANNA KINGSFORD AND EDWARD MAITLAND
(*The Perfect Way*)

EVOI, Father Iacchos, Lord God of Egypt, initiate thy servants in the halls of thy Temple;

Upon whose walls are the forms of every creature: of every beast of the earth, of every fowl of the air;

The lynx, and the lion, and the bull: the ibis and the serpent: the scorpion and every flying thing.

And the columns thereof are human shapes; having the heads of eagles and the hoofs of the ox.

The Ring of Return

All these are of thy kingdom; they are the chambers of ordeals, and the houses of the initiation of the soul.

For the soul passeth from form to form; and the mansions of her pilgrimage are manifold.

Thou callest her from the deep, and from the secret places of the earth; from the dust of the ground; and from the herb of the field.

Thou coverest her nakedness with an apron of fig-leaves; thou clothest her with the skins of beasts.

Thou art from of old, O soul of man; yea, thou art from the everlasting.

Thou puttest off thy bodies as raiment: and as vesture dost thou fold them up.

They perish, but thou remainest; the wind rendeth and scattereth them; and the place of them shall no more be known.

For the wind is the Spirit of God in man, which 'bloweth where it listeth, and thou hearest the sound thereof, but canst not tell whence it cometh, nor whither it shall go.'

Even so is the spirit of man, which cometh from afar off and tarrieth not, but passeth away to a place thou knowest not.

ANNA KINGSFORD
(*Hymn to Iacchos*)
(From *Clothed with the Sun*)

BEHOLD the manifold waves of the sea, which rise and sink, which break and are lost, and follow each other continually; even as these are the transmutations of the soul.

For the soul is one substance, as is the water of the deep, whose waves thou canst not number, neither tell their shapes, for the form of them passeth away; even as these are the incarnations of the soul.

ANNA KINGSFORD
(*Hymn to Poseidon*)
(From *Clothed with the Sun*)

A.D. 1700-1900

AN occultist or a philosopher will not speak of the goodness or cruelty of Providence; but, identifying it with Karma-Nemesis, he will teach that nevertheless it guards the good and watches over them in this as in future lives; and that it punishes the evil-doer, aye, even to his seventh re-birth, so long, in short, as the effect of his having thrown into perturbation even the smallest atom in the Infinite World of harmony has not been finally readjusted. For the only decree of Karma—an eternal and immutable decree—is absolute Harmony in the world of Matter as it is in the world of Spirit. It is not, therefore, Karma that rewards or punishes, but it is we who reward or punish ourselves, according to whether we work with, through, and along with Nature, abiding by the laws on which that Harmony depends, or—break them. . . .

We stand bewildered before the mystery of our own making, and the riddle of life that we will not solve, and then accuse the great Sphinx of devouring us. But verily, there is not an accident in our lives, not a misshapen day or a misfortune, that could not be traced back to our own doings in this or in another life.

H. P. BLAVATSKY
(*The Secret Doctrine*)

INTIMATELY, or rather indissolubly, connected with Karma, then, is the Law of Re-birth, or of the reincarnation of the same spiritual Individuality in a long, almost interminable, series of Personalities. The latter are like the various characters played by the same actor, with each of which that actor identifies himself and is identified by the public, for the space of a ew hours. The *inner*, or real Man, who personates those characters, knows the whole time that he is Hamlet only for a brief space of a few acts, which, however, on the plane of human illusion, represent the whole life of Hamlet. He knows also that he was, the night before, King Lear, the transformation in his turn of the

Othello of a still earlier preceding night. And though the outer, visible character is supposed to be ignorant of the fact, and in actual life that ignorance is, unfortunately, but too real, nevertheless the *permanent* Individuality is fully aware of it. . . .

The Delphic command ' Know thyself ' was perfectly comprehensible to every nation of old. So it is now, save to the Christians, since, with the exception of the Mussulmans, it is part and parcel of every Eastern religion, including the Kabalistically instructed Jews. To understand its full meaning, however, necessitates first of all belief in Reincarnation and all its mysteries. . . . Man must, in short, know who he was, before he arrives at knowing what he is.

H. P. BLAVATSKY
(*The Secret Doctrine*)

BUDDHISM does not believe in anything resembling a passage backwards and forwards between animal and human forms, which most people conceive to be meant by the principle of transmigration. . . . Buddhist writings certainly contain allusions to former births, in which even the Buddha himself was now one and now another kind of animal. But these had reference to the remote course of pre-human evolution, of which his fully-opened vision gave him a retrospect. Never in any authentic Buddhist writings will any support be found for the notion that any human creature, once having attained manhood, falls back into the animal kingdom.

Now, it is only by a return to physical existence that people can possibly be conceived to reap with precise accuracy the harvest of the minor causes they may have generated when last in objective life. Thus, on a careful examination of the matter, the Karmic law . . . will be seen not only to reconcile itself to the sense of justice, but to constitute the only imaginable method of natural action that would do this. The continued individuality running through successive Karmic rebirths once realised, and the corresponding chain of physical existences, intercalated between each, borne in mind, the exquisite symmetry of the whole system is in no way impaired by that feature which seems obnoxious to criticism at the first glance—the successive baths of oblivion through which the reincarnating spirit has to pass. On the contrary, that oblivion itself is in truth the only condition on which objective life could fairly be started afresh. Few earth-lives are entirely free from shadows, the recollection of which would darken a renewed lease of life for the former personality. And if it is alleged that the forgetfulness in each life of the last involves waste of experience and effort, and of intellectual acquirements, painfully or laboriously attained, that objection can only be raised in forgetfulness of the Devachanic life in which, far from being wasted, such efforts and acquirements are the seeds from which the whole magnificent harvest of spiritual results will be raised. In the same way, the longer the esoteric doctrine occupies the mind, the more clearly it is seen that every objection brought against it meets with a ready reply, and only seems an objection from the point of view of imperfect knowledge.

A. P. SINNETT
(*Esoteric Buddhism*)

THE way the law of Karma works when it is infringed in the first instance, as it constantly is being infringed, is by ultimate compensation. In everyday life, the action of anyone connected with us may impose suffering upon ourselves that we have not earned. People sometimes think that everything you suffer must have been earned by your own Karma. In the majority of cases probably that is true, but in a great number of cases it is not so, and all who want to understand the course of human life should bear that in mind. . . . The individual has many more lives than one, and if suffering is incurred in one life it is amply made up for in another. . . . I mean that if an ordeal is imposed upon you by no past sins of your own, and if you bear that ordeal with courage and without being in any way drawn aside from the path you want to tread, your success in passing through the ordeal claims a reward of a much higher order than one which would consist merely in the repayment to you on this plane of whatever you have been robbed of, if I may put it so. The higher reward is spiritual progress, and spiritual progress accomplished in that way, as compensation for ordeals passed through successfully on this plane, looked upon from above, is infinitely more important than a commonplace reward having to do with this one life or the next of the same order.

A. P. SINNETT
(*Theosophy and the Problems of Life*)

THY voice is like to music heard ere birth,
Some spirit lute touched on a spirit sea;
Thy face remembered is from other worlds.
It has been died for, though I know not when,
It has been sung of, though I know not where.
It has the strangeness of the luring West,
And of sad sea-horizons; beside thee
I am aware of other times and lands,
Of birth far back, of lives in many stars.

STEPHEN PHILLIPS
(*Marpessa*)

IF anything can keep us well within the thorny path that leads to happiness and virtue, it is the certainty that those who come after us will remember having been ourselves, if only in a dream. . . .

A.D. 1700-1900

Wherefore, O reader, if you be but sound in mind and body, it most seriously behoves you . . . to go forth and multiply exceedingly, to marry early and much and often, and to select the very best of your kind in the opposite sex for this most precious, excellent, and blessed purpose ; that all your future reincarnations (and hers), however brief, may be many.

GEORGE DU MAURIER
(*Peter Ibbetson*)

MY little-worlded self ! the shadows pass
In this thy sister-world, as in a glass,
Of all processions that revolve in thee :
Not only of cyclic Man
Thou here discern'st the plan,
Not only of cyclic Man, but of the cyclic Me. . . .
How many trampled and deciduous joys
Enrich thy soul for joys deciduous still,
Before the distance shall fulfil
Cyclic unrest with solemn equipoise !
. . . I do hear
From the revolving year
A voice which cries :
" All dies ;
Lo, how all dies ! O seer,
And all things too arise :
All dies and all is born ;
But each resurgent morn, behold, more near the Perfect Morn."

FRANCIS THOMPSON
(*From the Night of Forebeing*)

WHAT think we of thy soul ?
Which has no parts, and cannot grow,
Unfurled not from an embryo ;
Born of full stature, lineal to control ;
And yet a pigmy's yoke must undergo :
Yet must keep pace and tarry, patient, kind,
With its unwilling scholar, the dull, tardy mind ;

Must be obsequious to the body's powers,
Whose low hands mete its paths, set ope and close its
 ways;
 Must do obeisance to the days,
And wait the little pleasure of the hours;
 Yea, ripe for Kingship, yet must be
 Captive in statuted minority!

FRANCIS THOMPSON
(*Sister Songs*)

IN the doctrine of transmigration, whatever its origin, Brahminical and Buddhist speculation found, ready to hand, the means of constructing a plausible vindication of the ways of the Cosmos to man. . . . This plea of justification is not less plausible than others; and none but very hasty thinkers will reject it on the ground of inherent absurdity. Like the doctrine of evolution itself, that of transmigration has its roots in the world of reality; and it may claim such support as the great argument from analogy is capable of supplying.

PROFESSOR T. H. HUXLEY
(*Evolution and Ethics*)

GREAT music is a psychical storm, agitating to unimaginable depth the mystery of the past within us. Or we might say that it is a prodigious incantation—every different instrument and voice making separate appeal to different billions of pre-natal memories. There are tones that call up all ghosts of youth and joy and tenderness; there are tones that evoke all phantom pain of perished passion; there are tones that resurrect all dead sensation of majesty and might and glory—all expired exultations, all forgotten magnanimities. Well may the influence of music seem inexplicable to the man who idly dreams that his life began less than a hundred years ago! But the mystery lightens for whomsoever learns that the substance of Self is older than the sun. . . . To every ripple of melody, to every billow of harmony, there answers within him, out of the Sea of Death and Birth, some eddying immeasurable of ancient pleasure and pain.

LAFCADIO HEARN
(*Ghostly Japan*)

I SEEMED to understand as never before, how the mystery that is called the Soul of me must have quickened in every form of past existence, and must as certainly continue to behold the sun for other millions of summers, through eyes of other countless shapes of future being. . . . For thousands of years the East has been teaching that what we think or do in this life really decides—through some inevitable formation of atom-tendencies or polarities—the future place of our substance, and the future state of our sentiency. . . . Acts and thoughts, according to Buddhist doctrines, are creative. . . . What we think or do is never for the moment only, but for measureless time ; it signifies some force directed to the shaping of worlds—to the making of future bliss or pain.

What becomes of the dewdrop? By the great sun its atoms are separated and lifted and scattered. . . . Each one of them will combine again. . . . Even so with the particles of that composite which you term your very Self. Before the hosts of heaven the atoms of you were—and thrilled—and quickened—and reflected appearances of things. And when all the stars of the visible Night shall have burnt themselves out, those atoms will doubtless again take part in the orbing of Mind—and will tremble again in thoughts, emotions, memories—in all the joys and pains of lives still to be lived in worlds still to be evolved. . . . Your personality signifies, in the eternal order, just as much as the especial motion of molecules in the shivering of any single drop. Perhaps in no other drop will the thrilling and the picturing be ever exactly the same ; but the dews will continue to gather and to fall, and there will always be quivering pictures.

The very delusion of delusions is the idea of death as loss.

LAFCADIO HEARN
(*Kotto*)

HOW vain and dull this common world must seem
To such a One as thou, who shouldst have talked
At Florence with Mirandola, or walked
Through the cool olives of the Academe :
Thou shouldst have gathered reeds from a green stream
For Goat-foot Pan's shrill piping, and have played
With the white girls in that Phæacian glade
Where grave Odysseus wakened from his dream.

Ah ! surely once some urn of Attic clay
Held thy wan dust, and thou hast come again
Back to this common world so dull and vain,
For thou wast weary of the sunless day,
The heavy fields of scentless asphodel,
The loveless lips with which men kiss in Hell.

OSCAR WILDE
(*Phèdre :* To Sarah Bernhardt)

ALONG the garden ways just now
I heard the flowers speak ;
The white rose told me of your brow,
The red rose of your cheek ;
The lily of your bended head,
The bindweed of your hair :
Each looked its loveliest and said
You were more fair.

A.D. 1700-1900

I went into the wood anon,
  And heard the wild birds sing,
How sweet you were ; they warbled on,
  Piped, trilled the self-same thing.
Thrush, blackbird, linnet, without pause,
  The burden did repeat,
And still began again because
  You were more sweet.

And then I went down to the sea,
  And heard it murmuring too,
Part of an ancient mystery,
  All made of me and you.
How many a thousand years ago
  I loved, and you were sweet—
Longer I could not stay, and so
  I fled back to your feet.

ARTHUR O'SHAUGHNESSY
(*A Love Symphony*)

WAS I a Samurai renowned,
  Two-sworded, fierce, immense of bow ?
  A histrion angular and profound ?
A priest ? a porter ?—Child, although
I have forgotten clean, I know
That in the shade of Fujisan,
What time the cherry-orchards blow,
I loved you once in old Japan.

As here you loiter, flowing-gowned
And hugely sashed, with pins a-row,
Your quaint head as with flamelets crowned,
Demure, inviting—even so,
When merry maids in Miyako
To feel the sweet o' the year began,
And gardens green to overflow,
I loved you once in old Japan.

The Ring of Return

Clear shine the hills ; the rice-fields round
Two cranes are circling ; sleepy and slow,
A blue canal the lake's blue bound
Breaks at the bamboo bridge ; and lo !
Touched with the sundown's spirit and glow,
I see you turn, with flirted fan,
Against the plum-tree's blooming snow . . .
I loved you once in old Japan !

Envoy.

Dear, 'twas a dozen lives ago ;
But that I was a lucky man
The Toyokuni here will show :
I loved you—once—in old Japan.

W. E. HENLEY
(*Ballade of a Toyokuni Colour-Print*)

IT is evident that the universal repetition of idea in form throughout all nature, to which we have called attention, is but the expression of a deep and basic law. This law is that all existence proceeds in cycles, each having its objective and its subjective arc. . . . In the vegetable kingdom, this ebb and flow of conscious force is within material limits largely and easily studied. . . . All the beautiful imagery and design expressed in leaf, stalk, and flower perish as completely as though they had never existed. The life force has ebbed, yet not entirely. Root, rhizoma, or bulb hold in subjective embrace every detail, even to the most minute ; and when the subjective cycle is completed the inner, subjective entity thrills, expands, clothes itself again with its vestment of cells, and reproduces the dead plant in all its former perfection and beauty. Every such reproduction by a root or bulb is a genuine specific reincarnation of the same elemental centre of consciousness, or ' elemental soul,' in the same plant ; yet we fail to recognise this. . . .

A.D. 1700-1900

In the vegetable kingdom specific re-embodiment of plants takes place under the ebb and flow of the natural, cyclic laws known as the 'seasons.' In the animal, the metamorphosis of insects absolutely proves the reincarnation of the same conscious entity in an entirely different organism, under an inner subjective force, unaided by external conditions. . . . Now, if the individualisation of a tulip, even, has proceeded so far that nature has expressly provided for subjective cycles of the same individual, by the evolution of a bulb, how much more reasonable it is that the intense individualisation in man should also be conserved by subjective periods in his life-history. That the conditions limiting his consciousness in each state are different is no argument against these existing. The consciousness of a butterfly differs vastly from that of a caterpillar. . . . It logically follows, then, that the individualisation, carried to so marked an extent as it is in man, should be provided with subjective periods in which to assimilate and make its own the experiences of the last physical life.

DR. JEROME ANDERSON
(*Reincarnation: A Study of the Human Soul*)

"DEATH lies between us, my Beloved," she continued. "One line of shadow—only one little line! But thou mayst not pass it save when God commands—and I—I cannot! For I know naught of death—save that it is a heavy, dreamless sleep allotted to over-weary mortals, wherein they gain brief rest 'twixt many lives—lives that, like recurring dawns, rouse them anew to labour. How often hast thou slept thus, my Theos, and forgotten me? . . .

"Life after life hast thou lived, and given no thought to me—yet I remember and am faithful."

"Wouldst thou be willing to live again, Sah-lûma, if such a thing could be?"

The Ring of Return

"Friend, I would rather never die!" responded the Laureate, half playfully, half seriously. "But—if I were certain that death was no more than a sleep, from which I should assuredly awaken to another phase of existence—I know well enough what I would do!"

"What?" questioned Theos. . . .

"I would live a different life *now*! . . . so that when the new Future dawned for me, I might not be haunted or tortured by the remembrance of a misspent Past! For if we are to believe in any everlasting things at all, we cannot shut out the fatal everlastingness of Memory! Never to lose sight of one's own bygone wilful sins—this would be an immortal destiny too terrible to endure. For then, inexorable retrospection would for ever show us where we had missed the way, and how we had failed to use the chances given us. . . . Thus, if we indeed possessed the positive foreknowledge of the eternal regeneration of our lives, 'twould be well to free them from all hindrance to perfection here—while we are still conscious of Time and Opportunity."

MARIE CORELLI
(*Ardath: The Story of a Dead Self*)

OLD memories are mine once more,
I see strange lives I lived of yore;
With dimmed sight see I far-off things,
I feel the breath of bygone springs,
And ringing strangely in mine ears
I hear old laughter, alien tears
Slow falling, voices of past years.

None sees the slow sure upward sweep
By which the soul from life-depths deep
Ascends—unless, mayhap, when free
With each new death we backward see
The long perspective of our race,
Our multitudinous past lives trace,
Since first as breath of God through space

Each came, and filled the lowest thing
With life's faint pulse scarce quivering;
So ever onward, upward, grew,
And ever with each death-birth knew
An old sphere left, a mystic change—
A sense of exaltation strange
Thus through a myriad lives to range.

But even in our mortal lives
At times the eager spirit strives
To gain through subtle memories
Some hint of life's past mysteries—
Brief moments they, that flash before
Bewilder'd eyes some scene of yore,
Some vivid hour returned once more.

Each death is but a birth, a change—
Each soul through myriad by-ways strange,
Through birth and death, doth upward range.

WILLIAM SHARP (' FIONA MACLEOD ')
(*A Record*)

WHERE have I known thee, dear, in what strange place,
Midst what caprices of our alien fate,
Where have I bowed, worshipping this thy face,
And hunger'd for thee, as now, insatiate?
Tell me, white soul, that through those starry veils
Keepst steadfast vigil o'er my wavering spirit,
On what far sea trimm'd we our darkling sails
When fell the shadow o'er that we now inherit?
Two tempest-driven souls were we, or glad
With the young joy that recks of no to-morrow?
Or were we as now inexplicably sad
Before the coming twilight of new Sorrow?
Did our flesh quail as now this poor flesh quails,
Our faces blanch, as mine, as thine that pales!

WILLIAM SHARP (' FIONA MACLEOD ')
(From *A Sonnet-Sequence*)

The Ring of Return

STUDENTS of Gaelic will remember that Tuan—who under the grey cloud and by the whispering rushes of the west, gave out the same ancient wisdom as Pythagoras gave by Ionian Kroton, or as Empedocles gave by Sicilian Acragas—remembered his many transformations. He had been, he said, an eagle and a stag and a salmon in deep waters, and had known other changes. In like manner the Sicilian sophist remembered that he had been 'a youth and a maiden and a bush and a bird and a gleaming fish in the sea'; and the greatest of Greek mages declared that again and again he had lived in a changed body, as old raiment discarded or new raiment donned.

I think the soul knows. I think the soul remembers. I think that intuition is divine and unshakable. . . . I think we have travelled a long way, and have forgotten much, and continually forget more and more. The secret road of the soul is a long road. When, at last, we turn, looking backward so as at last to go forward, we shall see a long way off the forsaken homes of joy, and above these our inheritance behold the stars of our spiritual youth.

WILLIAM SHARP ('FIONA MACLEOD')
(*The Winged Destiny*)

WHEN from that world ere death and birth
He sought the stern descending way,
Perfecting on our darkened earth
His spirit, citizen of day—
Guessed he the pain, the lonely years,
The thought made true, the will made strong?
Divined he from the singing spheres
Eternal fragments of his song?

A.D. 1700-1900

Hoped he from dimness to discern
  The Source, the Goal, that glances through?
That one should know, and many turn—
  Turn heavenward, knowing that he knew?
Once more he rises; lulled and still,
  Hushed to his tune the tideways roll;
These waveless heights of evening thrill
  With voyage of the summoned Soul.

O closing shades that veil and drown
  The clear-obscure of shore and tree!
O star and planet, shimmering down
  Your sombre glory on the sea!
O soul that yearned to soar and sing,
  Enamoured of immortal air!
Heart that thro' sundering change must cling
  To dream and memory, sad and fair!

Sun, star, and space, and dark and day,
  Shall vanish in a vaster glow;
Souls shall climb fast their age-long way,
  With all to conquer, all to know:
But thou, true Heart, for aye shalt keep
  Thy loyal faith, thine ancient flame;
Be stilled an hour, and stir from sleep
  Reborn, rerisen, and yet the same.

F. W. H. MYERS
(*To Tennyson*)

WE commonly know that we are going to die, though we do not know that we are going to be born. But are we sure this is so? We may have had the most gloomy forebodings on this head and forgotten all about them.

The Ring of Return

Death is the dissolving of a partnership, the partners to which survive and go elsewhere. It is the corruption or breaking up of that society which we have called Ourself. The corporation is at an end, both its soul and body cease as a whole, but the immortal constituents do not cease and never will. The souls of some men transmigrate in great part into their children, but there is a large alloy in respect both of body and mind through sexual generation; the souls of other men migrate into books, pictures, music or what not; and everyone's mind migrates somewhere, whether remembered and admired or the reverse. . . .

Our mistake has been in not seeing that death is indeed, like birth, a salient feature in the history of the individual, but one which wants exploding as the end of the individual, no less than birth wanted exploding as his beginning.

Dying is only a mode of forgetting. We shall see this more easily, if we consider forgetting to be a mode of dying. So the ancients called their River of Death, Lethe—the River of Forgetfulness. They ought to have called their River of Life, Mnemosyne—the River of Memory.

I must have it that neither are the good rewarded nor the bad punished in a future state, but everyone must start anew quite irrespective of anything they have done here, and must try his luck again, and go on trying it again and again *ad infinitum.* Some of our lives, then, will be lucky and some unlucky. . . .

To die is to change, and to change is to die to what has gone before.

(From *The Note-Books of Samuel Butler*)

A.D. 1700-1900

YET for the great bitterness of this grief,
We three, you and he and I,
May pass into the hearts of like true comrades hereafter,
In whom we may weep anew and yet comfort them,
As they too pass out, out, out into the night,
So guide them and guard them Heaven and fare them well!

SAMUEL BUTLER
(*In Memoriam—to H. R. F.*)

The Ring of Return

RUSSIAN

I REMEMBER, O Fire,
How thy flames once enkindled my flesh,
Among writhing witches caught close in thy flame-woven mesh.
How, tortured for having beheld what is secret,
We were flung to the fire for the joy of our sabbath.
But to those who had seen what we saw,
Yea, Fire was naught.
Ah, well I remember
The buildings ablaze where we burned
In the fires we lit, and smiled to behold the flames wind
About us, the faithful, among all the faithless and blind.
To the chanting of prayers, the frenzy of flame,
We sang thy hosannahs, oh strength-giving Fire:
I pledged love to thee from the pyre!

Oh, Fire, I know
That thy light with an ultimate splendour our being shall drench;
It shall flare up before eyes that Death fain would finally quench.
With swift knowledge it burns, and with joy heaven-high
At the vastness of vistas unfolding afar.
Who has summoned these visions to being? And why?
Who has rayed them in colours befitting a star?
Beyond life is the answer.
Oh, thou heavenward heart of the element ever in flight,
On my twilight horizon let Death, necromancer,
Shed perpetual light!

KONSTANTIN BALMONT
(From *Hymn to Fire*)
(Translated by BABETTE DEUTSCH
and AVRAHM YARMOLINSKY)

A.D. 1700-1900

IN the land of Ra the flaming, by the shores of Nile's slow waters, where the roofs of Thebes were seen,
In the days of yore you loved me, as dark Isis loved Osiris, sister, friend and worshipped queen!
And the pyramid its shadow on our evening trysts would lean.

Oh, the mystery remember of our meeting in the temple, in the aisle of granite, dim and straight,
And the hour when, lights extinguished, and the sacred dances broken—each to each was sudden mate;
Our caresses, burning whispers, ardours that we could not sate.

In the splendour of the ballroom, clinging to me, white and tender—through Time's curtain reft in twain,
Did your ear not catch the anthems, mingling with the crash of cymbals, and the people's answering refrain?
Did you not repeat in rapture that our love awoke again?

Once before, we knew existence, this our bliss is a remembrance, and our love—a memory;
Casting off its ancient ashes, flames again our hungry passion, flames and kindles you and me—
As of old by Nile's slow waters, in the land beyond the sea.

VALERY BRUSOV
(*The Tryst*)
(Translated by AVRAHM YARMOLINSKY)

VI

THE TWENTIETH CENTURY

1900-1927

MYRTALÉ, when I am gone
(Who was once Anacreon),
Lay these annals of my heart
In some sacred shrine apart;
Into it put all my sighs,
All my lover's litanies,
All my vows and protestations,
All my jealous accusations,
All my hopes and all my fears,
All the tribute of my tears—
Let it all be there inurned.
All my passion as it burned;
Label it, when I am gone,
'Ashes of Anacreon.'

AUSTIN DOBSON
(*To Myrtalé*)

OUT of the depths of the Infinite Being eternal,
Out of the cloud more bright than the brightness of sun,
Out of the inmost, the essence of spirit supernal,
We issued as one.

First essence electric, concentric, revolving, subduing,
We throbbed through the ether, a part of the infinite germ,
Dissolving, revolving, absorbing, reforming, renewing,
The endless in term.

Spirit of growth in the rocks, and the ferns, and the mosses,
Spirit of growth in the trees, and the grasses, and flowers,

The Ring of Return

Rejoicing in life, unconscious of changes or losses,
Of days or of hours.

Spirit of growth in the bird and the bee, ever tending
To form more complex, its beauty and use combined,
Adapted perfection, the finite and infinite blending,
One gleam from One Mind.

Thus spirally upward we come from the depths of creation;
The man and the woman the Garden of Eden have found,
And are joined by the Lord in an endless and holy relation,
Ensphered and made round.

Obedience still is the law of each fresh emanation,
The prayer to the Father, 'Not my will, but Thy will be done';
Then deathless, immortal, we pass through all forms of creation,
The twain lost in One.

ELLA DIETZ
(*Emanation*)

SMALL wonder that his dreaming had seemed real to Charlie. The Fates that are so careful to shut the doors of each successive life behind us had, in this case, been neglectful, and Charlie was looking, though that he did not know, where never man had been permitted to look with full knowledge since Time began. . . .

It was no consolation that once in his lives he had been forced to die for his gains. I also must have died scores of times, but behind me, because I could have used my knowledge, the doors were shut. . . . One thing only seemed certain, and that certainty took my breath away for the moment. If I came to full knowledge of anything at all, it would not be one life of the soul in Charlie Mears's body, but half a dozen—half a dozen several and separate existences spent on blue water in the morning of the world!

RUDYARD KIPLING
(*The Finest Story in the World*)
(From *Many Inventions*)

STRANGERS drawn from the ends of the earth, jewelled and plumed were we.
I was Lord of the Inca race, and she was Queen of the Sea.
Under the stars beyond our stars where the new-forged meteors glow
Hotly we stormed Valhalla, a million years ago.

She with the star I had marked for my own—I with my set desire—
Lost in the loom of the Night of Nights—lighted by worlds afire—
Met in a war against the Gods where the headlong meteors glow,
Hewing our way to Valhalla, a million years ago!

They will come back, come back again, as long as the red Earth rolls.
He never wasted a leaf or a tree. Do you think He would squander souls?

RUDYARD KIPLING
(*The Sack of the Gods*)
(From *Naulahka*)

THINK not that the love thou enterest into to-day is for a few months or years:

The little seed set now must lie quiet before it will germinate, and many alternations of sunshine and shower descend upon it before it become even a small plant.

The Ring of Return

When a thousand years have passed, come thou again.
And behold ! a mighty tree that no storms can shake.

Love does not end with this life or any number of lives ; the form that thou seekest lies hidden under wrapping after wrapping ;

Nevertheless it shall at length appear—more wondrous far than aught thou hast imagined.

Therefore leave time : do not like a child pull thy flower up by the roots to see if it is growing ;

Even though thou be old and near the grave there is plenty of time.

EDWARD CARPENTER
(*When a Thousand Years have Passed*)

AFTER long ages resuming the broken thread—coming back after a long but necessary parenthesis,

To the call of the early thrush in the woods, and of the primrose on the old tree-root by the waterside—

Up with the bracken uncurling from the midst of dead fronds of past selves :

As of morning, and to start again after long strange slumber and dreams,

Beholding the beautiful light, breathing the dainty sweet air, the outbreath of innumerable creatures,

Seeing the sun rise new upon the world as lovers see it after their first night.

All changed and glorified, the least thing trembling with beauty—all old sights become new, with new meanings—

Lo ! we too go forth.

The great rondure of the earth invites us, the ocean-pools are laid out in the sunlight for our feet.

For now, having learned the lesson which it was necessary to learn, of the intellect and of civilisation—

Having duly taken in and assimilated, and again duly excreted its results—

Once more to the great road with the animals and the trees and the stars travelling to return—

The Twentieth Century

To other nights and days undreamt of in the vocabularies of all dictionaries
I inevitably call you.

Then after many years, after many thousands of years—
After many times lying down to sleep and rising again, after many times entering again into the mother's womb, after often passing through the gates of birth and death—the sleeper says to him that awakes him:
" Ah! beautiful one, ah! prince of love, so many times with thy fingers in vain touching my closed lids! . . .
Henceforth the long chain of births and deaths I abandon, I arise and go forth with thee—to begin my real life."

Centuries long in her antechambers tarrying,
Lost in strange mazes, wandering, dissatisfied—in sin and sorrow, lonely, despised and fallen—
At length the soul returns to Paradise. . . .
Through the great gates, redeemed, liberated, suddenly in joy over the whole universe expanding—after her many thousand year long exile,
At length the soul returns to Paradise.

EDWARD CARPENTER
(*After Long Ages*)

I SAW deep in the eyes of the animals the human soul look out upon me.

I saw where it was born deep down under feathers and fur, or condemned for awhile to roam four-footed among the brambles. I caught the clinging mute glance of the prisoner, and swore that I would be faithful.

Thee my brother and sister I see and mistake not. Do not be afraid. Dwelling thus and thus for a while, fulfilling thy appointed time—thou too shalt come to thyself at last. . . .

The Ring of Return

Come nigh little bird with your half-stretched, quivering wings—within you I behold choirs of angels, and the Lord himself in vista.

EDWARD CARPENTER
(*Have Faith*)
(From *Towards Democracy*)

THE important thing . . . is to see that undoubtedly various orders of consciousness do exist, *actually embedded within us*; and that the words I and Thou do not merely cover our bodily forms and the outlines of our minds as we habitually represent them to ourselves, but cover also immense tracts of intelligence and activity lying behind these and only on occasions coming into consciousness. . . . To command these tracts in such a way as to be able to enter in and make use of them at will, and to bring them into permanent relation with the conscious ego, will I think be the method of advance, and the means by which all these questions of the perduration and reincarnation of the ego, and of its real relation with other egos, will at length be solved. If we could by any means explore and realise what is meant by that letter ' I '; if we could travel inward with firm tread to its remotest depth, and find the regions where it touches close, so close, on the other forms of the same letter; if we could stand assured, and look around us, in that central land where it ceases to convey the sense of difference and only indicates unity; and if then with lightning swiftness we could pass to the extreme periphery where in its particular and invincible shape it almost rejoices to stand alone antagonising the rest of the universe—why, then, surely all would be clear to us, and Gladness and Beauty would be our perpetual attendants. . . .

Here in this perennial, immeasurable consciousness sleeping within us we come again to our Celestial City, our Home from which as individuals we proceed, but from which we are never really separated. . . . Every man feels doubtless that his little mortal life is very inadequate, and that to express and give utterance to all that is in him would need many lives, many bodies. Even what we have been able to say here shows that the deeper self of him—that which is the source of all his joy and inspiration—has had the experience of many lives, many bodies, and will have.

EDWARD CARPENTER
(*The Art of Creation*)

THE blue dusk ran between the streets: my love was winged within my mind,
It left to-day and yesterday and thrice a thousand years behind.
To-day was past and dead for me, for from to-day my feet had run
Through thrice a thousand years to walk the ways of ancient Babylon.
On temple top and palace roof the burnished gold flung back the rays
Of a red sunset that was dead and lost beyond a million days.
The tower of heaven turns darker blue, a starry sparkle now begins;
The mystery and magnificence, the myriad beauty and the sins
Come back to me. I walk beneath the shadowy multitude of towers;
Within the gloom the fountain jets its pallid mist in lily flowers.
The waters lull me, and the scent of many gardens, and I hear
Familiar voices, and the voice I love is whispering in my ear.
Oh real as in dream all this; and then a hand on mine is laid:
The wave of phantom time withdraws; and that young Babylonian maid,
One drop of beauty left behind from all the flowing of that tide,

Is looking with the self-same eyes, and here in Ireland
by my side.
Oh light our life in Babylon, but Babylon has taken
wings,
While we are in the calm and proud procession of eternal
things.

A. E.
(*Babylon*)

TO those who cry out against romance I would say, You yourself are romance. You are the lost prince herding obscurely among the swine. The romance of your spirit is the most marvellous of stories. Your wanderings have been greater than those of Ulysses. . . .

Looking back upon that other life through the vistas of memory, I see breaking in upon the images of this world forms of I know not what antiquity. I walk out of strange cities steeped in the jewel glow and gloom of evening, or sail in galleys over the silvery waves of the antique ocean. I reside in tents, or in palace chambers, go abroad in chariots, meditate in cyclopean buildings, am worshipper of the Earth-gods upon the mountains, lie tranced in Egyptian crypts, or brush with naked body through the long, sunlit grasses of the prairies. Endlessly the procession of varying forms goes back into remote yesterdays of the world. . . . Were not [these] . . . I ask myself, memories of the spirit incarnated many times?

A. E.
(*The Memory of the Spirit*)
(From *The Candle of Vision*)

EVEN the best men are not, when they die, in such a state of intellectual and moral perfection as would fit them to enter heaven immediately. . . . This is generally recognised, and one of two alternatives is commonly adopted to meet it. The first is that some tremendous improvement—an improvement out of all proportion to any which can ever be observed in life—takes place at the moment of death. . . . The other and more probable alternative is that the process of gradual improvement can go on in each of us after the death of our present bodies. . . .

And it seems to me that the natural inference . . . is that this life will be followed by others like it, each separated from its predecessor and successor by death and rebirth. For otherwise we should be limited to the hypothesis that a process of development, begun in a single life bounded by death, should be continued as an indefinitely long life not divided by birth and death at all. And to suppose, without any reason, such a change from the order of our present experience seems unjustifiable.

The doctrine of pre-existence does not compel us to deny all influence on a man's character of the characters of his ancestors. . . . But there is no impossibility in supposing that the characteristics in which we resemble the ancestors of our bodies may be to some degree characteristics due to our previous lives. . . . A man whose nature had certain characteristics when he was about to be reborn, would be reborn in a body descended from ancestors of a similar character. . . . It would be the character of the ancestors . . . and its similarity to his character, which determined the fact that he was reborn in that body rather than another. The shape of the head does not determine the shape of the hat, but it does determine the selection of this particular hat for this particular head.

A man who dies after acquiring knowledge—and all men acquire some—might enter his new life, deprived indeed of his knowledge, but not deprived of the increased strength and delicacy of mind which he had gained in acquiring the knowledge. And, if so, he will be wiser in the second life because of what has happened in the first. . . . So a man may carry over into his next life the disposition and tendencies which he has gained by the moral contests of this life, and the value of those experiences will not have been destroyed by the death which has destroyed the memory of them. . . . In the same way, if the whole memory of the love of a life is swept away at death, its value is not lost if the same love is stronger in a new life because of what passed before. . . . If love has joined two people in this life, we have reason for believing that their existences are bound up with one another, not for one life only, but for ever.

The prospect of a great number of lives—perhaps an infinite number, though this is not a necessary part of the theory—gives us the prospect of many dangers, many conflicts, many griefs, in an indefinitely long future. Death is not a haven of rest. It is a starting-point for fresh labours. But if the trials are great, so is the recompense. We miss much here by our own folly, much by unfavourable circumstances. Above all, we miss much because so many good things are incompatible. We cannot spend our youth both in the study and in the saddle. We cannot gain the benefit both of unbroken health and of bodily weakness, both of riches and of poverty, both of comradeship and of isolation, both of defiance and of obedience. We cannot learn the lessons alike of Galahad and of Tristram and of Caradoc. And yet they are all so good to learn. Would it not be worth much to hope that what we missed in one life might come to us in another? And would it not be worth much to be able to hope that we might have a chance to succeed hereafter in the tasks which we failed in here? . . .

And surely death acquires a new and deeper significance when we regard it no longer as a single and unexplained break in an unending life, but as part of the continually recurring rhythm of progress—as inevitable, as natural, and as benevolent as sleep. We have only left youth behind us, as at noon we have left the sunrise. They will both come back, and they do not grow old.

JOHN M. ELLIS MCTAGGART
(*Some Dogmas of Religion*)

O NEVER take those eyes away from me;
Such storms are mine, I have great need of stars;
For at such radiant shrines of mystery
Awhile I pray, forgetting prison-bars.
Where have we met before, that such delight
Thrills through mine inmost soul whene'er I meet
The gaze that pierces through heart's darkest night?
Beam in the wilderness to guide my feet
Where'er thy heart shall bid me stand or go,
In some far ancient shrine (this is my dream)
Still wert thou mine alone; full well I know
The channel of one life holds not that stream
Of love, which flows from one who vainly longs
To hymn a deathless love in mortal songs.

LILY NIGHTINGALE
(From *A Cycle of Sonnets*)

WE parted, and not a word was spoken, but at one and the same moment had we understood our inexpressible thought. . . . We have never met again. Perhaps centuries will elapse before we do meet again.

Much is to learn, and much to forget,
Through worlds I shall traverse not a few

before we shall again find ourselves *in the same movement of the soul* as on that evening: but we can well afford to wait.

MAURICE MAETERLINCK
(*The Invisible Goodness*)
(From *The Treasure of the Humble*)
(Translated by ALFRED SUTRO)

The Ring of Return

THE experience and memory of the past survive in our very organisation ; we are the product of evolution through the ages. Conscious memory may fail—does fail—but the effect of experience lasts.

What happened before earth-life we have forgotten—if we ever knew, we have forgotten. Our individual memory begins soon after birth. Before that we cannot trace identity. Perhaps we had none. Either we had none or we have forgotten. . . . The doctrine is old ; Plato taught it before the time of Christ, Wordsworth taught it early in the last century—the doctrine that when we enter into flesh we leave behind all memory of previous existences ; all, except for occasional dim and shadowy recollections which, though they may be stronger in infancy, occasionally surprise the grown man also. Dimly he may remember the days of his infancy,

> But he forgets the days before
> God shut the doorways of his head.

Crowds of unsuspected things are awaiting our discovery. . . . The doctrine of evolution—evolution of capacity for knowledge—is profoundly true with respect to the spirit of man.

SIR OLIVER LODGE
(*Reason and Belief*)

WE are not things of yesterday, nor of to-morrow. We do not indeed remember our past ; we are not aware of our future ; but, in common with everything else, we must have had a past, and must be going to have a future. Some day we may find ourselves able to realise both.

All we can cause or can observe is variety of *motion*—never creation or annihilation. And even the motion is *transferred* from one body to another, and transformed in the process ; it is not generated from nothing, nor can it be destroyed. Special groupings and appearances are transitory ; it is their intrinsic and constructive essence which is permanent. . . . We shall argue that personality or individuality itself dominates and transcends all temporal modes of expression, and so is essentially eternal wherever it exists.

No science asserts that our personality will cease a quarter of a century hence, nor does any science assert that it began half a century ago. Spiritual existence 'before all worlds' is a legitimate creed.

No science maintains that the whole of our personality is incarnate here or now ; it is, in fact, beginning to surmise the contrary, and to suspect the existence of a larger transcendental individuality, with which men of genius are in touch more than ordinary men. We may be all partial incarnations of a larger self.

SIR OLIVER LODGE
(*Man and the Universe*)

As regards Reincarnation, it is probably a mistake to suppose that the same individual whom we knew in bodily form is likely to appear again, at some future date. There may be exceptions, but as a rule that seems unlikely to happen. What may happen, however, is that some other portion of the larger self becomes incarnate ; and if so, it would be likely to feel a strong affinity, though often in a vague and puzzled way, with some other portion which had been embodied previously. And again, if this second incarnate portion happened to include some part of what had gone to make the previous individual, then there might not only be a sense of affinity, but some kind of reminiscence, some memory of places and surroundings which had previously been familiar. . . .

This idea seems to help us to contemplate the Platonic doctrine of Reminiscence as a possible reality in some cases. . . . Indeed, some such doctrine may be necessary to explain the aptitudes and powers and instincts both of animals and of children, especially when those children show signs of exceptionally early precocity. When they can calculate, for instance, or play a musical instrument, without having learnt. . . .

How large a subliminal self may be, one does not know, but one can imagine that in some cases it is very large, so that it contains the potentiality for the incarnation not only of a succession of ordinary individuals, but of really great men. It would be a mistake to suppose that Dante and Tennyson were reincarnations of Virgil, but one might, though presumptuously, imagine that all three were incarnations of one great Subliminal Self, which was able to manifest itself in different portions, having a certain family likeness, though without any necessary bodily consanguinity or inheritance in the ordinary sense.

The heredity link appears to be of quite different order from the subliminal link ; and mother and son need have no spiritual or subliminal relationship, in spite of their great similarity. The similarity of the bodily instrument would be sufficient, in that case, to account for the similarity of that portion of the son's larger self which automatically solicited this means of manifestation. And the importance of parenthood, in providing a suitable corporeal instrument or vehicle for the manifestation of a really great personality, can hardly be over-estimated. But the indwelling spirit need not come from the parents at all.

SIR OLIVER LODGE
(*The Making of Man*)

LONG, long ago you lived in Italy ;
You were a little princess in a state
Where all things sweet and strange did congregate,
And in your eyes was hope or memory
Or wistful prophecy of things to be ;
You gave a child's blank ' no ' to proffered fate,
Then became grave, and died immaculate,
Leaving torn hearts and broken minstrelsy.

But Love that weaves the years on Time's slow loom
Found you again, reborn, fashioned and grown
To your old likeness in these harsher lands;
And when Life's day was shadowed in deep gloom
You found me wandering, heart-sick and alone,
And ran to me and gave me both your hands.

LORD ALFRED DOUGLAS

WHAT is a span of ten thousand years, or ten times ten thousand years, in the history of time? It is as naught—it is as the mists that roll up in the sunlight; it fleeth away like an hour of sleep or a breath of the Eternal Spirit. Behold the lot of man! Certainly it shall overtake us, and we shall sleep. Certainly, too, we shall awake, and live again, and again shall sleep, and so on and on, through periods, spaces and times, from æon unto æon, till the world is dead, and the worlds beyond the world are dead, and naught liveth save the Spirit that is Life.

Time hath no power against Identity, though sleep the merciful hath blotted out the tablets of our mind, and with oblivion sealed the sorrows that else would hound us from life to life, stuffing the brain with gathered griefs till it burst in the madness of uttermost despair. . . . The wrappings of our sleep shall roll away . . . and the voices shall be heard, when down the completed chain, whereof our each existence is a link, the lightning of the Spirit hath passed to work out the purpose of our being; quickening and fusing those separated days of life, and shaping them to a staff whereon we may safely lean as we wend to our appointed fate.

SIR RIDER HAGGARD
(*She*)

"YOU know me and my story," I muttered at last. "No," he answered; "at least not more than I know that of many men with whom I chance to be in touch. That is, I have not met you for nearly eleven hundred years. A thousand and eighty-six, to be correct. I was a blind priest then, and you were the captain of Irene's guard."

At this news I burst out laughing, and the laugh did me good.

"I did not know I was so old," I said.

"Do you call that old?" answered Jorsen. "Why, the first time that we had anything to do with each other, so far as I can learn, that is, was over eight thousand years ago, in Egypt before the beginning of recorded history."

"I thought I was mad, but you are madder," I said.

"Doubtless. Well, I am so mad that I managed to be here in time to save you from suicide, as once in the past you saved me, for thus things come round." . . .

That was how I came to know Jorsen.

Sure knowledge has come to me about certain epochs in the past in which I lived in other shapes. . . .

They do not all come back to me with equal clearness, the earlier lives being, as one might expect, the more difficult to recover and the comparatively recent ones the easiest. Also they seem to range over a vast stretch of time, back indeed to the days of primeval, prehistoric man. . . .

To take a single instance of what I do know: once this spirit of mine, that now by the workings of destiny for a little while occupies the body of a fourth-rate auctioneer, and of the editor of a trade journal, dwelt in that of a Pharaoh of Egypt—never mind which Pharaoh. Yes, although you may laugh and think me mad to say it, for me the legions fought and thundered; to me the peoples bowed and the secret sanctuaries were opened that I and I alone might commune with the gods; I who in the flesh and after it myself was worshipped as a god.

I sat upon the borders of the Road . . . and watched the dead go by.

The Twentieth Century

There were many that night. Some plague was working in the East and unchaining thousands. . . . The knowledge which I have told me that one and all they were very ancient souls who often and often had walked the Road before, and therefore, although as yet they did not know it, were well accustomed to the journey. No, I am wrong, for here and there an individual did know. Indeed, one deep-eyed, wistful little woman, who carried a baby in her arms, stopped for a moment and spoke to me.

"The others cannot see you as I do," she said. "Priest of the Queen of queens, I know you well; hand in hand we climbed by the seven stairways to the altars of the moon."

"Who is the Queen of queens?" I asked.

"Have you forgotten her of the hundred names whose veils we lifted one by one; her whose breast was beauty and whose eyes were truth? In a day to come you will remember. Farewell till we walk this Road no more."

"Stay—where did we meet?"

"When our souls were young," she answered, and faded from my ken like a shadow from the sea."

SIR RIDER HAGGARD
(*The Mahatma and the Hare: A Dream Story*)

I SHALL return to thee,
Earth, O dearest
Mother of mine!
I who have loved thee with joy everlasting,
Endless discovery, newness diurnal;
I who with every delight of my heart,
As with strands of gold, have enwoven the fairest
Flowers of thy beauty, whose sorrows yearn for thee,
See, with no gesture
Of long resignation, of farewell eternal,
Now I depart,

But as to some new festival hasting
I bid them fall from me, disentwine
The withered garland, the worn vesture.

    Not as a warrior
    Lost and defeated,
    Out of thy legions
    Perished and gone,
Lady, I pass from the fight into regions
Hid from its roar—but the battered armour
Bruises the limbs, the sword is broken.
Loose me them gently, cast them undone,
    After thy manner,
Into the crucible, the seven-times heated.
I to the front, to thy face still addrest
Shall await the recall, shall watch for the token,
Leap at the word. I ask not for rest,
But a trustier steel—and back to the banner!

I shall still blindly fumble and wait
Till the true door open, the true voice call again;
And back to the human high estate,
Back to the whole of the soul, resurgent,
O Earth! O dearest! I shall return,
I shall return to thee, Earth, my mother.

MARGARET L. WOODS
(*Vale Atque Ave*)

A MAN has a soul, and it passes from life to life, as a traveller from inn to inn, till at length it is ended in heaven. But not till he has attained heaven in his heart will he attain heaven in reality.

Many children, the Burmese will tell you, remember their former lives. As they grow older, the memories die away and they forget, but to the young children they are very clear. I have seen many such. . . .

I met a little girl not long ago . . . about seven years old, and she told me all about her former life when she was a man. Her name was Maung Mon, she said, and she used to work the dolls in a travelling marionette show. It was through her knowledge of and partiality for marionettes that it was first suspected, her parents told me, whom she had been in her former life. She could even as a sucking-child manipulate the strings of a marionette doll. But the actual discovery came when she was about four years old, and she recognised a certain marionette booth and dolls as her own. She knew all about them, knew the name of each doll, and even some of the words they used to say in the plays. . . .

H. FIELDING HALL
(*The Soul of a People*)

RED Anarchy! what meaneth thy mad quest,
Through seas of blood, for some dim isle of rest—
Through hell's red pit, for heavens of the blest?

Hearken! O wild-eyed spirit of red hell!
The way to happiness is not where dwell
The grinning ghouls who toll the funeral bell!

Only with love can hate be overcome,
Time only solve Life's long perplexing sum,
And never till the dogs of war are dumb!

When the red flames engulf the works of man,
When the red knife cuts short life's little span,
Barbarians we, as when the world began!

Go, Anarchy! we hate thy awful name,
Thy red flag is a winding-sheet of shame—
Make one last fire and perish in its flame!

And we will slowly mount Life's spiral stair,
Evolving into worlds sublimely fair,
With natures fit to breathe Elysian air!

HERBERT THOMAS
(*To Mad Anarchy*).
(From *Ballads of Evolution*)

The Ring of Return

REINCARNATION unites all the family of man into a universal brotherhood. . . . It promotes the solidarity of mankind by destroying the barriers that conceit and circumstances have raised between individuals, groups, nations, and races. All are alike favoured with perfect poetic justice. The children of God are not ordained some to honour and others to abasement. There are no special gifts. Physical blessings, mental talents, and moral successes are the laborious result of long merit. Sorrows, defects, and failures proceed from negligence. The upward road to the glories of spiritual perfection is always at our feet, with perpetual invitations and aids to travel higher. The downward way into sensual wreckage is but the other direction of the same way. We cannot despise those who are tending down, for who knows but we have journeyed that way ourselves? It is impossible for us to scramble up alone, for our destiny is included in that of humanity, and only by helping others along can we ascend ourselves.

E. D. WALKER
(*Reincarnation: A Study of Forgotten Faith*)

LIFE presents us with many problems which, on any other hypothesis than this of reincarnation, seem utterly insoluble; this great truth does explain them, and therefore holds the field until another and more satisfactory hypothesis can be found. . . .

We understand that our present life is not our first, but that we each have behind us a long line of lives, by means of the experiences of which we have evolved from the condition of primitive man to our present position. Assuredly in these past lives we shall have done good and evil, and from every one of our actions a definite proportion of result must have followed under the inexorable law of justice. From the good follow always happiness and further opportunity; from the evil follow always sorrow and limitation. . . .

It is in reality a most comforting doctrine. . . .

Objectors chiefly found their protest on the fact that they have had so much trouble and sorrow in this life that they will not listen to any suggestion that it may be necessary to go through it all again. But this is obviously not argument ; we are in search of truth, and when it is found we must not shrink from it, whether it be pleasant or unpleasant, though, as a matter of fact, as said above, reincarnation rightly understood is profoundly comforting.

C. W. LEADBEATER
(*An Outline of Theosophy*)

ARRIVED from far, he trod the remembered ways
Of that grave town, where he was wont to be
With heroes old of far-resounding days,
Gathered for wandering wars of land and sea.

There, crumbling o'er a sculptured tomb, he found
The rusted armour he himself did wear,
Battling, long since at Troy, and underground
Lay his own body, long since crumbling there.

Even so, in wandering through the haunted nave
Of time's old church, I saw against a stone
A panoply of love, hung o'er a grave
Where lay a rigid body, once my own.

Why waste a thought on long-forgotten men,
Or spell the record of those fading lines?
Sweet life is sweeter to me now than then,
And round my heart a nobler armour shines.

H. W. NEVINSON
(*Pythagoras at Argos*)

THE doctrine of the ascensional life of the soul through series of existences is the common feature of esoteric traditions and the crown of theosophy. I will add that it is of the utmost importance to us. For the man of the present day rejects with equal scorn the abstract and vague immortality of philosophy and the childish heaven of an infant religion. And yet he abhors the dryness and nothingness of materialism. Unconsciously he aspires to the consciousness of an *organic immortality* responding at once to the demands of his reason and the indestructible needs of his soul.

Greek poetry, so profound and luminous in its symbolism, compared the soul sometimes to the winged insect, sometimes to the earth-worm, and again to the heavenly butterfly. How often has it been a chrysalis, and how often a winged creature of light? Though it will never know this, it still feels that it has wings!

The heavenly life of the soul may last hundreds or thousands of years, according to its degree or strength of impulse. It belongs, however, only to the perfect, to the most sublime souls, to those which have passed beyond the circle of generations, to prolong it indefinitely. . . . The rest are carried along by an inflexible law to reincarnation, in order to undergo a fresh trial, and to rise to a higher rung or to fall lower if they fail.

The spiritual, like the terrestrial life, has its beginning, its apogee, and its decline. When this life is exhausted, the soul feels itself overcome with heaviness, giddiness, and melancholy. An invisible force once again attracts it to the struggles and sufferings of earth. This desire is mingled with terrible dread and a mighty grief at leaving divine life. But the time has come; the law must be obeyed. The heaviness increases, a sensation of dimness is felt. The soul no longer sees its companions of light except through a veil, and this veil, ever denser and denser, gives a presentiment of the coming separation. It hears their sad farewells; the tears of the blest, the loved ones whom it is leaving, fall over it like heavenly dew which will leave in its heart the burning thirst of an unknown happiness. Then, with solemn oaths, it promises to *remember*—to remember the light when in the world of darkness, to remember truth when in the world of falsehood, and love when in the world of hatred. The return, the immortal crown, can only be acquired at this cost. It awakens in a dense atmosphere ; ethereal constellations, diaphanous souls, oceans of light—all have disappeared. And now it is back on earth, in the abyss of birth and death. . . .

Terrestrial birth is death from the spiritual point of view, and death is a celestial resurrection.

Lives follow without resembling one another, but a pitiless logic links them together. Though each of them has its own law and special destiny, the succession is controlled by a general law, which might be called the repercussion of lives. . . . There is no word or action which has not its echo in eternity, says a proverb. According to esoteric doctrine, this proverb is literally applied from one life to another.

What, then, is the final end of man ? After so many lives, deaths, rebirths, periods of calm, and poignant awakenings, is there any limit to the labours of Psyche ? Yes, say the initiates, when the soul has definitely conquered matter, when, developing all its spiritual faculties, it has found in itself the principle and end of all things, then, incarnation being no longer necessary, it will enter the divine state by a complete union with the divine intelligence. . . . The soul which has become pure spirit does not lose its individuality, but rather perfects it as it rejoins its archetype in God.

EDOUARD SCHURÉ
(*Pythagoras and the Delphic Mysteries*)
(Translated by FRED ROTHWELL)

The Ring of Return

[Behind them they left a heap of carnage to be shared by the black raven, with its dusky plumage and hooked beak, and the dun-coated, white-tailed eagle . . . and by that grey beast, the wolf of the forest.—*The Battle of Brunanburh;* N. Kershaw's translation.]

'TWAS a thousand years ago
(My mad dreaming knows it so)
When my fame was for the dinging of the lyre,
I was silenced in that battle
Where our foe was driven cattle.
But listen to the dead skald now.

From the mountain flew War's eagle,
Odin's wind-cleaving beagle,
To his feast near the billows of the sea.
He was white-tailed, and his breast
Shone with crimson from the West.
But listen to the dead skald now.

And the grey wolves of the wild,
Those defilers and defiled,
Sniffed carnage on a sudden salt wind.
Ere the moon allured the wave
They were feasting on the brave.
And those grey wolves are men-wolves now.

And the ravens flew in flocks
From the pine-woods on the rocks.
Croak, croak where the dead lay high!
So compassionless and loud
They wrought shame upon the proud.
God! save me from those ravens now.

HERBERT EDWARD PALMER
(*Various Reincarnations*)

The Twentieth Century

PRESENTLY I became aware that some communication was passing between my consciousness and the consciousness of the newly-arrived spirit. It did not take place in words but in thought, though only by words can I now represent it.

"Yes," said the other, "you do well to rest and be happy ; is it not a wonderful experience ?—and yet you have been through it many times already, and will pass through it many times again."

I suppose that I did not wholly understand this, for I said : "I do not grasp that thought, though I am certain it is true : have I, then, died before ?"

"Yes," said the other, "many times. It is a long progress ; you will remember soon, when you have had time to reflect, and when the sweet novelty of the change has become more customary. You have but returned to us again for a little ; one needs that, you know, at first ; one needs some refreshment and repose after each one of our lives, to be renewed, to be strengthened, for what comes after."

All at once I understood. I knew that my last life had been one of many lives lived at all sorts of times and dates, and under various conditions ; that at the end of each I had returned to this joyful freedom.

It was the first cloud that passed over my thought. "Must I return again to earth ?" I said.

"Oh, yes," said the other, "you see that ; you will soon return again—but never mind that now ; you are here to drink your fill of the beautiful things which you will only remember by glimpses and visions when you are back in the little life again."

And then I had a sudden intuition. I seemed to be suddenly in a small and ugly street of a dark town. I saw slatternly women run in and out of the houses ; I saw smoke-stained, grimy children playing in the gutter. . . . I knew in a sad flash of thought that I was to be born there, to be brought up as a wailing child, under sad and sordid conditions, to struggle into a life of hard and hopeless labour, in the midst of vice, and poverty, and drunkenness, and hard wage. It filled me for a moment with a sort of nervous dread, remembering the free and liberal conditions of my last life, the wealth and comfort I had enjoyed.

"No," said the other, for in a moment I was back again, "that is an unworthy thought—it is but for a moment; and you will return to this peace again."

But the sad thought came down upon me like a cloud. "Is there no escape?" I said. And at that, in a moment, the other spirit seemed to chide me, not angrily, but patiently and compassionately.

"One suffers," he said, "but one gains experience; one rises,"—adding more quietly: "we do not know why it must be, of course—but it is the Will; and, however much one may doubt and suffer in the dark world there, one does not doubt of the wisdom or the love of it here." And I knew in a moment that I did not doubt, but that I would go willingly wherever I should be sent.

A. C. Benson
(*The Thread of Gold*)

WHEN the time for birth comes, a body is chosen of a special type, suitable for the soul's acquirement of the experience needed at that special time. . . . It is not that the body by long-continued effort is wrought into the likeness of the soul, though there is some truth in this view also, but that the type of body is arranged beforehand to suit and express the type of Personality which requires manifestation during this earth-life. In short, the body is made to fit the Personality just as a suit of clothes is made to fit the body; and, since this is the case, it is not to be wondered at that the shape, size, structure, and contour of the body and its parts should show the character of the person who uses that body as a vehicle.

The Twentieth Century

The inner or real man is brought into touch with his physical environment by means of his physical body. . . . The not-yet-incarnate soul, descending towards birth, requires a physical body to bring it into touch with the physical world, and until it has acquired one the physical side of things can make no impression upon it. . . . The soul brings its various faculties with it when it is born upon this earth, but its possibility of using them efficiently depends upon the kind of body that is given to it. . . . We have apparently to see in body a kind of physical epitome or expression for the whole of the soul's character, or rather for so much of it as succeeds in manifesting during the space of one lifetime. . . . Body is a living mask which hides, and yet at the same time expresses, the man who wears it.

ALAN LEO
(*Esoteric Astrology*)

WHAT we are, what we have, all our good qualities, are the result of our own actions in the past. What we lack in physical, moral, or mental excellence may yet be ours in the future.

Exactly as we cannot do otherwise than take up our lives each morning where we laid them down the preceding night, so by our work in previous lives have we made the conditions under which we now live and labour, and are at present creating the conditions of our future lives. . . .

Genius is the hall-mark of the advanced soul. . . . It reveals a glimpse of the degree of attainment which will be the common possession of the Coming Race. . . .

The twin laws of Rebirth and Consequence solve, in a rational manner, all the problems incident to human life as man steadily advances towards the next stage in evolution—the Superman. . . .

Spirits incarnate only to gain experience ; to conquer the world ; to overcome the lower self—attain self-mastery. When we realise this we shall understand that there comes a time when there is no further need for incarnation, because the lessons have all been learned. . . .

A man who has evolved so far as to have an individual, separate soul cannot turn back in his progress and enter the vehicle of animal or plant, which are under a group-spirit. The individual spirit is a higher evolution than the group-spirit, and the lesser cannot contain the greater.

MAX HEINDEL
(*The Rosicrucian Cosmo-Conception*)

AND in the ecstatic void the vision of the whole cycle of my existence began to be revealed to me, rolling itself backwards into the unguessed deeps of the past, so that I might learn. I saw the endless series of my lives, recurring and recurring in sequences of three—the imprisonment in the double envelope, the partial freedom of the single radiant envelope, and the freedom. The last an ageless realisation, the second a long purgation, the first an ordeal brief but full of fate! . . . I ceased to be Morrice Loring, and became a legion. These lives flashed up before me, one anterior to another, mere moments between the vast periods that separated them. . . . And one life was not more important to me than another. All were equally indispensable and disciplinal. The variety of those imprisonments seemed endless. Some were fevers of desire; others had almost the calmness of a final wisdom. Some were cruel; some were kind. In some the double barriers were so thin that the immortal prisoner shone through them, and men wondered. And in the next the walls might be hopelessly thick again. . . . Undulations in the curve of evolution.

But as the remoter past swam towards me in this vision, the development of that prisoner which was I showed unmistakable. He had seemed to be helplessly isolated in the prison named Morrice Loring, but in the light of comparison it was not so. Far back in the chain his captivity had far more closely resembled death, and his powers had far more closely resembled utter impotence.

And still at each dissolution of the prison a radiant envelope escaped, and the prisoner escaped from the radiance into the uncoloured light, and ultimately gazed amid an invisible splendour, as now he gazed, at the spectacle of his evolution, to gather the harvest of experience.

ARNOLD BENNETT
(*The Glimpse*)

" I CAN see no wisdom or purpose in anything now but to get to one's journey's end as quickly and as bravely as one can. And even then, even if we do call life a journey, and death the inn we shall reach at last in the evening when it's over ; that, too, I feel will be only as brief a stopping-place as any other inn would be. Our experience here is so scanty and shallow—nothing more than the moment of the continual present. Surely that must go on, even if one does call it eternity. And so we shall all have to begin again. . . . There are so many of us, so many selves, I mean ; and they all seem to have a voice in the matter."

" But surely," she began in a low voice, still steadily sewing, " that was our compact last night—that you should let me help, that you should trust me just as you trusted the mother years ago who came in the little cart with the shaggy, dusty pony to the homesick boy watching at the window. Perhaps," she added, her fingers trembling, " in this odd shuffle of souls and faces, I *am* that mother, and most frightfully anxious you should not give in." . . . " What worlds we've seen together, you and I. And then—another parting. . . .

The Ring of Return

It has all, my one dear, happened scores of times before —mother and child and friend—and lovers that are all these too, like us."

WALTER DE LA MARE
(*The Return*)

"ARCHDALE has been endowed with tremendous gifts. If I believed in reincarnation, I should be willing to admit that he is 'one of the best,' that, in short, his amazing pre-eminence would indicate—how shall I put it?—evidence of an accumulation of talents and rewards."

Thellusson laughed and shrugged his shoulders.

"You represent accumulations also."

"I do—I do. It's amazing. And if one knew a little more——"

"Happiness is as contagious as influenza; probably more so. But, mind you, I could not have been really happy had I not believed in reincarnation. The doctrine permeates nearly all philosophies and has been accepted by the greater portion of the human race. To me it explains adequately the mysteries of sin and suffering, and the apparent injustice involved in lives widely and cruelly differentiated."

H. A. VACHELL
(*The Other Side*)

OLD is the soul, and otherwhere
Read once with shining eyes
The Word's compounded meanings rare
And her own mysteries.

FROM the deeps within ourselves,
Above the common interests of sense,
Strange pasts at times well up, of leaf and bud,
And we who know not truly what we are
Know also not, yet guess, what once we were.

The Twentieth Century

'TIS scarcely true that souls come naked down
To take abode up in this earthly town,
Or naked pass—all that they wear denied:
We enter slip-shod and with clothes awry,
And we take with us much that by and by
May prove no easy task to put aside.

A. E. WAITE
(*Collected Poems*)

IF it be admitted that the soul of the savage is destined to live and to evolve, and that he is not doomed for eternity to his present unjust state, but that his evolution will take place after death and in other worlds, then the principle of soul-evolution is conceded, and the question of the place of evolution alone remains. . . . The Ancient Wisdom teaches, indeed, that the soul progresses through many worlds, but it also teaches that he is born in each of these worlds over and over again, until he has completed the evolution possible in that world. The worlds themselves, according to its teaching, form an evolutionary chain, and each plays its own part as a field for certain stages of evolution. Our own world offers a field suitable for the evolution of the mineral, vegetable, animal, and human kingdoms, and therefore collective and individual reincarnation goes on upon it in all these kingdoms. Truly, further evolution lies before us in other worlds, but in the divine order they are not open to us until we have learned and mastered the lessons our own world has to teach.

Just as the memory of some of the present life is indrawn beyond the reach of the waking consciousness . . . so is the memory of the past lives stored up out of reach of the physical consciousness. It is all with the Thinker, who alone persists from life to life; he has the whole book of memory within his reach, for he is the only 'I' that has passed through all the experiences recorded therein. . . . The difficulty of memory does not lie in forgetfulness, for the lower vehicle, the physical body, has never passed through the previous lives of its owner ; it lies in the absorption of the present body in its present environment, and in its coarse irresponsiveness to the delicate thrills in which alone the soul can speak. . . .

Memory of their own past lives, however, is possessed by a considerable number of people who . . . have learned how much richer life becomes when memories of past lives pour into it, when the friends of this brief day are found to be the friends of long ago, and old remembrances strengthen the ties of the fleeting present. Life gains security and dignity when it is seen with a long vista behind it, and when the loves of old reappear in the loves of to-day. Death fades into its proper place as a mere incident in life, a change from one scene to another, like a journey that separates bodies but cannot sunder friend from friend. The links of the present are found to be part of a golden chain that stretches backwards, and the future can be faced with a glad security in the thought that these links will endure through days to come and form part of that unbroken chain.

With reincarnation man is a dignified, immortal being, evolving towards a divinely glorious end ; without it, he is a tossing straw on the stream of chance circumstances, irresponsible for his character, for his actions, for his destiny.

ANNIE BESANT
(*The Ancient Wisdom*)

THE right way of looking on Reincarnation is that it is a theory of immortality, a theory of the way in which the human spirit unfolds his powers in an endless life. . . . The experience gained in one life, according to this theory, is carried through the gateway of death . . . the man passing from life to life gathering experience, and, out of the body in which experience is gathered, assimilating the whole of it, so that it becomes the faculties of the soul. . . . Such a theory is eminently just. It puts no one man at a disadvantage over against another. And it makes everyone's position depend, first, on the time that lies behind him—a necessary factor—and then on the effort that he makes to lead the human rather than the animal life. . . . Looked at thus, the highest genius is only the victor in innumerable combats ; the noblest saint is only the conqueror in innumerable battles. The character that a man brings with him at birth is the character that he has made during his past. Emphatically everyone is self-made, made from within, building character life after life.

You have forgotten your childhood, though you have the same physical brain now. In another life you had a different brain. . . . It is only the Spirit which passes from life to life, with its three great qualities of Will, Cognition, and Activity. The whole of the rest of you is new with each birth, and before the Heavenly Life is over all the experience which has been changed into character is handed on to the Spirit that dies not. . . . If, then, you are to remember, you must reach the memory of the Spirit.

ANNIE BESANT
(From a Lecture on *Reincarnation*)

I HOLD that when a person dies
His soul returns again to earth ;
Arrayed in some new flesh-disguise,
Another mother gives him birth.
With sturdier limbs and brighter brain
The old soul takes the road again.

The Ring of Return

Such is my own belief and trust;
  This hand, this hand that holds the pen,
Has many a hundred times been dust
  And turned, as dust, to dust again;
These eyes of mine have blinked and shone
In Thebes, in Troy, in Babylon.

All that I rightly think or do,
  Or make, or spoil, or bless, or blast,
Is curse or blessing justly due
  For sloth or effort in the past.
My life's a statement of the sum
Of vice indulged, or overcome.

I know that in my lives to be
  My sorry heart will ache and burn,
And worship unavailingly
  The woman whom I used to spurn,
And shake to see another have
The love I spurned, the love she gave.

And I shall know, in angry words,
  In gibes, and mocks, and many a tear,
A carrion flock of homing-birds,
  The gibes and scorns I uttered here.
The brave word that I failed to speak
Will brand me dastard on the cheek.

And as I wander on the roads
  I shall be helped and healed and blessed;
Kind words shall cheer and be as goads
  To urge to heights before unguessed.
My road shall be the road I made,
All that I gave shall be repaid.

So shall I fight, so shall I tread,
  In this long war beneath the stars;

The Twentieth Century

So shall a glory wreathe my head,
So shall I faint and show the scars,
Until this case, this clogging mould,
Be smithied all to kingly gold.

JOHN MASEFIELD
(*A Creed*)

IT is, I think, a really consoling idea that our present capacities are determined by our previous actions, and that our present actions again will determine our future character. It seems to liberate us from the bonds of an external fate and make us the captains of our own destinies. If we have formed here a beautiful relation, it will not perish at death, but be perpetuated, albeit unconsciously, in some future life. If we have developed a faculty here, it will not be destroyed, but will be the starting-point of later developments. Again, if we suffer, as most people do, from imperfections and misfortunes, it would be consoling to believe that these were punishments of our own acts in the past, not mere effects of the acts of other people, or of an indifferent nature over which we have no control. The world on this hypothesis would at least seem juster than it does on the positivist view, and that in itself would be a great gain.

Of all the dawns that I have watched in the mountains, never was one like that I saw to-day. I forgot the glacier, and was aware only of the stars. Through the chinks in my prison wall they blazed brighter and brighter, till where they shone it fell away, and I looked out on the Past. I knew myself to be more than myself, an epitome of the generations ; and I travelled again, from the source, my life which is the life of Man. I was a shepherd pasturing flocks on star-lit plains of Asia ; I was an Egyptian priest on his tower conning the oracles of the sky ; I was a Greek sailor with Boötes and Orion for my guides; I was Endymion entranced on mountains of Arcady. I saw the star of Bethlehem and heard the angels sing; I spoke with Ptolemy, and watched the night with Galileo. A thousand times I had died, a thousand times been born. By those births and deaths my course was marked through the night of Time.

PROFESSOR G. LOWES DICKINSON
(*Religion and Immortality*)

WHILE I gaze
I seem to watch unfold
Some long-forgotten life I lived of old
In beauty-worshipping Athenian days.

O godlike voice of wisdom! Master-Sage!
Break from the dream that binds thee now; return
Here to this earth and all the hearts that yearn.
The world is waiting, worn: redeem this age—
Ah, quench the bitter thirst with which we burn;
And with thy wisdom make us re-aspire
To all things high and beautiful and strong;
Bring back the joy that we have lost so long—
Teach us to love, and with thy spirit of fire
Cleanse the whole world;—or, if this may not be,
Gather about thyself some ardent few
That seek the Good, the True,
As in those garden-lawns that here we see,
And once, two thousand years ago, we knew.

CLIFFORD BAX
(*The School of Plato*, written after seeing the great fresco,
L'Ecole de Platon, by Jean Delville)

EARTH is the great primeval revelation
Set for the soul, considering, to divine,
And we, too slow for wise interpretation,
Take now from earth our sign;

The Twentieth Century

Take now assurance of that Pervading Spirit,
  At Whose word April with impulsive breath
Stirs the white world, how all things here inherit
  Alternate life and death.

Wherefore shalt thou, new-born in after ages,
  Weave of new words a second golden fleece,
As once he taught, the kingliest of all sages,
  In the noon-time of Greece.

Yea, the mute lyre that we have heard, have cherished,
  Again shall make man brother to sea and earth—
A little while sleep on! Thou art not perished,
  Not dead, but waiting birth.

CLIFFORD BAX
(*Threnody on the Death of Swinburne*)

THIS, the unageing spirit, alone
Divines a glory that none has known,

For only with eyes of eternal youth
Does any gaze on beauty or truth.

Itself unshaken by death and birth,
It looks through time at the soul on earth,

And, like one tale among many, hears
The dream that moves her to joy or tears.

Was it a single dream that wrought
This I, this tangle of sense and thought?

Though all but the last may lie unguessed,
The immortal self is a palimpsest

That many a hand in many a clime
Covered with tragic or laughing rhyme.

The Ring of Return

Death shall close the outward eyes,
But nothing which can see death dies.

CLIFFORD BAX
(*The Traveller's Tale*)

WHAT though I vaunted that I could prove any proposition to which I then subscribed? Poetry, like the sea, undermined those intellectual sand-castles; and when I read

Oh, light our life in Babylon, but Babylon has taken wings,
While we are in the calm and proud procession of eternal things,

I might still have adduced objections to the theory of reincarnation, but something within me had apprehended that it is true.

A man became for me now the protagonist of a stupendous saga. . . . Behind him I saw innumerable lives that stretched far back beyond even the first ages of the earth, an endless record of slow descent into matter, a chain of cause and effect that had its origin only in the Darkness Thrice Unknown from which the whole universe had once been emanated: and before him I saw the unborn æons through which he should travel on the 'homeward way'; life after life rising like a vision of mountain-peaks beheld from the top of the Apennines, and fading into the dim bloom of a distance immeasurably withdrawn, until at last, transformed from a filth-eating fool to a spirit of unimaginable beauty, he should put on the gnostic 'Robe of Glory' and be lost in the central light.

CLIFFORD BAX
(*Inland Far*)

GUEST: It's not only the poor it pays to be careful with. You can't say for a certainty, who any man might have been in his last existence, nor what he is doing on earth.

Leah: Grandmother, every one of us is born to a long life of many many years. If he die before his years are done, what becomes of the life he has not lived, do you think? What becomes of his joys and sorrows, and all the thoughts he had not time to think, and all the things he hadn't time to do . . . ? No human life goes to waste. If one of us dies before his time, his soul returns to earth to complete its span, to do the things left undone and experience the happiness and griefs he would have known. . . .

Messenger: The souls of the dead *do* return to earth, but not as disembodied spirits. Some must pass through many forms before they achieve purification. (*Leah listens with ever-increasing attention.*) The souls of the wicked return in the form of beasts, or birds, or fish—of plants even, and are powerless to purify themselves by their own efforts. They have to wait for the coming of some righteous sage to purge them of their sins and set them free. Others enter the bodies of the newly-born, and cleanse themselves by well-doing.

Leah: (In tremulous eagerness) Yes . . . Yes. . . .

Messenger: Besides these, there are vagrant souls which, finding neither rest nor harbour, pass into the bodies of the living, in the form of a Dybbuk, until they have attained purity.

Rabbi Azrael: Every day of a man's life is the Day of Atonement, and every word he speaks from his heart is the name of the Lord. Therefore the sin of any man, whether of commission or of omission brings the ruin of a whole world in its train. (*His voice becomes weaker and weaker.*) Through many transmigrations, the human soul is drawn by pain and grief, as the child to its mother's breast, to the source of its being, the Exalted Throne above. But it sometimes happens that a soul

The Ring of Return

which has attained to the final state of purification suddenly becomes the prey of evil forces which cause it to slip and fall. And the higher it has soared, the deeper it falls.

S. ANSKY
(*The Dybbuk*)
(Translated from the Yiddish by
HENRY ALSBERG and WINIFRED KATZIN)

LONG ere from immanent silence leapt
Obedient hands and fashioning will,
The giant god within us slept,
And dreamt of seasons to fulfil
The shaping of our souls that still
Expectant earthward vigil kept ;
Our wisdom grew from secrets drawn
From that far-off dim-memoried dawn.

JOHN DRINKWATER

THERE is a certain amount of valuable evidence on the subject of reincarnation memories, quite apart from the plausibility of the hypothesis on general grounds. I would not, however, suggest that evidence of this kind has ever been put together sufficient, either in quantity or quality, to afford anything like conclusive proof. The most important argument must still remain that from the *à priori* probabilities of the case. The position claimed is that reincarnation explains the problems of life as no other solution propounded has ever yet done, that it is neither inconsistent with the most advanced theories of science, nor with religion in its highest form, that it offers a stimulus to human effort which we look for in vain elsewhere, and that, at a time when the materialistic hypothesis has hopelessly broken down, it stands before the world as the only coherent and rational alternative to this hypothesis that so far, at any rate, has been submitted for approval to the considered judgment of mankind.

HON. RALPH SHIRLEY
(*The Occult Review*, May 1913)

DEEP Womb of Promise! back to thee again
And forth, revivified, all living things
Do come and go,
For ever wax and wane into and from thy garden;
There the flower springs,
Therein does grow
The bud of hope, the miracle to come,
For whose dear advent we are striving, dumb
And joyless: Garden of Delight
That God has sowed!
In thee the flower of flowers,
The apple of our tree,
The banner of our towers,
The recompense for every misery,
The angel-man, the purity, the light
Whom we are working to, has his abode:
Until our back and forth, our life and death
And life again, our going and return
Prepare the way: until our latest breath,
Deep-drawn and agonised, for him shall burn
A path: for him prepare
Laughter and love and singing everywhere;
A morning and a sunrise and a day!

JAMES STEPHENS
(*A Prelude and a Song*)

HIS body lying very still, he began to remember, but it was remembering with a deeper and fuller pulse than was ordinarily the case. He remembered that younger brother who was dead, and not him alone, but many another, kindred and friends and associates.

The Ring of Return

The past lived again, but lived with a difference. What multitudes of kindred, and friends, and associates! The meeting went deep and wide. Had he touched all those in one life, or had it been in many lives? . . . However it might be, it was a world transmuted and without pain.

"And when the last human being has crossed?"

"Then will the others come on into humanity—they that we call the animals. And those behind them will lift to where they were. But our wave goes on into the spiritual world that is the world of subtler matter, vaster energy, understanding at last, love at last, beauty at last."

As Curtin rode he thought that he faintly remembered all the forests of the world. "Is it infectious? Is it because in some sort Drew remembers, or is it because I have been—and surely I *have* been—in all the forests of the world?"

The momentary outlines shifted. There fell a sense of having done this times and times and times, a sense of hut and cave, so often, so long, in so many lands, that there was a feel of eternity about it. Rain and the cave and the fire, and the inner man still busied with his destiny! There was something that awed in the perception that ran from one to another, that held them in a swift, shimmering band. 'How old—how old! How long have we done this?'

The rhythm of the storm, the rhythm of the room, the rhythm of the fire, passed into a vast, still sense of ordered movement. 'Of old, and now, and to-morrow —everywhere and all time—until we return above time and place, and division is healed.'

MARY JOHNSTON
(*Sweet Rocket*)

The Twentieth Century

WE piled the crackling brushwood sticks,
  With the dead brown stalks of fern,
Into a heap, and lighted six
  Matches to make it burn.

And I stood on the windward side,
  And you upon the lee;
The blue smoke drifted like a tide
  Ebbing to you from me.

Through eddying wreaths I saw your eyes
  Narrowed, as if you were
In mirth, or pain, or sharp surprise,
  Or fear too keen to bear.

The hazel leaves had a stir and thrill
  As if they watched men die;
And the centuries tumbled at a shrill,
  Sharp, long-forgotten cry.

The lit twigs cracked, the flame put out
  A quivering glutton's tongue;
The cruel beech-trees pressed about
  To see you burn so young.

The red fire leapt and lit your face;
  I winced—you were so white
To have come once more to the ancient place
  Of red pain and black night.

But sudden the flaming gates of hell
  That had opened, closed again;
For, breaking through the still trees, fell
  Big-dropped, the blessed rain.

The Ring of Return

And hell's door and time's door
  They both crashed to together,
And the devil's oven was no more
  Than a bonfire spoilt by weather.

The great drops hurrying through the trees
  Were like the noise of feet,
As if back through the centuries
  A strayed hour beat retreat.

I heard you speak from miles away—
  A strange, far, hollow sound.
You said it was no use to stay,
  The bonfire was quite drowned.

ROSE MACAULAY
(*The Door*)

NO planet knows that this
    Our wayside planet, carrying land and wave,
  Love and life multiplied, and pain and bliss,
Bears, as chief treasure, one forsaken grave.

    Nor, in our little day,
May His devices with the heavens be guessed,
His pilgrimage to thread the Milky Way,
Or His bestowals there be manifest.

    But in the eternities,
Doubtless we shall compare together, hear
A million alien Gospels, in what guise
He trod the Pleiades, the Lyre, the Bear.

    O, be prepared, my soul!
To read the inconceivable, to scan
The million forms of God those stars unroll
When, in our turn, we show to them a Man.

ALICE MEYNELL
(*Christ in the Universe*)

The Twentieth Century

IF those shape-changings yet may be
  That Ovid and his kindred sing,
    Make me a broad bird-haunted tree,
  Earth-rooted, yet with heart to spring
So heavenly high that, when the glades
  Hold it as truth that all is right,
I may assert above their shades
  The flouted legend of the light.

If those shape-changings may be still
  That Ovid and his kindred sang,
Make me a calm exalted hill
  Where secret-symbolled curtains hang
So thick that mortals travel-proud
  In vain my sky-tranced summit seek,
But judge by its enfolding cloud
  The hidden stature of the peak.

JAMES H. COUSINS
(*Metamorphoses*)

IN the dusky path of a dream I went to seek the love who was mine in a former life.

Her house stood at the end of a desolate street.

In the evening breeze her pet peacock sat drowsing on its perch, and the pigeons were silent in their corner.

She set her lamp down by the portal and stood before me.

She raised her large eyes to my face, and mutely asked, " Are you well, my friend ? "

I tried to answer, but our language had been lost and forgotten.

I thought and thought ; our names would not come to my mind.

Tears shone in her eyes. She held up her right hand to me. I took it and stood silent.

Our lamp had flickered in the evening breeze and died.

RABINDRANATH TAGORE
(*The Gardener*)

The Ring of Return

THOSE who, by means of meditation, rise to that which unites man with spirit are bringing to life within them the eternal element which is limited by neither birth nor death. Only those who have had no experience of it themselves can doubt the existence of this eternal element. Thus meditation becomes the way by which man also attains to recognition and contemplation of his eternal, indestructible, essential being. . . . Gnosis and Theosophy tell of the eternal nature of this essential being, and of its reincarnation. The question is often asked : 'Why does a man know nothing of those experiences which lie beyond the borders of birth and death ?' Not thus should we ask, but rather : 'How may we attain to such knowledge ?' The entrance to the Path is opened by right meditation.

RUDOLF STEINER
(*The Way of Initiation*)

THE comings out and the goings into matter are no more than the systole and diastole of the ego-heart ; and, speaking from the standpoint of eternity, they are relatively as brief. To you a lifetime is a long time. It used to seem so to me, but it does not seem so now. . . .

You should get away from the mental habit of regarding your present life as the only one, get rid of the idea that the life you expect to lead on this side, after your death, is to be an endless existence in one state. . . .

Many people resent the idea that the life after death is not eternal, a never-ending progression in spiritual realms ; though few who so object have much of an idea what they mean when they talk of spiritual realms.

Life everlasting is possible to all souls—yes ; but it is not possible to go on for ever in one direction. . . . Unless you are willing to go in and out of dense matter, you will never learn to transcend matter. There are those who can stay in or out at will, and, relatively speaking, as long as they choose ; but they are never those who shrink from either form of life.

I used to shrink from what I called death. There are those on this side who shrink from what *they* call death. Do you know what they call death? It is rebirth into the world. Yes, even so.

Letters from a Living Dead Man
(Written down by ELSA BARKER)

THE darkness draws me, kindly angels weep
Forlorn beyond receding rays of light,
The torrent of the earth's desires sweep
My soul through twilight downward into night.

Once more the light grows dim, the vision fades ;
Myself seems to myself a distant goal ;
I grope among the bodies' drowsy shades,
Once more the old Illusion rocks my soul.

Once more the Manifold in shadowy streams
Of falling waters murmurs in my ears ;
The One Voice drowns amid the roar of dreams
That crowd the narrow pathway of the years.

I go to seek the starshine on the waves,
To count the dewdrops on the grassy hill ;
I go to gather flowers that grow on graves ;
The world's will closes round my prisoned will.

Yea, for the sake of the wild western wind,
The spherèd spirit scorns her flame-built throne ;
Because of primroses in time of mind,
The Lonely turns away from the Alone.

Who once has loved the cornfield's rustling sheaves,
Who once has heard the gentle Irish rain
Murmur low music in the growing leaves,
Though he were god, comes back to earth again.

The Ring of Return

Oh earth, green wind-swept Erin, I would break
  The tower of my soul's initiate pride
For a gray field and a star-haunted lake,
  And those wet winds that roam the country-side.

I who have seen am glad to close my eyes,
  I who have soared am weary of my wings;
I seek no more the secret of the Wise,
  Safe among shadowy, unreal human things.

Blind to the gleam of those wild violet rays
  That burn beyond the rainbow's circle dim,
Bound by dark nights, and driven by pale days,
  The sightless slave of time's imperious whim;

Deaf to the flowing tide of dreams divine
  That surge outside the closèd gates of birth,
The rhythms of Eternity, too fine
  To touch with music the dull ears of Earth—

I go to seek with humble care and toil
  The dreams I left undreamed, the deeds undone,
To sow the seed and break the stubborn soil,
  Knowing no brightness whiter than the sun—

Content in winter if the fire burns clear,
  And cottage walls keep out the creeping damp,
Hugging the old Illusion, warm and dear,
  The Silence and the Wise Book and the Lamp.

EVA GORE-BOOTH
(*Re-incarnation*)

IN the days of Atlantis, under the wave,
  I was a slave, the child of a slave.

When the towers of Atlantis fell
I died, and was born again in hell.

The Twentieth Century

From that sorrowful prison I did escape,
And hid myself in a hero's shape.

But few years had I of love or joy,
A Trojan, I fell at the siege of Troy.

I came again in a little while,
An Israelite slave on the banks of the Nile.

By the Ganges I was an outcast born,
A wanderer and a child of scorn.

By the waters of Babylon I wept,
My harp among the willows slept.

In the land of Greece I opened my eyes
To reap the fields of Plotinus the wise.

When the great light shattered the world's closed bars,
I was a shepherd who gazed at the stars.

For lives that were lonely, obscure, apart,
I thank the Hidden One in my heart.

That always and always under the sun
I went forth to battle and never won.

One thing I have learnt the long years through,
To know the false words from the true;

The slave who toiled on the banks of the Nile
With wisdom gladdened his long exile;

From Buddha at eve at the Ganges' side
An outcast learnt the worth of the world's pride;

Amongst the stars on a Syrian night,
A shepherd found the Light of Light;

The Ring of Return

From dream to dream, o'er valley and hill,
I followed the Lord Christ's wandering will.

Behold there are kings who would change with me
For love of the ancient mystery.

Shepherd and reaper and slave I have been,
There are few who have seen what I have seen.

Beggar and reaper and shepherd and slave,
I am one who rests not in any grave ;

I will follow each stormy Light divine,
And the secret of all things shall be mine.

These things have I seen. Would you bid me mourn
That I was never an Emperor born ?

EVA GORE-BOOTH
(*The Vagrant's Romance*)

EVERY spiritual vibration in the self is immortal, therefore the inner spiritual essence of the self, the real Ego in us, of eternal life, cannot die, and continues from one 'generation,' or birth, to another. But every false vibration dies out. The whole self is like a plant cut down to its roots to grow again next year. The plant grows again, altered in many ways by different weather and earth conditions. It is the same in tendency, modified by different stimuli. The new psyche is what belongs to one by right ; it is the result of every one of one's will vibrations in the Universal Element. Therefore the new psyche holds, in unconsciousness, the whole history of one's past psychic and spiritual living. Will is, of course, the sum of millions of vibrations of desire in a given direction, so that the sum of one's desires seems to be the material out of which one's animal life is built, now, and in the future.

Thus to know yourself is to gain knowledge of the vibrations of past lives. . . .

These vibrations are the temptations to evil within us; they are also what we call our natural good instincts, as they form our natural characters: and their inter-relations with the desires of other lives work out into the circumstances and events of our lives. . . .

It is only in this life that we suffer the results of our mistakes in living . . . there is no pain in eternal or real life, the life of lives. . . . On its negative side, this eternal life that Christ offers to all men, now at once, is a deliverance from reincarnation, from the life and death circle of this earthly living, not from any torments of a bodiless state, but simply from the body of this death.

The suggestion of the idea of a form of reincarnation as a substitute for the hell of the Middle Ages, and as explanation of those strange sentences in which Christ seems to attach conditions to the attainment of Eternal Life, will doubtless seem unfamiliar and even forbidding to modern readers, though to the Jews and the Greeks such an idea would be familiar enough. The Church doubtless cast it out as a heresy, perhaps because of its connection with Greek philosophy as well as Jewish tradition. But then so strong was their horror of anything connected with the heathen world, that the early fathers also condemned washing, presumably because of the association of the baths with the immoral everyday life of heathen Rome. . . . But there is so very much in the New Testament that seems to give colour and authenticity to such a doctrine, that I would appeal to followers of Christ to overcome any shrinking from a conception usually associated with Pagan thought, and give the suggestion full and honest consideration in their study of the Gospels and Epistles. . . .

The idea of a succession of lives and deaths, following one another, for those who have not yet attained real life—are not yet Sons of God and children of the Resurrection—seems to illuminate, in a curious way, some of

Christ's most profound and seemingly paradoxical teaching on the destiny and the hope, the life or death, of the human psyche.

EVA GORE-BOOTH
(*A Psychological and Poetic Approach to the Study of Christ in the Fourth Gospel*)

DEATH is the absence of Love. Love brings us back to life, again and again, through Reincarnation, till in the end Love gains that great response from the love in us, which flings us into the circle of transmuting Force that is in God, and we are raised to Eternal Love, Truth, and Life.

At the beginning of each incarnation we have the wine of youth, a beautiful and joyous thing. But what is that to the Wine of Eternal Life, at the end of all incarnations, the noble or beautiful wine, as St. John called it?

EVA GORE-BOOTH
(*The Inner Kingdom*)

HOW all the stars did glitter and gleam
Through the gate of ivory, open wide,
Last time I died,
Cradled in the soft arms of a dream.

Through the gate of horn in mercy and ruth,
May the One Light shine from a blue sky
Next time I die,
Clasping the feet of the Beautiful Truth.

Love, all our little lives forgive,
On pain and failure be Thy radiance shed,
Raise Thou the Dead,
Give Truth to all the world, that all may live.

EVA GORE-BOOTH
(*Yesterday and To-morrow*)
(From *The Shepherd of Eternity*)

The Twentieth Century

THE souls that united in a common work in Greece scattered and have since gone forth into many nations. The sculptors and painters reincarnated in the middle ages in Italy as the great masters of painting; the architects appeared as the great cathedral builders of France, Germany, and Italy. A few of her dramatists were the Elizabethan dramatists of England; and in many countries of Europe the souls that co-operated in the Renaissance were mainly egos from Greece. Every so often individual Greeks still appear in the nations, and their temperament is unmistakable. Goethe, Schiller, and Lessing in Germany, and Byron, Keats, and Shelley in England, are typical of these returned Greeks. But there is no reincarnation of the Periclean Greeks as a body, making a separate nation; Greece was as a forcing-house, and her brilliant egos were selected out of all nations, and were returned to their normal homes to carry back with them the leaven that Greece gave.

Nations come and nations pass away; but nations are reborn too. By what we do in them now to serve them we earn the right to be their inspirers and leaders in their future transformations. Time may pass us by, and we grow old and 'die'; but that is only an illusion. We are immortal souls, and the world's history is only the alphabet of our speech, and we fashion the future as we will to fashion it. . . .

For this is the power the Divine Wisdom gives to all who love her—to greet life in all time not as the elders of the sunset, but as the children of the dawn.

C. JINARAJADASA
(*History and Reincarnation*)
(From *Theosophy and Modern Thought*)

THE man is an Ego, an imperishable circle in the sphere of Divinity; 'long, long ago, indeed, he had his birth, he verily is now within the germ.' He has lived on earth in many a past life, and there thought and felt and acted both good and evil; he has set in motion forces that help or hinder both himself and others. He is bound and not free. But he lives on from age to age to achieve an ideal, which is his Archetype. Just as for plant and animal life there are archetypes of the forms, so are there archetypes for the souls of men. One shall be a great saint of compassion, another a teacher of truth, a third a ruler of men; artist and scientist, doer and dreamer, each has set before him his archetype, that thought of God Himself of what each man shall be in the perfection of his God-given temperament. And each Ego achieves his archetype by finding his work. For this it is that we, as Egos, come into incarnation—to discover our work and to release the hidden powers within us by battling with circumstances as we achieve our work. . . .

Helps and handicaps, joys and pains, opportunities or privations, are the bricks of the Ego's own making for his temporary habitation; the Lords of Karma add nothing and take nothing away; they but adjust the forces of the soul's making so that his ultimate destiny, his archetype, shall be achieved as swiftly as may be as he treads the round of births and deaths.

C. JINARAJADASA
(*The Problem of Heredity*)
(From *Theosophy and Modern Thought*)

ALL my life I have had an awareness of other times, and places. I have been aware of other persons in me. . . . I, whose lips had never lisped the word 'king,' remembered that I had once been the son of a king. More—I remembered that once I had been a slave and a son of a slave, and worn an iron collar round my neck. Still more, when I was three, and four, and five years of age, I was not yet I. I was a mere becoming, a flux of spirit not yet cooled solid in the mould of my particular flesh and time and place. In that period all that I had ever been in ten thousand lives before strove in me, and troubled the flux of me, in the effort to incorporate itself in me and become me.

I, like any man, am a growth. I did not begin when I was born nor when I was conceived. I have been growing, developing, through incalculable myriads of millenniums. All these experiences of all these lives have gone to the making of the soul-stuff or the spirit-stuff that is I. . . . I am this spirit compounded of the memories of my endless incarnations. . . .

I am all of my past, as every protagonist of the Mendelian law must agree. All my previous selves have their voices, echoes, promptings in me. My every mode of action, heat of passion, flicker of thought is shaded, toned—infinitesimally shaded and toned—by that vast array of other selves that preceded me and went into the making of me. . . .

I am man born of woman. My days are few, but the stuff of me is indestructible. I have been woman born of woman. I have been a woman and borne my children. And I shall be born again. Oh, incalculable times again shall I be born ; and yet the stupid dolts about me think that by stretching my neck with a rope they will make me cease.

JACK LONDON
(*The Jacket*)

THE antipathies and sympathies of To-day, the sudden affinities like falling in love at sight, and the sudden hostilities that apparently had no sense—all were due to relationship in some buried Yesterday, while those of To-morrow could be anticipated, and so regulated, by the actions of To-day. Even to the smallest things.

Le Vallon lived in eternal life. He knew that it stretched infinitely behind his present 'section,' and infinitely ahead into countless other 'sections.' The results of what lay behind he must inevitably exhaust. Be that harvest painful or pleasant, he must reap what he had sown. But the future lay entirely in his own hands, and in his power of decision; chance or caprice had no word to say at all. And this consciousness of being in eternal life now, at the present moment, master of fate, potentially at least deific—this has remained a part of me, whether I will or no.

To Julius Le Vallon the soul was indeed unconquerable, and man master of his fate. Death lost its ugliness and terror; the sense of broken, separated life was replaced by the security of a continuous existence, whole, unhurried, eternal, affording ample time for all development, accepting joy and suffering as the justice of results, but never as reward or punishment.

ALGERNON BLACKWOOD
(*Julius Le Vallon*)

'OLD Souls' and 'Young Souls' was a classification that ruled my mind in this period. . . . In the Old lay innate the fruits, the results, the memories of many, many previous lives, and the ripeness of long experience showed itself in certain ways—in taste, in judgment, in their standard of values, in that mysterious quality called tact: above all, perhaps, in the type and quality of goods they desired from life. Worldly ambitions, so-called, were generally negligible in them. What we label to-day as the subconscious was invariably fully charged; also, without too much difficulty, accessible. It made them interesting, stimulating, not easily exhausted. Wide sympathies, spread charity, and understanding were their hall-marks, and a certain wisdom, as apart from intellect, their invariable gift; with, moreover, a tendency to wit, if not that rare quality wit itself, and humour, the power of seeing, and therefore laughing at, oneself. The cheaper experiences of birth, success, possessions, they had learned long ago; it was the more difficult, but higher values they had come back to master, and among the humbler ranks of life they found the necessary conditions. Christ, I reflected, was the son of a carpenter. The Young Souls, on the other hand, were invariably hot-foot after the things of this world—Show, Riches, and Power stuck like red labels on their foreheads. The Napoleons of the earth were among the youngest of all; the intellectuals, those who relied on reason alone, often the prosperous, usually the well-born, were of the same category. Rarely was 'understanding' in them; a brilliant cleverness could never rank with that wisdom which knows that *tout comprendre c'est tout pardonner*. To me the Young Souls were the commonplace and uninteresting ones. They were shallow, sketchy, soon exhausted, the *Dutzend-menschen*: whereas the others were intuitive, mature in outlook, aware of deeper values and eager for the things of the spirit.

ALGERNON BLACKWOOD
(*Episodes before Thirty*)

I LAID me down upon the shore
And dreamed a little space;
I heard the great waves break and roar;
The sun was on my face.

My idle hands and fingers brown
Played with the pebbles grey;
The waves came up, the waves went down,
Most thundering and gay.

The pebbles, they were smooth and round
And warm upon my hands,
Like little people I had found
Sitting among the sands.

The Ring of Return

The grains of sand so shining-small
  Soft through my fingers ran ;
The sun shone down upon it all,
  And so my dream began.

How all of this had been before :
  How ages far away
I lay on some forgotten shore
  As here I lie to-day.

The waves came shining up the sands,
  As here to-day they shine ;
And in my pre-Pelagian hands
  The sand was warm and fine.

I have forgotten whence I came,
  Or what my home might be,
Or by what strange and savage name
  I called that thundering sea.

I only know the sun shone down
  As still it shines to-day,
And in my fingers long and brown
  The little pebbles lay.

FRANCES CORNFORD
(*Pre-existence*)

CERTAINLY the human personality which covers the period from birth to death of the body is destined to perish and to have an end as it had a beginning ; but the real ' individuality,' that which is the essential being, keeps and assimilates to itself, deeply graves in its memory, all states of consciousness of the transitory personality. When, conformably to the palingenesis of which Schopenhauer speaks, it builds up another living personality, it brings to the latter all its permanent gains, and is further enriched by those of the new objectification. It is thus that the will, originally unconscious, becomes a conscious will.

The Twentieth Century

Against this inference of rebirth, no objections of a scientific kind can be raised. We may seek in vain for a single one in the whole stock of knowledge.

It will evidently be wise to take account only of facts and reasoned deductions from facts in constructing a philosophy of individual evolution. It is on them only that the sovereign beauty and the shining truth of evolution by palingenesis should be based. It needs no other revelation.

Collective evolution, like individual evolution, may be summed up in the formula—transition from the unconscious to the conscious.

The visible person, subject to birth and death, limited in powers, ephemeral in duration, is not the real being, he is only its attenuated, fragmentary, and illusory representation.

The real being, learning little by little to know itself and the universe, is the divine spark on the way to realise its divinity, of unlimited potentialities, creative and eternal.

Ignorance of the past is as great a blessing as ignorance of the future. Only the ideally evolved being will find no drawback in knowing all the vast accumulation of experience—sensations and emotions, efforts and struggles, joys and pains, loves and hates, high and low impulses, self-sacrificing or selfish acts—all, in fact, which has gone to build him up through the multiple personalities which have each specialised in some particular way.

If the commonplace man had but a flash of this knowledge, he would be dumbfounded by it. His present errors and anxieties are as much as he can bear. . . . Remembrance of the past could but impede present effort. . . .

For animals, and men of very low grade, the phase of existence which follows on death is short and dark. . . . The call of matter asserts itself with irresistible power, and the mystery of rebirth is soon brought about.

But for the more highly evolved man, death bursts the narrow circle within which material life has imprisoned a consciousness which strained against the bounds imposed by profession, family, and country. He finds himself carried far beyond the old habits of thought and memory, the old loves and hatreds, passions and mental habits.

To the degree that his evolutionary level permits, he remembers his past and foresees his future. He knows the road by which he has travelled ; he can judge of his conduct and his efforts. Many things which, in life, appeared to him very important, now, seen from a higher point of view, seem small and petty.

Great joys and great sorrows, mental storms out of all proportion to their causes, the passions which devastate a life, and the ambitions which consume it—all these are reduced to their true values, and hold but a very small place in the chain of remembrance.

Some of the links with the past are easily broken ; they pass away like the mists of dawn. Some are strong ; they are part of the unbreakable chain of destiny, and can be unwound only little by little.

There are good days and bad days, good lives and bad lives ; days and lives which are profitable ; days and lives that are lost. A single day and a single life cannot be appraised apart from preceding days and lives : they form a chain of consequences. . . . Lives as well as days are separated from one another by a period of seeming repose which is, nevertheless, one of useful assimilation and preparation ; and as on waking we find many problems solved as if by magic, so it is at the dawn of another life. . . .

Thus, from one existence to another, the Self comes

slowly, and by the vast accumulation of stored and assimilated experiences, to the higher phases of life that are reserved to the complete development of its consciousness—to the complete consciousness that realises all.

GUSTAVE GELEY
(*From the Unconscious to the Conscious*)
(Translated by STANLEY DE BRATH)

HOW can I leave the garden that I made,
The flowers I planted,
And the paths I laid;
The cedar through whose boughs the sunbeams slanted
On summer mornings, while the blackbird played
A golden flute, whose melodies enchanted
Drew dancing angels down from heaven's glade,
Till all the grass by starry feet was haunted,
And dew-bright wings fled, gleaming, thro' the shade?

How shall I bear it when my blossoms fade,
When lost are all the treasures that I vaunted,
And Death's dark Hand the Balance down has weighed?

Nay, rather ask, how shall I bear to leave
Those other Gardens of Immortal Wonder,
Where human heart is never left to grieve,
But long may dream and ponder
'Neath God's o'ershadowing Heart, and can achieve
No deeper joy than listening to the thunder
Of that great Pulse, whose rhythmic beatings weave
Chains of star-jewels that go circling under
His Throne, and from His Eyes their light receive?

How from that resting-place shall I retrieve
My spirit, when the moment comes to sunder
From heaven's delights, and there is no reprieve?

EVA MARTIN
(*Death and Rebirth*)
(From *The White Road*)

The Ring of Return

Part I *The Garden of Eden*

THE *Serpent:* " The serpent never dies. Some day you shall see me come out of this beautiful skin; a new snake with a new and lovelier skin. That is birth. . . . I made the word dead to describe my old skin that I cast when I am renewed. I call that renewal being born."

Eve: " Born is a beautiful word."

The Serpent: " Why not be born again and again as I am, new and beautiful every time? "

Part II *The Twentieth Century*

Savvy: " I believe the old people are the new people, reincarnated, Frank. I suspect I am Eve. I am very fond of apples; and they always disagree with me."

Conrad: " You *are* Eve in a sense. The Eternal Life persists; only It wears out Its bodies and minds and gets new ones, like new clothes. You are only a new hat and frock on Eve."

Franklyn: " Yes. Bodies and minds ever better fitted to carry out Its eternal pursuit."

Lubin (with quiet scepticism): " What pursuit, may one ask, Mr. Barnabas? "

Franklyn: " The pursuit of omnipotence and omniscience. Greater power and greater knowledge: these are what we are all pursuing even at the risk of our lives and the sacrifice of our pleasures. Evolution is that pursuit and nothing else. It is the path to Godhead. A man differs from a microbe only in being further on the path."

George Bernard Shaw
(*Back to Methuselah*)

The Twentieth Century

JOAN: And now tell me: shall I rise from the dead, and come back to you a living woman?

What! Must I burn again? Are none of you ready to receive me?

O God that madest this beautiful earth, when will it be ready to receive Thy saints? How long, O Lord, how long?

GEORGE BERNARD SHAW
(*Saint Joan*)

THERE are three things that I love,
Yea, four there be that make my heart to leap within me;
The breaking of a wave upon the beach,
The moorland that stretches immeasurably northward from the Grampians,
And the coming of dawn upon the mountains.
The coming of the dawn I love,
When the peewits for a moment are still,
And the moor-cock
For the moment forgets to cry to his mortal enemy
In the next-door corrie;
And the moorland I love;
And the sea I love;
But of all things upon this earth
I love most the smile of the beloved.

O my beloved, world-wise, world-old,
How can you be so young, and smile so oldly?
There is all the sea in your smile;
The dawn upon the mountains is there,
And the purple, brown, interminable moorland.

The Ring of Return

You have the whispering of pines,
And the glamour of the mirage of the Arabian deserts,
The hidden treasures of Ind,
The wondrous carved work of Cathay,
Lacquer of azure upon gold
Giving richly clothed figures
In willow-hung gardens ornamented with pagodas.

How can you have all these things, beloved,
In that strange, rich smile of yours?
How can you have gathered into that smile
So many treasures of so many lands?
Sometimes I hear the tinkling of guitars
Beneath Moorish balconies
In Moorish Cordova;
Sometimes the grinding of Arctic floes,
When the Samoyede peoples
Hurriedly pack their smoke-stained tents,
And fly for the southern pastures.
And yet,
Why should you not have all of the sea within you,
And the magic of the dawn,
And the crying of peewits upon the interminable moorlands?
Within
The little circle of those lips
Why may there not be gathered
All the magic and the remembrance of the world,
Best beloved?

We have lived with each other,
And loved each other,
And fled from each other,
And followed each other,
So many, many times;

Back and forth, back and forth,
For richer or poorer,
In sickness or health,
Until death did us part ;
And back we came,
Back and back to play the old, old game through,
Loving and leaving and leaving and loving,
Until—why, my beloved,
There must be scarce one acre of this weary, bad old
earth
We have not trod together
Some time !

And now—
Though you have forgotten,
Yet every now and then,
Like the lightning that flickers on summer nights
Low down on the horizon,
There comes that smile,
Comes and goes.

Some day, perhaps, you will remember ;
And then you will know
Why it is that of all things on this earth
I love best the smile of my Margaret, my beloved.

J. CALDWELL-JOHNSTON
(*La Bien Aimée de Tout le Monde*)
(From *The Book of the Beloved*)

WHEN the question is asked, 'Where were we before we were born ? ' we have a definite answer in the system of slow development by incarnation, with long intervals of spirit rest between, while otherwise we have no answer, though we must admit that it is inconceivable that we have been born in time for eternity. Existence afterwards seems to postulate existence before. As to the natural question, 'Why, then, do we not remember such existences? ' we may point out that such remembrance would enormously complicate our present life, and that such existences may well form a cycle which is all clear to us when we come to the end of it, when perhaps we may see a whole rosary of lives threaded upon one personality. The convergence of so many lines of theosophic and Eastern thought upon this one conclusion, and the explanation which it affords in the supplementary doctrine of Karma of the apparent injustice of any single life, are arguments in its favour, and so perhaps are those vague recognitions and memories which are occasionally too definite to be easily explained as atavistic impressions.

SIR ARTHUR CONAN DOYLE
(*A History of Spiritualism*)

" I HAVE had a dream, a whole lifetime, two thousand years ago! . . . A lifetime—childhood, boyhood, manhood. . . . I have lived through a whole life in that old world. . . .

" As it happened, death came early enough for me to die with a living love still in my heart." . . .

" To live again," said Sunray very softly.

" And love again," said Sarnac, patting her knee.

" That tale," said the guest-master stoutly, " was no dream. It was a memory floating up out of the deep darkness of forgotten things into a living brain—a kindred brain."

Sarnac thought. " What is a personality but a memory? If the memory of Harry Mortimer Smith is in my brain, then I am Smith. I feel as sure that I was Smith two thousand years ago as that I was Sarnac this morning. Sometimes before this in my dreams I have had a feeling that I lived again forgotten lives. Have none of you felt like that? " . . .

The Twentieth Century

" When children have dreams of terror, of being in the wild with howling beasts, of long pursuit and hair-breadth escapes, perhaps it is the memory of some dead creature that lives again in them ? " asked Starlight. . . . " Maybe life from its very beginning has been spinning threads and webs of memories. Not a thing in the past, it may be, that has not left its memories about us. Some day we may learn to gather in that forgotten gossamer, we may learn to weave its strands together again, until the whole past is restored to us, and life becomes one. . . . And however that may be, and however these things may be explained, I can well believe without any miracles that Sarnac has touched down to the real memory of a human life that lived and suffered two thousand years ago." . . .

" And I too believe that," said Sunray. . . . " I do not question for a moment that Sarnac lived that life."

" It was a life," said Sarnac, " and it was a dream, a dream within this life; and this life too is a dream. Dreams within dreams, dreams containing dreams, until we come at last, maybe, to the Dreamer of all dreams, the Being who is all beings. Nothing is too wonderful for life and nothing is too beautiful."

H. G. Wells
(*The Dream*)

YOU sing to me, and I have heard that call
Played upon flutes two thousand years ago.
Delicate flutes whose music's rise and fall
Drew all the dancers' feet within a snare
Where mine more wildly stepped to it than all.

The Ring of Return

Through empty groves the summer winds now blow,
And all that youth will no more heed your call,
But I who perished too can hear it yet.
Who love it now as then the best of all.

EDWARD STORER
(*Narkissos*)

REINCARNATION resolves every human problem. It accounts for the astonishing and often heart-breaking contrasts between individuals . . . by the declaration that these varying individuals are at higher or lower stages in the evolution of the race, some having been through a greater number of lives than others, or made better use of their opportunities. And without reincarnation there is no accounting at all for differences between individuals, nor can the fact of contrast between noble and base be denied by any impartial observer. Unless many individuals are to be born again, perhaps many times, they must be written down as God's hopeless failures, glaringly imperfect miscreations. . . . Our life stretches back into the dim and distant past, when we were ape, tiger, bat, insect, bird, plant, creeping slime, or mineral in the depths of the earth. Our life stretches forward into the veiled but glorious future, through life after life of growth, development, lessons learned through joy and pain, lives on the earth and lives in the glorious angel-worlds, until at length, after millions of years, we pass into the perfect rest of spiritual perfection. . . . Not only once, in the earth-life which we know at present, have we laboured, and suffered, and perhaps fallen, and risen again; not only once have we cherished our dear ones, toiling for their sakes, seeking their happiness. . . . We are age-long friends, companions since the birth of time, companions since the Divine Being begot our psychic individualities in spiritual worlds long ago. The memory of our past has dropped from us for a time, in order that we may endure the discipline of temporary separation from our spiritual origins and thus learn our mutual interdependence, and our absolute dependence upon the spiritual world and upon God, and also in order that each new life which we live here on earth may indeed be a new life, a fresh beginning; without the actual recollection of the past—for that would render useless the gates of birth and death—with the fruits of experience carried over in our character and its spiritual powers. . . . Reincarnation is the only solution to life's riddles, for without it life has no rational purpose.

G. BASEDEN BUTT
(*Modern Psychism*)

TRIVIALITIES. Disproportions. Emptiness. She was impatient of it all.

(She did not know that we create our own surroundings; it is so long a process that no one life can bear witness that we do.)

She fled away, and wrenched open the Gates. But she wasn't ready for what her eyes fell on—

The fullness of Light, the illimitable Distance; the great, luminous Calm.

It was like to have slain her; and she lay as for dead.

'*All Thy waves have passed over me*'

Yet it was good that she had tired of these former things.

The little boat will wait.

She will look again through the Gates some day, and her eyes, and her heart, and her whole being, will be satisfied.

PAMELA GREY
(*The Gates*)
(From *The Vein in the Marble*)

The Ring of Return

BRIEF were my days among you, and briefer still the words I have spoken.

But should my voice fade in your ears, and my love vanish in your memory, then I will come again,

And with a richer heart and lips more yielding to the spirit will I speak.

Yea, I shall return with the tide,

And though death may hide me, and the greater silence enfold me, yet again will I seek your understanding. . . .

Know, therefore, that from the greater silence I shall return. . . .

What was given us here we shall keep,

And if it suffices not, then again must we come together and together stretch our hands unto the giver.

Forget not that I shall come back to you.

A little while, and my longing shall gather dust and foam for another body.

A little while, a moment of rest upon the wind, and another woman shall bear me. . . .

If in the twilight of memory we should meet once more, we shall speak again together and you shall sing to me a deeper song.

And if our hands should meet in another dream we shall build another tower in the sky.

KAHLIL GIBRAN
(*The Prophet*)

THE man sprang to his feet beholding that his life and the tree's were of one stuff. Yea, from such had sprung his body and his soul—out of the dust and dew and heat of a million years, out of unnumbered births and deaths, out of the ancient work of things which lived in sunken continents and seas that are no more. In the white-oak he beheld the Dryad, the tree-soul, which, as the Greek divined, has in it something of humanity. . . .

He thought of thought, finer action of the all-potential

sap, forcing its way to finer fibres, the *will* of successive races and æons moulding delicate organs for itself, giving the tree-soul memory at last, and voice and vision; housing it at last in the marvellous, unrooted body of man.

Through veil of soul and moon and tree, he saw the unseen Universal Will, the One which binds, includes, and is all things.

SUSAN GLASPELL
(*The Road to the Temple*)

STRANGE that your brow should wear,
Long borne unconscious there,
Signs of a quest that ended when I came.
Strange that my uttered word
Fell not on ears that heard
Until I learned to call you by your name.

Worn as a garment new,
Hiding yourself from view,
Feature and form I saw but did not know.
Yet at the words you spoke
Deep-sleeping thoughts awoke;
Thus did our hearts unite, our minds conflow.

Haply some ancient page,
Scribed in an earlier age,
Tells of our trystings when a world was young.
So, in far years to be,
Again you'll come to me,
Singing our old songs in a later tongue.

OLIVER DOUGLAS
(*Recognition*)

WHEN that caressing light forgets the hills
That change their hue in its evolving grace
When, harmony of swaying reeds and rills,
The breeze forgets its music, and the face

The Ring of Return

Of Nature smiles no longer in the pond,
  Divinity revealed! When morning peeps
Above earth's rim, and no bird-notes respond;
  When half a world in mellow moonlight sleeps,
And no peace glistens on the cooling air;
  When dew brings no wet wonder of delight
On jewelled spider-web and scented lair
  Of drone and hue and honey; when the night
No longer shadows the retreating day,
  Nor purple dawn pursues the greying dark;
And no child laughs, and no wind bears away
  The bursting glory of the meadow-lark;
Then—then it may be—never until then
  May death be dreadful, or assurance wane
That we shall die awhile, to waken when
  New morning summons us to earth again.

'We live as long as we are useful, and as long as it is good for us to live. Thereafter we die, which is another form of living, even as ice and water and rain and dew are the same thing in different aspects. When the appointed time comes, we return, as the rain returns to the earth it has left for a season. . . . There is a balance in the universe, and an Intelligence that governs it. No man can escape the consequences of his own act, though it take him a million lives to redress the balance. Justice is inevitable. Evil produces evil, and is due to ignorance. But justice being infinite in all its ways, there is a middle way by which we may escape from ignorance. I, who saw the world increasing its downward impetus while it believes itself to be progressing upward through the invention of new means for exploiting selfishness; I, who saw the ruins of Egypt, and of Babylon; of Rome and Greece; of Jerusalem; of Ceylon; of India; I, who have lived for fifty years within a stone's throw of a city ten times older than Babylon; I *knew* that day follows night, and I waited for the dawn, not knowing the hour. I waited.

The Twentieth Century

'I knew there are those who have won merit in their former lives, whose time comes to be born again. I knew that the key to evolution is in character—not in numbers or material increase—in the character of the soul, my Son! I knew that at the right time those would begin to be born whose character would influence the world, as mine could not. And I waited.'

TALBOT MUNDY
(*Om*)

EVEN the observant Masonic student is made aware by the formula used at Lodge-closing, that by some great Warden of life and death each soul is called into this objective world to labour upon itself, and is in due course summoned from it to rest from its labours and enter into subjective celestial refreshment, until once again it is recalled to labour. For each the 'day,' the opportunity for work at self-perfecting, is duly given; for each the 'night' cometh when no man can work at that task; which morning and evening constitute but one creative day in the soul's life, each portion of that day being a necessary complement to the other. Perfect man has to unify these opposites in himself; so that for him, as for his Maker, the darkness and the light become both alike.

The world-old secret teaching upon this subject, common to the whole of the East, to Egypt, the Pythagoreans and Platonists, and every College of the Mysteries, is to be found summed up as clearly and tersely as one could wish in the *Phædo* of Plato, to which the Masonic seeker is referred as one of the most instructive of treatises upon the deeper side of the science. It testifies to the great rhythm of life and death above spoken of, and demonstrates how that the soul in the course of its career weaves and wears out many bodies, and is continually migrating between objective and subjective conditions, passing from labour to refreshment and back again many times in its great task of self-fulfilment. And if Plato was, as was once truly said of him, but Moses speaking Attic Greek, we shall not be surprised at finding the same initiate teaching disclosed in the words of Moses himself. Does not the familiar Psalm of Moses declare that man is continually 'brought to destruction,' that subsequently a voice goes forth saying 'Come again, ye children of men!' and that the subjective spiritual world is his refuge from one objective manifestation to another? What else than a paraphrase of this great word of comfort is the Masonic pronouncement that, in the course of its task of self-perfecting, the soul is periodically summoned to alternating periods of labour and refreshment? It must labour, and it must rest from its labours; its works will follow it, and in the subjective world every Brother's soul will receive its due for its work in the objective one, until such time as its work is completed and it is 'made a pillar in the House of God and no more goes out' as a journeyman-builder into this sublunary workshop.

W. L. WILMSHURST
(*The Masonic Initiation*)

SNOWFLAKES of pureness unalloyed,
That in dark space
Are built, and spilt from out the teeming void
With prodigal grace,
Air-quarried temples, though you fall scarce felt
And all your delicate architecture melt
To tears upon my face,—

I too am such encrystalled breath
In the void planned
And bodied forth to surge of life and death;
And as I stand
Beneath this sacramental spilth of snow,
Crumbling, you whisper: 'Fear thou not to go
Back to the viewless hand;

The Twentieth Century

'Thence to be moulded forth again
Through time and space,
Till thy imperishable self attain
Such strength and grace,
Through endless infinite refinement passed
By the eternal Alchemist, that at last
Thou see Him face to face.'

W. L. WILMSHURST
(*Nox Nivosa*)

ONLY two explanations of human inequalities can be forthcoming. Either individuals come into existence already variously endowed—some possessing wonderful gifts—and join the great stream of evolution at different points of its course, or a long past must lie behind each one during which the present capacities have been gradually acquired. The first implies the special creation of a spirit for every fresh body, but, just as special creation is rejected as an explanation of variety in form and structure, so must it ultimately be rejected as an explanation of human differences. The second involves the idea of reincarnation, which implies that man is the result of his own past, being what he has made himself. Viewed from this standpoint, the differences which characterise people are no longer a problem. They are the summed-up results of the experiences of previous incarnations. The birth of a genius, a saint, a sage, those remarkable differentiations from the average stock that so puzzle the observer of life, can thus easily be accounted for; for they are seen as the product of accumulated endeavour and work carried over a period of many lives; they but reveal the finer possibilities and powers that lie dormant in others. In them is witnessed a flowering of the Spiritual Ego.

OLIVE STEVENSON HOWELL
(*Heredity and Reincarnation*)

The Ring of Return

I STILL have my own ideas of a future state. It is this—that if we are hunted and pursued in this life by malicious enemies, so, in the life to come, it is we that will be the hunters and our enemies the hunted. This idea comes from no vindictive spirit. . . . It comes from the knowledge that I have never wilfully done harm to anyone on earth. My capacity for taking punishment has been tremendous, but the spirit to inflict it on another was not given to me at birth. But in this new life to come, it will be the decree of the reigning powers that I shall ride on the backs of my enemies, and they will live in fear of me from hour to hour. This will go on until we die again and enter into another new state of life. For there is probably more states of life than one or two ; and even in our next life to this we will not be much wiser than we are now, to know what extraordinary life will be the end of all.

W. H. DAVIES
(*Later Days*)

JUST as the evolution of form shows our own physical form to be the outcome of a long process of physical evolution, so in the evolution of life, the life within us is seen as the outcome of an age-long evolution from the very simplest manifestations to ever higher and higher stages, until in the great Rhythm of Creation the separate life has regained the unity of the Divine from which it came. The dynamic view of the universe applied to the human soul, to our own life, to the consciousness within us, produces as its result the doctrine of Reincarnation, of the many lives on earth through which we have reached our present stage of evolution, the doctrine of Karma by which our different lives are causally connected, and the doctrine of the Perfection or Deification of man, in which that life reaches its perfection.

J. J. VAN DER LEEUW
(*The Fire of Creation*)

The Twentieth Century

ONE vision of the Eternal does not satisfy ; one vision opens up another, and so it goes on through life after life. Evolution does not suddenly begin at a certain moment, nor stop at a given moment, nor after one life ; it is an endless road.

J. KRISHNAMURTI
(*The Kingdom of Happiness*)

THE principle . . . is indestructible. It continues to act objectively, from reincarnation to reincarnation, on both sides of the grave, in some unknown sense. The bearers of this principle change, and they do not guess, or, if so, only faintly, that their essence is eternal. The rare man, who succeeds in anchoring his consciousness in true Being, knows himself to be immortal, and death no longer signifies an end to him. . . .

He who seeks progress first will never attain to perfection. It is wonderful how plastically the myth of the transmigration of souls expresses the truth of this relation : the man who has faithfully fulfilled his dharma in a lowly position in life will be reborn in a higher one ; he who has entered upon the path of saintliness will gain, through incarnation upon incarnation, more advantageous circumstances.

Benares is overflowing with the diseased and the infirm. . . . And yet I have never felt less compassion. These sufferers suffer so little ; they have, above all, no fear whatever of death. . . . As to their infirmity—well, that must be endured ; it will not take very long anyhow. And some old sin is no doubt scored off in the process. The faith of the Indians is said to be pessimistic. I know of none which is less so. It believes in a scheme of the world in which every being rises upward inevitably, in which, at most, one man in millions of millions succeeds in falling lower. The whole processes of the world bear him along in so far as he progresses, and he must overcome all resistance before he can deteriorate. The aim of this ascent is, of course, not one which may seem desirable to the Westerner. His soul is still too young to strive after liberation. But it is certain that to the Hindu liberation means the same state of bliss as Heaven does to the Christian.

COUNT HERMANN KEYSERLING
(*The Travel Diary of a Philosopher*)
(Translated by F. HOLROYD REECE)

IF the deep wood is haunted, it is I
Who am the ghost ; not the tall trees,
Nor the white moonlight slanting down like rain,
Filling the hollows with bright pools of silver.

A long train whistle serpentines around the hill,
Now shrill, now far away.
Tell me, from what dark, smoky terminal
What train sets out for yesterday ?

Or, since our spirits take off and resume
Their flesh as travellers their cloaks, O tell me where,
In what age and what country you will come,
That I may meet you there.

ROBERT HILLYER
(*Nocturne*)

FORGET not Memphis and the evening lights
Along the shore, the wind in the papyrus,
The sound of water through the glass-green nights,
The incense curling upward to Osiris.
Forget not Athens and the starry walks
Beside Ilissus under the cool trees,
The Master's garden, and the quiet talks
Of gods and life to come. Forget not these.

And in the after years, forget not this :
How in a withered world allied to death,

The Twentieth Century

When love was mocked and beauty deemed amiss,
 We met and pledged again the ancient faith.
For this, of all our loves the loveliest,
 So thwarted and so strong, will seem the best.

ROBERT HILLYER
(*Sonnet*)
(From *The Halt in the Garden*)

THE psychology of to-day tries to build up the mind of the individual from the racial mind of the past. It has to deal in masses, for it has not the Buddhist secret of rebirth. The psychology of to-morrow will investigate the past of the individual—the last little bit of that past; and it will find itself up against the Buddhist doctrine of rebirth. The next step will be to inquire into the psychology of our future—into what *we* rise up as, when *we* discard this body, the whence of that new body and the nature of it. It is no idle quest, but of tremendous practical importance. Few of us will urgently need to wireless to the Antipodes, much less to Mars. But we all die, and very soon. Are we always going to be so childish as to be content, not only with creeds, but with sciences that leave us in ignorance of death, and so in the fear of death?

MRS. C. A. F. RHYS DAVIDS
(*Buddhist Psychology*)

THE doctrine of Reincarnation, in its simplest possible outline, is this: That the Immortal Ego in man, that part which is divine, seeks experience in a succession of mortal physical bodies, with intervals of varying length spent on other planes of being between its incarnations. This is sometimes expressed by saying that the Individuality lives through many personalities. . . . The acceptance of the theory does not involve the assertion that all Egos came into evolution simultaneously; some may be much older than others, e.g. the philosopher may be conjectured to be probably an older soul than the society butterfly or the primitive savage. It does imply that at the start of their evolution all souls had equal potentialities, and that their present positions represent exactly the result of the use they have made of the time and opportunities they have had so far.

HUGH ROSCOE
(*Occultism and Christianity*)

JOY awaits the successful candidate in the mystic meditation, who, by the action of the Paraclete, conquers the life centres, and enters the realm of spiritual realities and becomes a Master of the Gnostic Science. Little wonder that the work has to be pursued with patience through many years and lives until the consummation, but even in its early stages the memory of the eternal life remains unbroken, and knowledge becomes a certainty.

D. N. DUNLOP
(*The Path of Attainment*)

I CAN only remember my life on earth, and that not very well, but I have a feeling that I existed before that. Sometimes the feeling is quite strong. It connects me with Eastern lands. When on earth I felt drawn to Eastern art and life. I still feel as if there were a link. I can't tell for certain, and it does not matter—besides, it is only a bit of me. Could *parts* of us have been in existence elsewhere?

I also feel that this life is a growth towards a finer state of being.

I am content to lie in the tides of life and time and be carried whither they will.

A Message from H. D. LOWRY, author of *The Hundred Windows*, *Wreckers and Methodists*, etc.; given by MRS. C. A. DAWSON SCOTT in *From Four who are Dead*.

The Twentieth Century

I PERCEIVE the imprisoned lightnings in all things. I perceive the Light which is dull—the savage; the Light which is bright—the man evolved; the Light which is glory—the superman, the master.

I perceive an Apotheosis of Death. There is no death, only change, and always change with purpose, change to a greater end. Death is re-creation, renewal, the dropping of fetters, the casting aside of a vehicle which has ceased to suffice. Death is in very truth a birth into a fuller and larger life, or a dipping down into matter under the law of readjustment. Progress always, and progress towards Unity. We come ever nearer to each other and to the Real through death. If only we could realise this!

GEORGE S. ARUNDALE
(*Nirvana*)

SPIRIT may be thought of as the nucleus of the reincarnating ego.

Blavatsky taught reincarnation, and the theory was immediately seized upon by great numbers of intelligent persons who saw in it the only logical explanation of certain problems of existence, which formerly had defied solution, and which made of life not an ordered, coherent, and absolutely just scheme of evolution, but a wild chaos of hideous cruelty and injustice. . . .

In countless cases, during those early years, I have seen the acceptance of reincarnation turn the atheist and agnostic into a reverent worshipper of the Absolute.

What of the countless undeveloped millions who live and die with no conception of there being any other object in life save keeping soul and body together?

Are they to be judged by a record of three score years and ten? 'Their chance will come in the next world,' was the old-fashioned reply. Those of the clergy who do not openly preach reincarnation would rather leave the subject in darkness than proffer a reply which ordinary intelligence has long since rejected as utterly childish reasoning. It is a case of quiet agnosticism, or an eager grasping of the logical suggestion of a multiplicity of lives through which evolving man may gradually unveil the God within, and rise in time to a destined perfection.

The coming of the Dictator in so many parts of the world is a most interesting phenomenon. Reincarnation is throwing up men from the humblest families who are revolutionising their several countries as kings seem powerless to do.

There are now frequent cases of what students term 'third or fourth race savages in fifth race bodies.' The savage tribes of the earth are being so rapidly exterminated that it is hard for the primitive reincarnating ego to find suitable savage conditions. They therefore take birth in the lowest available bodies, and in the slums of their conquerors.

Without Reincarnation there is nothing but chaos to be made of human existence. The further back one plunges into history, the more hopeless does elucidation become, unless we use as the key to unlock the mysteries a multiplicity of lives during which the evolution of humanity proceeds on its God-appointed way.

VIOLET TWEEDALE
(*Mellow Sheaves*)

The Twentieth Century

THEN the proud grey joss in the corner stirred ;
On his wrist appeared a grey small bird,
And this was the song of the grey small bird :
" Where is the princess, loved forever,
Who made Chang first of the kings of men ? "

And the joss in the corner stirred again ;
And the carved dog, curled in his arms, awoke,
Barked forth a smoke-cloud that whirled and broke.
It piled in a maze round the ironing-place,
And there on the snowy table wide
Stood a Chinese lady of high degree,
With a scornful, witching, tea-rose face . . .
Yet she put away all form and pride,
And laid her glimmering veil aside
With a child-like smile for Chang and for me.

The walls fell back, night was aflower,
The table gleamed in a moonlit bower,
While Chang, with a countenance carved of stone,
Ironed and ironed, all alone.
And thus she sang to the busy man Chang :
" Have you forgotten . . .
Deep in the ages, long, long ago,
I was your sweetheart there on the sand—
Storm-worn beach of the Chinese land ?
We sold our grain in the peacock town
Built on the edge of the sea-sands brown—
Built on the edge of the sea-sands brown . . .
When all the world was drinking blood
From the skulls of men and bulls,
And all the world had swords and clubs of stone,
We drank our tea in China beneath the sacred spice-trees,
And heard the curled waves of the harbour moan.
And this grey bird, in Love's first spring,
With a bright-bronze breast and a bronze-brown wing,
Captured the world with his carolling.

The Ring of Return

Do you remember, ages after,
At last the world we were born to own?
You were the heir of the yellow throne—
The world was the field of the Chinese man,
And we were the pride of the sons of Han.
We copied deep books and we carved in jade,
And wove blue silks in the mulberry shade . . ."

"I remember, I remember
That Spring came on forever,
That Spring came on forever,"
Said the Chinese nightingale.

VACHEL LINDSAY
(*The Chinese Nightingale*)

WITH a heavy heart I asked him, "And whither does my way take me, Iza Bekchi?"

"Towards rebirth," he answered, and over his unspeakably beautiful face there again passed rays of light.

"And death?"

"That which is immortal returns to God." The voice sounded triumphantly.

"The immortal part of every man?" I asked, stretching out my hands to him.

"Of every man."

"So everyone shall be born again, O Evli!" Sweet hope descended on me.

"Rebirth may be twofold," he said, and his voice was deep as the sound of bells. "Unconscious and conscious."

I was outside my body. My corpse lay on the guillotine. . . .

I was a spirit, among many other spirits that floated in space. But I had consciousness. I was aware of my ego, and I had a purpose and a desire.

The Twentieth Century

I sought to find a new dwelling for myself, a new dwelling equipped with the instruments of sense so that I might receive from without and give back what comes from within: thoughts in the garb of words. I was seeking for a human body. . . . The will for reincarnation was the one impulse that dominated me. . . .

A crystalline, cold, clear air poured into my lungs. Many-coloured, confused rays struck my eyes, mingled sounds caught my ear. All those things happened to me which accompany the entry of a young being into this world. There I was. I had returned, an Evli.

My name was Sennon Vorauf.

I had a father, a mother, and other people who were fond of me. I learned to talk and to walk. I was a child as other children. Everything was new to me, everything a revelation—until I acquired the faculty of recalling my former existence. . . .

By slow degrees I became capable of classifying and putting together these recurrent and changing dreams. By and by I realised that they were the fragments of the life of Melchior Dronte, my previous self.

PAUL BUSSON
(*The Man who was Born Again*)
(Translated by PRINCE MIRSKI
and THOMAS MOULT)

I HEAR my husbands marching
The æons all adown:
The shepherd boys and princes—
From cavern unto crown.

I hear in soft recession
The praise they give to me;
I hear them chant my titles
From all antiquity.

The Ring of Return

But never do I answer,
  I might be overheard;
Lose Love's revised illusions
  By one unhappy word.

I sit, a silent siren,
  And count my cavaliers;
The men I wed in wisdom,
  The boys who taught me tears.

To some I gave devotion,
  To some I kinked the knee;
But there was one old wizard
  Who laid his spells on me.

He showed me like a master
  That one rose makes a gown;
That looking up to Heaven
  Is merely looking down.

He marked me for the circle,
  Made magic in my eyes;
He won me by revealing
  The truth in all his lies.

So, when I see that wizard
  Among the marchers dim,
I make the full court curtsy
  In fealty to him.

NATALIA CRANE
(*My Husbands*)

INDEX

Index

Index

Index

Index

Library of the Mystic Arts

A LIBRARY OF ANCIENT AND MODERN CLASSICS

APOCRYPHA, The. Intro. by Morton Enslin, Professor of Biblical Languages and Literature, St. Lawrence University. Size 7¼" x 11", xv + 239pp., bound in white and gold, 3-color slipcase. 62-12335. $15.00 REL

"A good book, like a virtuous woman, can be valued for a number of qualities. This makes its initial appeal through the beauty of its binding and printing. Only after one has admired these qualities does he read the familiar passages and move back to the excellent Introduction.

"In 1924 the Nonesuch edition of the Apocrypha appeared, limited to 1325 copies. This new edition is an almost exact facsimile of that very beautiful work, bound in a most attractive cover with stamped gilt design, and boxed. Most marked of its changes from the original, and one that enhances the value of the work considerably, is an Introduction by the editor of this Journal, Dr. Morton S. Enslin, who in brief, concise paragraphs provides excellent prefaces to the work as a whole and to each of the books individually. He places the Apocrypha in its proper context in biblical literature, indicates the inappropriateness of the name when applied to the books as a whole, and shows how it was that Luther split off these writings and placed them 'in the limbo between the Old Testament and the New.' The individual introductions serve to provide the backgrounds, probable datings, and general contents of each of the fourteen pieces. This is a valuable work for both the biblical scholar and the lover of fine books."—*J. Calvin Keene,* JOURNAL OF BIBLICAL LITERATURE

BIRREN, Faber. Color: A Survey in Words and Pictures: From Ancient Mysticism to Modern Science. index. 250 illus. 7⅝" x 10½", slipcased. 224pp. 62-18889. $15.00 PSYCH

In this marvelous encyclopedia of color facts and fancies, Faber Birren, leading consultant in America on the subject, offers a kaleidoscope of information for both the users of color in industry and science and the many who are intrigued by color artistically and psychologically. His contributions to the development of color application in government and industry have influenced us all. Here he offers the results of a lifetime devoted to his studies.

Illustrating his survey with more than two hundred and fifty illustrations in color, Mr. Birren conducts the reader on a leisurely stroll through primitive, ancient, medieval, and modern color conceptions, explaining color's mystic function, its many religious uses, the significance of gem stones, the relation of color to marriage and fertility.

A stimulating section on heraldry precedes an examination of color symbolism today. Color in medicine, from ancient cures to modern diagnoses, is dwelt upon at length, and medieval theories of alchemy are discussed.

The author includes an amusing account of the feud between Goethe and Sir Isaac Newton on color theory, and continues on to a consideration of modern spectroscopy and the wonders of human vision. The human aura is scrutinized, and the language of color, with charming and sometimes unexpected word derivations, dealt with extensively.

The relation of color to music, perhaps less well-known, is the subject of an unusual chapter, giving the history of color scales and color organs. In art, Renaissance artists, Impressionism, and Modern Painting are detailed with excellent illustrations.

CHANG, Garma C. C. Teachings of Tibetan Yoga. Introduction by John C. Wilson. 128pp. 62-22082. $5.00 YOGA

The author-translator who gave us the translation of *The Hundred Thousand Songs of Milarepa* now provides an introduction to the spiritual, mental, and physical exercises of his religion. Tibetan Yoga, or Tantrism, is summarized by the author in the following words: "The divinity of Buddahood is omnipresent, but the quickest way to realize this truth is to discover it within one's body-mind complex. By spiritual exercises and the application of Tantric techniques one can soon realize that his body, mind, and the 'objective world' are all manifestations of the divine Buddahood."

DINGWALL, Eric J. Some Human Oddities: Studies in the Queer, the Uncanny and the Fanatical. ill. bibliog. 198pp. 62-14948 $6.00 PSYCH

DINGWALL, Eric J. Very Peculiar People: Portrait Studies in the Queer, the Abnormal and the Uncanny. ill. index. bibliog. 224pp. 62-14949. $6.00 PSYCH

"These reissues of two fascinating books, originally written in 1946 and 1951 respectively, will be welcomed by all the lovers of true tales of the weird, strange and abnormal. Here are stories, scholarly written and scientifically analyzed, of visionary mystics like Emanuel Swedenborg, masochistic saints like St. Mary Magdalene de Pazzi, flying friars like Joseph of Copertino, mediums *extraordinaires* like D. D. Home and Eusapia Palladino, pornographers de luxe like Hadrian Beverland, transvestites like James Allen, and many others."—M.D. PUBLICATIONS

"Dr. Dingwall recounts some real-life stories that rival fiction for strangeness. He views and interprets the lives of these queer folk through the eyes of a psychic researcher—one of great note, indeed, and one with a sound academic background. The author has combined his talents as historian, psychologist and psychic researcher to produce a work for the scholarly with a taste for the macabre."—MEDICAL JOURNAL OF AUSTRALIA

FLOURNOY, Theodore. From India to the Planet Mars; Intro. and final chapter by C. T. K. Chari. xxxvi+469 pages. 63-16228. $10.00 PSYCH

The passing years have served to confirm the eulogistic estimates of those best fitted to judge this work of the author, who was professor of psychology at the University of Geneva and died in 1921. F. W. H. Myers' *Human Personality* called Flournoy's book, "a model of fairness throughout." William McDougall's *Outline of Abnormal Psychology,* summed up the merits of the book: "Among the many cases of the trance-medium type, one stands out preeminent by reason of the richness and variety of the phenomena presented, of the thoroughness and competence with which it was studied, and of the success attending the endeavor to throw the light of science upon its complexities; I mean the case of Hélène Smith most admirably studied and reported by Th. Flournoy." William James praised it in equally high terms. Recent research into extra-sensory perception and the problems of survival and reincarnation has given a new and decisive importance to this classic. Flournoy's gift for narrative is unquestionable. One learns from him that a popular treatment is consistent with scientific carefulness.

The medium he studied became famous especially for two of her most convincing and most bizarre "incarnations." In the one she re-lived the life of a queen in 15th century India. In the other she was allegedly transported to Mars and described and drew pictures of its flora, fauna and intelligent beings, and wrote in the "Martian language."

Flournoy's critical studies of this medium demolished most of the claims made for her. But what he left standing is amazing enough. Some of what he left is now taken away by the new studies contributed to this volume by Professor Chari, a professor of philosophy and an eminent parapsychologist in India. Even he, however, must testify to the extraordinary verisimilitude of the medium's "memories" of 15th century India.

FOX, Oliver. Astral Projection: A Record of Out-of-the-Body Experiences. xiii + 160 pages. 62-19195. $5.00 OCCULT

The noted psychic researcher, Dr. Hereward Carrington, reports in one of his works: "The only detailed, scientific and first-hand account of a series of conscious and voluntarily controlled astral projections which I have ever come across is that by Mr. Oliver Fox, published in the *Occult Review* for 1920." The articles were expanded into a book. This is its first publication in the United States.

The literature of psychic research includes many instances in which a person has an out-of-the-body experience. Sometimes it arises out of a very serious accident. Sometimes it comes in the course of a profound illness. At other times it results from the shock of tragic information or a harrowing experience. A considerable amount of material on out-of-the-body experiences is found in other books published by us: F. W. H. Myers' *Human Personality and its Survival of Bodily Death,* Mrs. Sidgwick's *Phantasms of the Living,* G. N. M. Tyrell's *Science & Psychical Phenomena & Apparitions.*